Handmade Music

Handmade
Midrash

Jo Milgrom

The Jewish Publication Society

PHILADELPHIA   NEW YORK   JERUSALEM

5752 / 1992

Library of Congress Cataloging-in-Publication Data
Milgrom, Jo, 1928–
    Handmade Midrash / Jo Milgrom. — 1st ed.
       p.   cm.
    Includes bibliographical references.
    1. Bible. O.T. Genesis I–IV, 2—Study. 2. Bible. O.T. Genesis XXII,
1–19—Study. 3. Midrash—Study and teaching. 4. Isaac (Biblical
patriarch)—Sacrifice—Study and teaching. 5. Activity programs in Jewish religious
education. 6. Bible. O.T.—Illustrations. I. Title.
BS1239.H55   1991
296.6'8—dc20   91–29181
ISBN 0–8276–0394–0 (cloth)   CIP
ISBN 0–8276–0406–8 (paperback)

Wilfred Owen: *The Collected Poems of Wilfred Owen*. Copyright © 1963 by Chatto &
Windus Ltd. Reprinted by permission of New Directions Publishing Corp.

The English renderings of passages from the Hebrew Bible conform generally to
Tanakh: The Holy Scriptures (JPS, 1985). In some cases, however, an alternative
translation has been used by the author.

Designed by Adrianne Onderdonk Dudden

Publication of this volume has been subvented by
the Center for the Arts, Religion, and Education,
Berkeley, California

Dedicated to my *Minyan Plus* grandchildren:

    To Talia, Noam, Yaron, and Lior,

    To Kinneret, Maor, and Ma'ayan,

    To Jonathan, Sara, and Hannah,

    To Asher's yet to be . . .

In the bright prospect that the late-blooming of Savta Jo will animate them,
like the sh'kedia, to early and lasting flower and fruit.

    And to Andrée Picard,

my model of age, vitality, and dignity . . . ,

and to the living memory of Fred Picard.

Contents

ILLUSTRATIONS IN COLOR

Preface

"Handmade midrash" is visual theology. It is an approach to biblical narrative that draws on the traditional study of Bible, midrash (rabbinic commentaries), and the cognate disciplines of literature, history, archaeology, and linguistics. However, it moves beyond these to form a new synthesis with comparative symbolism, art history, and psychology—to create a new discipline. This study was provoked by the limitations of academic study of Scripture in addressing present-day spiritual needs. Its intended audience is not only teachers and students of the university; it is also widely applicable to the continuing education of adults and to secondary schools as well.

The format of the book is a series of chapters that present workshops in which a biblical text, its midrashic expansions, and its art historical parallels are integrated into an individual handmade exercise whereby related spiritual issues become whole with the academic study.

The thesis of this book has been influenced by Carl Jung's observations that a patient's attitude toward religion is critical to healing in therapy. Jung discovered that the psyche spontaneously produces images with a religious content and is "by nature religious" and that many disturbances spring from a disregard of its religious nature, particularly during the second half of life.

In addition, my research has been enriched by the application of Jungian thought to the study of Scripture in the works of Edward Edinger and others; by the science of *Synectics* (creative problem solving) of William J. J. Gordon; and by Betty Edwards, *Drawing on the Artist Within,* from whom I learned much about making thought visible.

Why is handmade midrash important? It is an original interdisciplinary approach that relates biblical knowledge to inner personal development while continuing to support the contributions of historical criticism to classical biblical study. It is also ground-breaking in its dual use of art materials by those untrained in art. Finally, the joining of these several disciplines touches an integrative life principle that brings together the scattered and opposing parts of oneself.

Whereas a discipline normally demands expertise, our use of art materials to give visual form to thought invites neither skill nor training. As a result, one's awkward slowing down allows a reconsidering of "the obvious that wants to know more," the self-knowledge and symbolic meanings of life's ordinary encounters. The bottom line and startling irony of this method are that the vulnerability and insight achieved in the unskilled tactile activity are precisely what gives newfound personal relevance to the academic disciplines and make them more accessible.

Although handmade midrash did not officially come into being until my postdoctoral period, it germinated many years earlier in a flash of insight stimulated by my daughter Shira's sixth-grade class. Shira's excitement led me to see how Mrs. Smith at the Mary Munford Elementary School in Richmond, Virginia, taught ancient history using the primary sources of art and archaeology. I knew then that I would teach Bible emphasizing the visual image as the other side of the word.

The methodology of handmade midrash developed during my faculty years at the Graduate Theological Union, Berkeley, where I found a fertile environment for ecumenical thinking and creative work in my chosen field, religion and art. Jane Dillenberger guided me as both a personal and professional model; Dean Claude Welch found a place for me within the faculty of the GTU with the assistance of the Skaggs Foundation, Lou Stein, of blessed memory, of the Swig Foundation, Micha Taubman, and other benefactors unknown to me; Duane Christensen, of the American Baptist Seminary of the West, has become my disciple in the use of handmade midrash in an interfaith setting; Doug Adams at the Pacific School of Religion continues to be a staunch supporter.

Eduardo Rauch, co-director of the Melton Center of the Jewish Theological Seminary of New York, provided my first opportunity to present this material to my peers in the field of Jewish education. The *Melton Journal* was first to publish my initial experiments.

Sheila Segal, my editor, knew that this was a book before it was a book. I remember my tentative visit to her office, demonstrating to her how a handmade midrash worked and pointing to a fat folder containing the manuscript draft. I felt her catch my excitement. Sheila midwifed it.

Art therapists in two worlds have counseled me, Ofra Bruno in Jerusalem and Margaret Frings Keyes in California. The wise and noble spirit of Galit Hasan-Rokem keeps me from excessive pride. My many students have been the gift bearers of this project, with special gratitude to Joanna Percival, Susan Cafarelli, Sister Margaret McGovern, and Caroline Goeser. The most recent supporter of and influence on my thinking has been Colette Aboulker-Muscat of Jerusalem, whose imagery courses have resulted in greater personal integration and stronger affirmation of my path.

And, of course, during the lonely years of production, working out the new methodology, these years of writing, mailing, waiting, editing, photographing, writing more, cutting out and pasting in, Jacob, my faithful scholar husband, unfailingly integrated our souls, wafting his left brain encouragement into my right brain studio.

Jo Milgrom
Berkeley, September 1990

Handmade Midrash

Introduction

This book is about making a deep, living connection between the narratives of the Bible and the most important aspects of our personal experience. It is addressed to those who sense, in their transmission of values, that events have many levels of meaning. The symbolic thinking that connects these levels characterizes the midrashic spirit and the religious seeker of all faiths.

Handmade Midrash has drawn inspiration from the many disciplines that have enriched biblical interpretation to date—among them comparative religion, linguistics, literary analysis, history, and archaeology. It is nurtured by the rich materials of art history, art therapy, and psychology. It draws from the vast reservoir of traditional Jewish commentaries and, of course, from the midrash itself.

The term *midrash* describes both a method and a genre of literature in which imaginative interpretation discovers biblical meanings that are continually contemporary. Its classical period extended from the third to the twelfth centuries, but midrash is found even within the Bible, and as this book affirms, it continues to flourish creatively today.

The goal of the handmade midrash exercises is to awaken and nourish each individual's capacity for the creation of midrash by introducing to the study of Bible and religion a visual language that is parallel but antecedent to the language of words. To be truly creative, one must set aside normal modes of thought to see things in a new way. Research on creativity suggests that verbal language can be inappropriate for certain creative tasks and that words at times can even hinder thinking and discovery. Although this book has no need to discredit verbal language in order to champion the visual/nonverbal, it demonstrates how both can work together and enrich each other in biblical and religious studies.

Between Word and Image

From the very beginning of the biblical tradition there has been an awkward tension between the visual and the verbal. This is because the Second Commandment (Exod. 20:4, 5a) can be understood to forbid the making of any figural image: "You shall not make for yourself a sculptured image, or any likeness of what is in the heavens above or on the earth below, or in the waters under the earth. You shall not bow down to them or serve them."

These words can only be viewed quizzically in light of the Divine grace bestowed upon Bezalel, the resident artist of the Torah, whose very name means "in the shadow of God." Bezalel was commissioned to build the desert sanctuary and its furnishings, an artistic project par excellence (Exod. 25ff.). Fear and fascination centered on the sculpted cherubim that decorated the sanctuary. These were the only "images" of anything divine in Israel's visual experience. The text tells us that the cherubim are composite creatures with a human face, the body of a lion, the feet of an ox, and the wings of an eagle. They guarded the entrance to the most sacred precincts and were harnessed to the Divine chariot-throne.

The cherubim were of course nothing more than creative metaphors for God's omnipresence. How, then, can we explain the intensity of the Second Commandment's prohibition? The explanation lies in the palpable fear that Israel, only newly freed from idolatrous slavery, would mistake a part for the whole—the real meaning of idolatry—and thus be seduced by the visible attributes of the gods of the neighboring peoples.

How did Bezalel handle the cherubim crisis? Enveloped in clouds of incense behind the curtains of the Holy of Holies, the cherubim were, so to speak, out of sight and out of mind. A more comprehensive interpretation of the Second Commandment solves the problem by forbidding not the making but the worshiping of figural images. And so centuries later, in a more established religious climate, many cherubim decorated Solomon's Temple. The tension continues in the texts of the midrash. One might even say that what was explicit in the surrounding culture became implicit in the midrashic culture. Just as difficulties in the Bible invited resolution in the midrash, so the seeds of layered imagery in midrash continue to invite full flowering in a visual parallel.

The language of lines and visual images can access direct perception, a different kind of seeing that is essential to thinking and therefore to the creative process. How can a person acquire this language? Betty Edwards, in *Drawing on the Artist Within,* provides the cogent example of one who has never learned to read and write but can nevertheless use language. Such a person can speak with humor, intelligence, and understanding.

But important uses of literacy will be blocked off: access to written work of the present or of past centuries, the ability to fix ideas into writing for others to use, and the ability to increase knowledge through reading. Almost everyone will agree that learning to read and write makes a qualitative difference in terms of thinking.[1]

So it is with seeing, which is another kind of literacy. Training in perceptual skills is comparable to training in literacy. Just as one learns to read and write not necessarily to create works of literary art, one learns to see like an artist not necessarily to create art but simply to see and think better.

Another startling statement by Edwards is the idea that the lines of a drawing have inherent meaning.

> Marks on paper—with or without recognizable images—can be read like a language and can reveal to the person making the marks (as well as to the viewer) what has been going on in the mind of the mark maker; marks on paper . . . represent pure expression, devoid of any realistic or symbolic images . . . (and) can reveal thoughts of which even the thinker is unaware.[2]

Is it possible, I asked myself, hardly able to suppress the excitement that this notion aroused, to apply this principle of making and interpreting "marks on paper—with or without recognizable images" to the midrashic process? Could people make "marks on paper—with or without recognizable images" to interpret biblical passages? Could these marks then be set up parallel, side by side, with analytic verbal interpretation to constitute a more integrated and comprehensive understanding of the text?

Why was this insight so seminal to me? Why was it so vital for me to be able to give words a physical, visible existence, to make thought visible? It is because as a younger learner I myself was negatively affected by the remote language bred of specialized scientific learning and the resulting poverty of symbols. Thus driven to recover symbolic access to the biblical process itself, I have sought and found ways to bring access to others through the creation of the Handmade Midrash Workshop.

The Search for the Hidden

What actually happens in the workshops described in this book? How can the aforementioned principles be applied to the study of Scripture and to the enhancement of one's spirituality and personal creativity? Specific directions and detailed development of these truly simple activities unfold in the succeeding chapters.

Each Handmade Midrash Workshop brings together people of all backgrounds in a process of informal study and dialog regarding a biblical passage or another aspect of Jewish life and learning. The text is augmented by illustrations that present a visual aspect of the words, an opportunity to see how the visual can interpret the verbal.

References to Carl Jung,[3] specifically his concepts of "archetypes" and the process of "individuation," may lead the reader to think that these workshops are exercises in psychotherapy requiring the presence of a trained facilitator. This is not so. The teacher or facilitator and the participant explore and discover together. Whatever insights and healing take place are the result of the interaction, experienced by each person, between the biblical text and his or her own visual symbols and emotional needs.

The nonverbal imagination of the participants is engaged through simple art activities for those untrained in art, such as tearing and pasting construction paper or muslin, working with clay, or penciling various kinds of lines to explain a text more fully. The goal is to help the interfering ego stand aside and allow fragments of fantasy to emerge into consciousness. Natural inhibitions are disarmed by the utter simplicity of the task, the absence of expectations, and the honoring of ordinary materials of daily living. Thus the participant embarks on an inner journey in search of what Erich Neumann calls "the hidden treasure that in humble form conceals a fragment of the Godhead."[4]

One of my favorite representations of this process is its Hasidic migration: the search far and wide for the treasure that is close by. One such story is that of Reb Eisik, whose faith in God was unshaken, even after many years of poverty. One night Reb Eisik dreamed that he was to look for a treasure in the city of Prague, under the bridge that led to the king's palace. After the dream recurred a third time, he set out for Prague, located the bridge, but was unable to find a time when it was not carefully guarded. One day the captain of the guards, who had noticed him, asked him kindly whether he was looking for something or waiting for someone. When Reb Eisik told him about the dream and his faraway journey, the captain burst into laughter. "As for faith in dreams," he said, "if I had such faith I would have had to do the same stupid thing that you did, for I once had a dream that told me to go to Cracow and dig for treasure under the stove in the house of a Jew named Eisik son of Yekel. What a name! I can just imagine going to Cracow, knocking on every door where half the Jews are named Eisik and the other half Yekel."[5] Reb Eisik bowed silently and took his leave. He traveled back to Cracow and dug up the treasure beneath his stove.

As Carl Jung wrote, "The creative activity of imagination frees man . . . and raises him to the status of one who plays." As Schiller put it,

> Man is completely human only when he is at play: What is really required . . . is the attitude of the child at play. The hardest things for adults to learn about play is to take it seriously. They usually feel they can indulge in play only after having taken care of serious business. Yet play is a serious matter for the child, who continually creates, destroys, and recreates new worlds. Recognizing the importance of this kind of play is essential for active imagination.[6]

These forms, produced through innocent, childlike (as opposed to the pejorative "childish") play, speak to those who have made them and to everyone present in the language of symbols. They always mean something, irrespective of aesthetics or value judgments. These drawings, sculptures, or collages cannot be wrong, bad, or ugly. Their meanings are processed first in the actual doing, then in writing, in small-group dialog, and sometimes in a second writing. Often these works can be directly related to existing midrashim and art, providing evidence of the common reservoir of timeless human images and concerns.

In one Handmade Midrash Workshop, a young man, struggling to concretize what it felt like to encounter God on Mt. Sinai, tore black and white construction paper to create a visual metaphor for radiance and awe and placed a human figure within an eye. Was it God or Moses in the eye? he asked himself. He resolved the tension when he realized that the more centered he was, the greater his awareness that the human self perceives and reflects the Divine Self both inside and outside. Unknown to this person was the surrealist painting by Salvador Dali "Moses after Michelangelo," in which the head of Michelangelo's radiant Moses in the Church of St. Peter in Chains rests inside an eye.

Symbol: The Thing and Its Opposite

Something else happens in the Handmade Midrash Workshop. The study ceases to be only cognitive and academic. It becomes personal, sometimes even intimate, as the strangers in the group become known to one another through the expression of their individual concerns and dilemmas. They recognize the commonality of the human condition. One may also engage in the "handmade midrash" exercises as a private meditative activity, as part of a journaling process, alone or with a spiritual counselor, in a classroom setting, or in a retreat encampment. The full extent of its effect can never be fully known or anticipated.

One striking example is the young poet who, despairing of her nonproductiveness, released herself from writer's block through a series of handmade midrash exercises based on selected psalms. Sometimes she would read a psalm aloud in both Hebrew and English. At other times we would read to each other, alternating lines. She might then meditate on a specific image that the psalm evoked. How does it feel to be that thing? I asked. How does it feel, and what does it look like to be the prison in Psalm 142? She then translated the verbal image into a visual analog by tearing and pasting a collage of colored construction paper. Finally, she wrote about the new image.

The verbal images of the psalmist achieved pre-verbal power through the torn and pasted paper collage. The original words of the psalmist had said one thing; the visual forms created new metaphors, which translated back into words, freed the flow of language for the poet. The notion that the prison contained its own means of release emerged from meditation on the word *masger,* which means "prison" in Psalm 142 and "locksmith" in modern Hebrew. Thus, on a symbolic level, words often reveal their paradoxic opposites. Similarly, focusing on the Tree of the Knowledge of Good and Evil (Gen. 2–3) made us both poignantly aware that one is not conscious of life without awareness of death.

New Meanings from the Biblical Text

Through handmade midrash one learns to recognize that biblical phenomena and events occur at many levels of meaning. Symbolic thinking connects these levels and adds infinite richness to experience. As hidden forms and feelings surface, new meanings of the biblical text emerge. A counterpoint starts to resonate between the ancient text made intelligible and the individual's current life situation.

Archetypal motifs emerge from the text.[7] Pain is allowed to speak. Reconciliation and healing can then take place. The biblical text or the religious experience is understood in new and authentic ways, which brings release from ways of knowing and seeing that have become stale and oppressive. This method incorporates strategies in creative thinking and problem solving that are related to the search for meaning via a religious tradition. It affirms that people can effect change in their lives, for the whole point of seeing something differently is to do something about it.

In the Handmade Midrash Workshop, religion is viewed beyond its narrow, sectarian confines. It is seen as a fundamental human hunger to discover the Divine image in oneself and as a commitment to finding it mirrored in other human beings.

My Own Journey

Each workshop presented in this book contains three elements: verbal, visual, and symbolic. These elements are introduced through textual study, which is followed by an art history presentation and then linked to an elementary art exercise. They culminate in personal synthesis directed toward active growth and change.

A year ago I wrote: "The deeper connection between chapters is the movement toward greater complexity in relationships. Thus the first chapters deal with the individual confrontation between creativity and creation, between self and God. Subsequent chapters add the essential familial and worldly elements of interpersonal relationships." Last year I wrote this statement confidently. Today I look at it again, carefully. How could I say, or even think, that interpersonal relationships are more complex than one's relationship between self and God? Last year I wasn't that much younger.

The deeper connection between the chapters of this book is my own personal movement toward individuation.[8] My own journey, like that of my students, is parallel with that of Creation, followed by the story of Adam and Eve, then the test of Abraham. Yes, the first chapters deal with the confrontation between creation and creativity, with self and God, with Eden and exile. Subsequent chapters add elements of interpersonal relationships, aging, faith, and aloneness. The complexity grows all the time, for all relationships are really, as Jung says, "in a state of fluidity, change and growth, where nothing is eternally fixed and hopelessly petrified."[9] Will that work as a definition of individuation? For this year, at least, it does.

Handmade Midrash: The Basic Recipe

The chapters of this book describe variations of the Handmade Midrash Workshop and provide specific instructions for each exercise and related activities. The following general material is adaptable to each one and is relevant throughout the book.

The General Structure

Each workshop requires approximately three hours and has three parts: (1) biblical text study, often including midrashic texts; (2) slides relating the texts to matters of art history; and (3) hands-on creative art play, which we hereon call "handmade midrash." Thus the handmade midrash does not stand by itself but follows a more formal study period that combines word and image. The creation of a handmade midrash constitutes the final third. If, for whatever reason, there is no art history component, the art activity then constitutes the entire second half of the workshop. The techniques involved have been tested successfully with individuals and groups ranging from high-school age through mature adulthood.

The creation of handmade midrash is always linked to the study of a sacred text. The creative process moves the participant from the text to a personal experience of some aspect of its essence. The participant then returns to the text with a new and deeper knowledge of both text and self. A workshop therefore should be experienced in its entirety. As with a mystery film, it is unthinkable to arrive late and ridiculous to leave early.

Art for the Untrained

Many participants worry that they are going to have "to do art" and that they may make fools out of themselves in the process. "But I don't do art," many protest, to which I respond with expressions of relief. All the better. Neither do I. Handmade midrash is not art for art's sake; it is form for symbol's sake. Rough, untutored shapes responding to a biblical passage, shapes resembling something or nothing—these will be invested with whatever meaning the maker gives them. There is no right or wrong. The idea is to give the hands autonomy, to be a child, to allow the soul to play and to make shapes that the rational mind may at first consider worthless. Once those forms find their voice, they can become powerful personal metaphors resonating the individual's very nature and embodying a deep personal experience of the text.

Workshop participants are given assignments with specific instructions and materials: for example, to interpret the binding of Isaac (Gen. 22) by tearing forms out of four sheets of colored construction paper without using scissors. In this case, the instructions are to represent Abraham, Isaac, the ram, the altar, and the Divine Presence, gluing them in a relationship to a background sheet of paper.

Some people respond to the assignment by thinking and planning; others start to tear almost immediately. The forms may be figural; they may be geometric or abstract; or they may be amorphous blobs. It doesn't matter what they look like. All that matters is the meaning that the maker ascribes to them. It makes no difference whether there is a plan or not; the hands assert autonomy as they create a collage-assemblage, either flat (two-dimensional) or sculptural (three-dimensional), in about twenty minutes.

What is really going on? The process lifts the participant out of logic and sequential time, drawing on imaginative life to relate to a biblical passage with forms that surface in the mind's eye, even before one can think of the associated words. These shapes reflect the synectic principle at work: Creative analogy makes the familiar strange in order to see it in a new way. It's like looking at the world upside down from between your legs. Defining biblical concepts (the familiar) through creative metaphor (the strange) is the raw material of midrash.

At each level of the Handmade Midrash Workshop something new surfaces. Therefore, no part can be omitted. I once discovered, after a particular workshop, that writing a second time, after several days of reflection, could be even better than writing only once. So when you are finished, or when you have decided you can't do any more, or don't want to do any more, form small groups of two to six people, depending on the size of the total group. Describe to each other what you have done and what it means. Ask someone else to describe what she or he sees in what you have done. Tell what was the hardest, or the easiest, form to make and why. Discuss the role that color plays. What about sizes, proportion, movement? How do the parts relate to one another? In the Akedah Exercise (the binding of Isaac), you might ask what your handmade midrash says about parent/child relationships or about the nature of God. What does your altar mean? Would you like to add a sixth element of your choosing? Would you like to change any part of your collage? Where are you in your representation of the Akedah? Do you identify with any particular element of it? The group leader should allow each participant three or four minutes to talk and to receive input.

The Small-Group Experience

When the discussion is over, at least for the time being, it is time for the participants to write, using as many of the following approaches as they wish:

Writing a Synthesis

1   Free-associate, allowing strange images and thoughts to surface and be expressed.

2   Depolarize by bringing opposites together. For example, think of love and hate as closely related rather than as poles apart. Bridge a gap between two things that seem different but, from a different point of view, may be closely related.

3   Find correspondences between what is happening in the picture and in your inner feelings and thoughts.

4   Look for a balance of feeling, form, and concept. Does one figure dominate or emerge from the background? Does the total configuration obscure the parts? Can you see the whole through a part, thus deriving a universal concept from the particular? The bottom line is your personal application.

Both in writing and in group discussion, address how the visual experience of handmade midrash has affected your earlier interpretations. Reflect on the most important thing that happened to you in the workshop.

Closure

One of the most exciting aspects of these workshops is that participants unknowingly come up with concepts or images to be found in the classical midrashim or in the history of art, as well as elements common to other religious traditions. This affirms my belief in the collective unconscious. It also makes ordinary people feel very much part and partner with the noblest expressions of art and thought.

Notes

1. Betty Edwards, *Drawing on the Artist Within* (New York: Simon & Schuster, 1986), 40.

2. Ibid., 50.

3. Carl G. Jung (1875–1961) was a physician, psychiatrist, and scholar in comparative mythology, alchemy, and the psychology of religion. His immense *Collected Works* (twenty volumes) have inspired and augmented the findings of many leading creative scholars of our time. Evidence of this is found in the forty-odd volumes already published in the continuing *Eranos-Yahrbuch* series, in which some two hundred major scholars have responded to the cultural-historical studies of Jung.

Jung offered a psychology that acknowledges the reality of the psyche as the medium through which we perceive our inner and outer worlds. He affirmed the individual's own experience of unconscious material as an open system of unlimited potential for growth and decay, good and evil, order and chaos. Jung regarded the psyche as an inherently self-regulating system, with a tendency toward balance and wholeness. Thus the aim of one's life, psychologically speaking, should not be to suppress or repress, but to come to know one's other side, and so both to enjoy and to control the whole range of one's capacities—that is, in the full sense to "know oneself."

4. H. I. Champernowne, "Creative Expression and Ultimate Values," in *American Journal of Art Therapy* 16 (October 1976):5, quoting Erich Neumann, *Art and Creative Unconscious* (London: Routledge & Kegan Paul, 1971), 168.

5. Martin Buber, Hasidism and Modern Man (New York: Horizon, 1958), 170–171.

6. Janet Dallett, "Active Imagination in Practice," in *Jungian Analysis*, Murray Stein (ed.) (Boulder, Colo.: Shambhala and London, 1984), 179.

7. Archetypes are nuclei of energy or instincts based on our common human biological structure that determine our patterns of perception and behavior (summarized from Dallett, n. 5). According to Jung: "The concept of the archetype . . . is derived from the repeated observation that . . . the myths and fairytales of world literature contain definite motifs which crop up everywhere . . . in the fantasies, dreams, deliria, and delusions of individuals living today. These typical images and associations are what I call archetypal ideas . . . they have their origin in the archetype, which in itself is irrepresentable, unconscious, preexistent form that seems to be part of the inherited structure of the psyche and can therefore manifest itself anywhere at any time." C. G. Jung, *Memories, Dreams, Reflections* (New York: Random House, 1965), 392.

8. According to Jung, individuation is "not only a conscious relationship to the archetypal world, but also a conscious relationship to interpersonal reality and social collectivity. It includes developing the ability for introspection no less than for experiencing, playing with, feeling for, and fulfilling one's calling in outer reality." Stein, *Jungian Analysis*, 340.

9. Ibid., 39.

The
Workshops

Workshop 1

The Sensory Aleph

Our first workshop introduces the Hebrew alphabet as a symbol set by which we may see, hear, and quantify a personal connection with God. In Jewish mysticism, the letter *aleph,* normally modest and silent, plays a dramatic role when the Torah is given. Through selections from the Kabbalah, the *aleph* becomes the vehicle by which we can deal artistically with the transcendent God, thereby experiencing God as close and personal.

After viewing an exhibition of my students' Aleph creations, my friend and colleague Daniel Matt was prompted to share with me a mystical interpretation of the following lines from Psalm 100: "Acknowledge that the Lord is God. He made us and we are His." In the Hebrew text, the word *His* is spelled לֹא , meaning "not," which renders the lines meaningless: "He made us and we are not." However, an asterisk in the Masoretic Hebrew text leads our eyes down to a footnote that advises us to read the word as if it were "correctly" spelled לוֹ , meaning "His." The *Sepher Bahir,* a mystical text that first appeared in the late twelfth century in southern France, suggests that we retain the *aleph* but translate the word לֹא in yet another way: "He made us and we belong to the Aleph." This rendering not only preserves the original form but also reminds us of how long ago our Aleph obsession began.

In the Aleph Workshop, the first Hebrew letter becomes the vehicle through which the individual may see, hear, and quantify a connection with God. These three actions—to see, to hear, and to quantify—indicate that there is a graphic, a phonic, and a numerologic tradition in Jewish thought and art. This is true of all language and culture: There is the printed word in all its calligraphic glory; there is the language heard in its infinite varieties; and there is mathematics, by which letters are given numerical equivalents. One example in Judaism is the tradition that requires a specific numerical sequence for the fringes of a prayer shawl: 10, 5, 11, 13. The equation $10 + 5 = 15$ stands for the numerical value of God's name: *yod* (10) + *hey* (5) = 15. The number 11 stands for the last two letters of God's name: *vav* (6) + *hey* (5) = 11. The number 13 is the sum total of the letters that spell out *Ehad* (or "One"): *aleph* (1) + *het* (8) + *dalet* (4). Thus the wearer of the tallit, holding its fringes during the recitation of the *Sh'ma,* is meditating on the Oneness of God.

Although Jews often play the game of numerical equivalents known as *gematria,* they were not the originators of it. Such games were known earlier to the Greeks and to the Babylonians before them. The earliest example we have dates back to an inscription of Sargon II (727–707 B.C.E.) stating that the king built the wall of Khorsabad 16, 283 cubits long to correspond to the numerical value of his name. The difference is that in Jewish usage the letters play a sacred role in the work of creation and in bringing God's presence to the attention of the world. In this drama the letter *aleph* is the star.

Some other letters in the Hebrew alphabet run a close second to the *aleph,* particularly those that compose the name of God, YHVH (*yod, hey, vav, hey*). After that, the rest of the letters start to clamor, and we begin to hear about names of God that have twenty-two, forty-five, and even seventy-two letters. Thus we realize that we are only tapping the surface of a rich tradition.

The *aleph,* normally modest and silent, plays a stunning role on Sinai when the Torah is given. The *aleph* is a kind of distilled essence of the need for a sensory experience of God, of the need to see and hear revelation. With the help of selections from the Kabbalah and the visual arts, we can experience the *aleph* as a means to enter into a palpable relationship with a transcendent God. Our opening exercise with the *aleph* will also elicit some of the recurring motifs of this book: the duality of word and image, of matter and spirit; the struggle of language to connect us to God; and the search for metaphor that reveals the many levels of meaning in a single event.

My immediate goals are that this small-scale project will enable each participant to experience sanctity through the modest materials and acts of daily life; that language be recognized as a potential means of Divine–human communication; that a splintered Jewish community come to know its essential oneness. I also hope that the performance of handmade midrash exercises within a multidenominational group can enhance the religious life of non-Jews as well as Jews. I hope that it will contribute to the creation of an ecumenical community.

An ancient fragment from the Book of Creation (*Sefer Yetsirah,* 3rd–6th century, C.E.) presumes a conversation that took place between the Holy One and the Torah as God prepared to embark on the work of Creation. Speaking in metaphor, or in midrashic language, God says to the Torah, "I request laborers," to which the Torah replies, "I put at your disposal twenty-two laborers, namely, the twenty-two letters in the Torah." Between the third and sixth centuries of the Common Era, these twenty-two letters have established their status as God's tools in creation: "Twenty-two letters He engraved, hewed out, weighed, changed, combined, and formed out of all existing forms and all forms that may in the future be called into existence."[1]

The significance of this fragment of text for us is the idea that language creates reality. In other words, one's view of self and of the world is determined by the language one uses. This principle is important in neurolinguistic programming, which is one of the off-shoots of psychotherapy. We will see shortly how it works in Jewish thought. For now, let us return to the letters of the alphabet as they are summoned to participate in the giving of the Torah so that God's presence may be known on earth. Remembering that the alphabet has a graphic, a phonic, and a numerological aspect, we are ready for a sensory experience of God's appearance, the theophany.

A Vision of Sinai: Black Fire on White Fire

Moses ben Nahmanides (Ramban), a thirteenth-century Kabbalist, gives us a clue to the experience of revelation in the introduction to his commentary on the Torah. Invoking an image that goes back to the Palestinian Talmud, Nahmanides says that the Torah was written in black fire on white fire.[2]

We understand the association of light with God. But how can we see white fire against a light sky? Can we make out anything in a blizzard? Might we say, then, that black fire represents human endeavor, the recording in black ink on white parchment of what we believe is God's word in order to make it visible, to give it human reality? Is it not also true that the more we write down the black fire, the more white fire is revealed in the relationship of the background to the figure? Thus it is human effort that makes God's presence real on earth. We see that God is in need of humanity. We are mutually dependent.

A striking visualization of "black fire on white fire" is Ben Shahn's graphic entitled *The Alphabet of Creation,*[3] which is based on the tale told by Abraham Abulafia, a thirteenth-century wandering Kabbalist (fig. 1.1). The tale, in turn, is based on the earlier midrash that God used the letters of the Torah to create the world. The letters, thus personified, vie in turn for the first position in Creation. Each one presents herself as the embodiment of a particular quality that is essential for Creation, beginning with the last letter of the alphabet, the *tav*.

The *tav* presents herself as Torah, then *shin* as Shaddai (Almighty), and so forth. But God rejects them all one by one, canceling each positive quality with a negative one. Torah loses because *tav* is also the X that marks the doomed man; Shaddai, because it is also *sheker*, meaning "falsehood." This process of negation illustrates the illusive duality and the inherently contradictory nature of language.

The Irresistible Bet

The countdown continues until the twenty-first letter, the irresistible *bet*, takes the stage. *Bet* represents *bracha*, meaning "blessing." It is clearly the winner, or so it seems. Could creation be represented by any more appropriate quality than blessing? No negative aspect even dares a whimper. And so God begins the Torah with the *bet* of *Bereshit*, "In the beginning." The modest and silent *aleph*, the last letter in the countdown, is mollified with second place: *Aleph* is chosen to begin the Ten Commandments—*Anokhi*, "I am." Thus the *aleph*, apparently the understudy, becomes the star of revelation.

If one concentrates not on the letters themselves (the figure) but on the spaces between the letters (the ground), the letters become hazy and a new configuration emerges, that of the white fire. As we begin to expand our knowledge of Torah, seeking its larger framework, we begin to get those unexpected, elusive flashes of white fire. This is also true in music: The sound is possible only because of the rests, the silences in between. It is also true about people: If we look only at a person and not at the context, spatial and otherwise, our view of the person is distorted, incomplete.

Another artist who is particularly successful in conveying this concept of black fire on white fire is Mark Podwal in *A Book of Hebrew Letters*. To illustrate the letter *nun*, Podwal uses *navi*, a "prophet," who is in a figure-to-ground relationship that parallels the Torah (fig. 1.2). Thus the Torah and the prophet are reflections of each other, like shadow and light, human and divine, black fire and white fire.[4]

Aleph: The Sound of Revelation

Another clue about revelation comes to us from Gershom Scholem,[5] who focuses on the theophany at Sinai as an issue in the relationship between authority and mysticism. The authority is clear: Israel received a set of doctrines whose direct, specific meaning denies any mystical formula that has infinite interpretation. But the mystical aspect arises when we ask what was divine about the revelation. What

fig. 1.1. Ben Shahn, *Alphabet of Creation*. (Copyright © Estate of Ben Shahn/VAGA, New York, 1991. Reprinted with permission.)

fig. 1.2. Mark Podwal, *Prophet/NAVI*. (*From* Mark Podwal, *A Book of Hebrew Letters*. Philadelphia: The Jewish Publication Society, 1978, page *nun*. Reprinted with permission.)

was actually heard at Sinai? Some traditions say that Israel heard all the Commandments; others, that Israel heard only the first two commandments and was so terrorized by the Divine Presence that Moses was implored to mediate the remaining eight.

Rabbi Mendel Torum of Rymanov (d. 1814) had a different idea. For him, revelation was both an acoustic and a linguistic challenge. What could God possibly sound like? He concluded that Israel heard only the first letter of the first word of the first utterance, namely, the *aleph* of the word *Anokhi*, "I am." Even a beginning student in Hebrew would be instantly perplexed, since *aleph* is a silent letter. Scholem explains that the *aleph* may be said to denote the source of all articulate sound, the "potential sound of the divine larynx, as it were, about to speak." Imagine hearing only the *aleph*, the latent possibility of all sound. In this way Rabbi Mendel transformed the revelation at Sinai into a mystical revelation "pregnant with infinite meaning but without specific meaning." According to Scholem, the concept that the word of God made itself heard through the medium of human language is one of the most important legacies bequeathed by Judaism to the religions of the world. This concept establishes the connection between us and God.[6]

One last phonic aspect of the *aleph* was suggested in the thirteenth century by Yaakov ben Yaakov HaCohen: "As the *aleph* works effortlessly, like a breath of air, so the Creator, though all powerful, creates without a show of power." *Aleph*, we recall, is the gateway to vowel sounds that make language audible. The pointed vowels as we know them today came into being only as recently as the tenth century of our own era. A thousand years earlier, vowels in the Bible were represented by four consonants that did double duty: *aleph, hey, vav,* and *yod.* These four were called "mother letters" (*matres lectiones*) because they gave birth, so to speak, to the breath that makes sound possible. These very letters compose two of God's names, EHYEH, "I am that I am," and the Tetragram YHVH (Yahweh), with the essential meaning of "being." These letters thus combine the features of Divine Being and Divine breath. Since they are generously sprinkled on all words (which would be unpronounceable without them), they have come to symbolize the Divine substance in language.

There is an easy association between the sound of breath in the wind/spirit of God's presence hovering in Genesis 1 and the sound of breath as the wind/spirit of the vowels that make possible the miracle of human language. Because the silent *aleph* is the first letter, and because it is the mysterious pause between nonsound and sound, we can understand why "the kabbalists regarded the *aleph* as the spiritual root of all of the others, encompassing in its essence the whole alphabet, hence all other elements of human discourse."[7]

Aleph: *An Axis Mundi*

We have "heard" the inaudible *aleph* and "seen" the unseeable letters of Torah etched in black fire on white. Now it remains to examine how the *aleph* operates graphically as the Divine connection par excellence.

Let us begin with a short and puzzling statement by historian of religion Mircea Eliade that "communication with the gods happens via an opening."[8] In *The Sacred and the Profane,* Eliade reminds us that space is not homogeneous. Sacred space is a sanctuary; it is not your living room. However, Eliade also says that it is possible to locate a patch of sacred space wherever you happen to be standing—even in your own living room.

By way of example, Eliade writes about primitives who perceived a sacred being and sacred space as "up there" and believed that they could reach it, literally, by poking a hole in the apex of their tent and running a pole through it, reaching into the heavens. Eliade calls that pole an "axis mundi," an axis of the world. It is a vertical connector between ordinary space and sacred, or "other," space. Examples of vertical connectors are found in cultures of greater sophistication as well. In the Bible, there is Jacob's ladder, the Tree of Life in the Garden of Eden, and Mt. Sinai—mountains being a favorite spot for Divine manifestations. The spires of the great cathedrals are also vertical connectors. We can also say that every act of scaling a great height—be it a tower or a mountain—reflects a primeval impulse to encounter "the other."

Along with the image of a vertical connector, there usually is an opening. Thus Jacob, deeply shaken, cried out, "How awesome is this place. This is none other than the abode of God, and that is the gateway to heaven" (Gen. 28:17). And when Adam and Eve ate from the magic tree, they were unceremoniously ushered out of the Garden of Eden while cherubim brandishing a revolving sword blocked the sacred portal.

Admittedly, the preceding examples involve extraordinary situations. How is it possible, in a more personal and mundane situation, to locate a patch of sacred space and connect with it when you are spiritually needy but engulfed in the secular space at the kitchen sink, where neither ladder nor mountain is available? Such a connection is accomplished in a metaphoric instant: Poke a finger into space and reach for it—fully conscious and filled with desire. Communication with God begins through a tiny opening and is completed through a vertical axis. The *aleph* is a graphic symbol of this connection.

The *aleph* is composed of three strokes: two tiny *yod* apostrophes in the upper right and lower left corners and a diagonal stroke in the opposite direction. Even though the diagonal is not exactly upright, it operates symbolically like a vertical *vav*. One may speak of the upper *yod* apostrophe, which is scarcely more than a dot, as the breakthrough of the Divine Presence, the first position in the Tetragram.

Thus the *yod* dot is the source of all visible language and a physical, spatial connection with God. All forms in space start with it. To get from our ordinary space to that sacred dot—the *yod*—the religious part of us must find a way to transcend ordinary space. In this we may learn from our ancestors, who knew intuitively how to bridge the gap. They would reach up, poke a tiny *yod*-like hole in space, and connect with the wholly "other" essence. "On the most archaic level of culture," Eliade explains, "transcendence is expressed by various images of an opening. Communication with the gods happens via an opening."

In the field of comparative religion, there is a variety of terms for that tiny opening and the implanting of the connection: *hidden seed, divine egg, root of roots,* to name just a few. In Kabbalah it is the *yod* that is the opening and the visual source of linguistic movement. It can be written as two coincident right-angled apostrophes: wings that evolve from the original point and movement. This *yod* point is the initial upper flag stroke of the *aleph*.

Before moving on to the experience of creating a personal *aleph*, it is helpful to consider how three artists have used the symbols discussed previously. In the example by Benn (fig. 1.3), the *yods*, which are parts of the *aleph*, are shown as God's signature. In Mark Podwal's Torah pointer (fig. 1.4), the *vav* operates as an axis mundi, a world axis, connecting us with God.[9] Similarly, a workshop participant named Ted focused on the *yod* in God's name as the means of making his own personal connection.

fig. 1.3. Benn, *He Bent the Heavens and Came Down (Ps: 18.10). (From* Benn, *Visions of the Bible: 52 Drawings.* Tel Aviv: Sinai, 1954, p. 34. Reprinted with permission.)

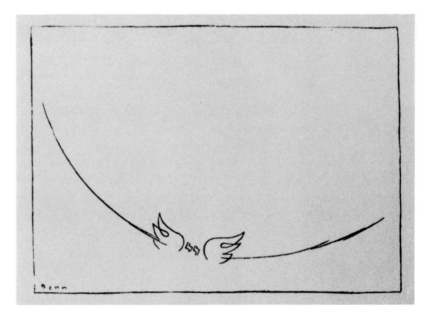

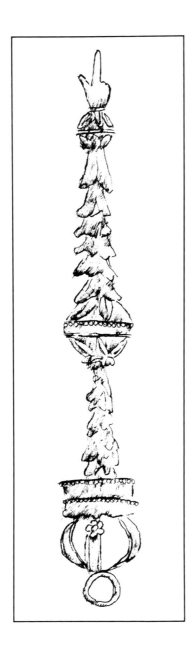

fig. 1.4. Mark Podwal, *Torah Pointer as Vov.* (*From* Elie Wiesel, *The Golem.* New York: Summit, 1983, p. 101. Reprinted with permission.)

Student Ted Virts, learning Hebrew with a calligraphy pen, did a series of *yods* followed by *kavvanot*, meditations directing the heart. Ted opens a dialogue with God as he concentrates on the *yod* of God's signature:

TED:

Meditation on the Yod

(fig. 1.5)

The breaking through of light, the first view of the Holy One, Blessed be S/he, is quite irregular. Without control, without recognition. I'm not sure what I am seeing; am I seeing at all? Perhaps God's attempts

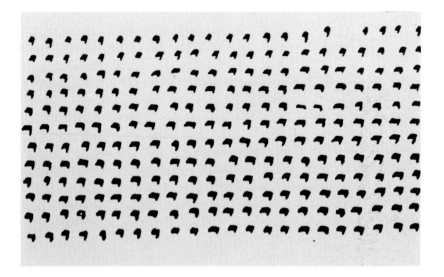

fig. 1.5. Ted Virts,
Meditation on the Yod.

are small because S/he fears us. Perhaps it is because God cares and knows how little we understand of light.

How tight my hand becomes trying to grasp the simple stroke. When I relax, the image comes easier. How tight I become in trying to grasp God. Would that I could relax and let the light come to me.

Each yod is different yet recognizable. God may be the same, but each of us sees differently. Or perhaps God is different to each of us so that we know God from the place where we are able to know.

Yod is always a question of balance. Too slow and the ink blurs; too fast and the image is not complete. Too much pressure and movement is gone; too little, and the picture is scattered. Too much control, or too little concentration, and the letter is distorted. God remains elusive, except in those times of harmony.

But even when the effort is not sufficient, there is always another chance. Even when the hand is not successful, the heart may be successful.

Even when I am not satisfied, others may see my intent. God may be recognized in my mistakes. God may be recognized in my successes.

Writing is an act of an individual; meaning is an act of the community. Without meaning, there is no writing; without writing, there is no meaning.

The Handmade Aleph

There are three variations for the Sensory Aleph Workshop: (1) an *aleph* drawn with pencil lines, based on Betty Edwards's concept of the "language of lines"; (2) a simple *aleph* collage made of torn and pasted pieces of colored construction paper; and (3) an *aleph* to be made at home, in any mode or materials, and brought to a follow-up session. The examples reproduced in this chapter represent all three variations.

Participants might keep in mind that the upper *yod* represents some attribute of the Divine and the lower *yod* might be a corresponding attribute of the participant, created in the Divine image. The *vav* stroke represents the way in which the participant is connected with God. Thus the *aleph* becomes an abstract portrait of the Divine–human connection. The lithograph by Hasidic artist Michoel Muchnik illustrates these very concepts, although the methodology for our handmade Aleph is very different.[10]

The creation of the handmade Aleph requires no special skill, talent, or training since the goal of this activity is not to create a beautiful work of art but to make a vital, meaningful work whose forms speak to the individual. At the outset the participant may not know what he or she is going to do, which can be somewhat worrisome. But the process is not unlike speech: Often you don't know exactly what you are going to say until the words tumble out of your mouth. Somehow speech engenders thought, which in turn engenders more speech; similarly, these exercises—once begun—stimulate free artistic play. Whether you try to think it through rationally or jump in and let your hands work without conscious direction, at a certain point intuition tells you to give your hands autonomy and put your mind in neutral gear.

Although the task is serious, one must approach it with lightness, with a spirit of free play, peering over the rim of childhood. When you have completed the exercise, look with curious pleasure upon what you have created. Interact with each individual part. Write about the process. Talk with other participants. Continue to write.

The true task of the *aleph*-maker is defined by George Orwell's suggestion that "each of us has an outer and an inner mental life: the former expressed in the ordinary language we use every day, and the latter in another form of thought (perhaps 'thought about feelings') that rarely surfaces because ordinary words cannot express its complexity."[11] Our goal is to make the thoughts of that inner world visible by using an alternative visual language.

The first step is to recognize that all of us draw all the time. We draw when we sign our names, and within these drawings we convey a quantity of visual information. Each letter says something unique about our psyche, physiology, and history. Betty Edwards makes this clear by instructing her students to write (i.e., draw) their names four different ways: (1) the way they always write it; (2) with the other hand; (3) with the normal hand but backwards; (4) with the other hand, in the

Preliminary Exercises in the Language of Lines

fig. 1.6. Denise, *Analog drawing in the "language of lines."*

normal direction, but without looking. Each of these signatures is a picture of the individual—perhaps confident and assertive, wobbly and awkward, or nervous and uncertain. It would take a string of adjectives to define verbally what the eye instantly grasps concerning the impact of this set of signatures. This exercise has a powerful first-time impact on the initiate seeking visual literacy.

In a second preparatory exercise, participants divide a sheet of typing paper into eight sections by folding it in half, then in half again, and finally a third time. Seven of the squares are then labeled with the following emotions or human characteristics—joy, anger, tranquility, depression, energy, illness, femininity (fig. 1.6). The word that goes in the eighth square is up to the individual. Using a pencil, the participant makes a visual representation of each of the eight words in the corresponding squares. The drawing may be made with one line or many, heavy pressure or light; it may fill all or only part of the space or be made with the point of the pencil, the side, or a combination. The eraser can be used if desired.

There is one restriction; you may not draw pictures or use recognizable symbols. Thus, no hearts and flowers, no lightning or raindrops, no question marks. How, then, do you draw anger, for example? Betty Edwards suggests thinking back to the last time you were angry and, without labeling the event or the reason, feel within yourself what the anger was like. Imagine you are feeling the emotion again, that it flows first from deep inside, then into your arm, down into your hand, and into your pencil, where it emerges from the point to record marks that are equivalent to the feeling, marks that look like the felt emotion. These marks can be adjusted, changed, or erased until they feel right as the image of that emotion. Allow the image to emerge in its own way—to state for itself what it means to say. The drawings that result are analogs; they make the subjective objective by giving it visible form[12] (see fig. 1.6).

Carl's *aleph* (fig. 1.7), accomplished in minutes, is minimal in form and eloquent in understatement: a disarmingly simple collage of three pieces of torn construction paper, whose two smaller segments are subtly placed against the *vav* axis to illustrate the angle of tension between the Divine and the human.

The remaining *alephs* were done at home. Using the language of lines, Denise creates her *aleph* (fig. 1.8) with the visual equivalent of its feeling content. Alice's *aleph* of clay and sewing notions emphasizes sanctity in the modest materials of daily living. The *alephs* of Jeff—photo collage (fig. 1.9), Franz—nature photography (fig. 1.10), Helen—rice grains (fig. 1.11), and Andy—linoleum block (fig. 1.13) show a range of creative materials and processes. Amy (fig. 1.12) and David express the painful predicament of Jews who are uncertain of their Jewish identity. In the final student sampling of *aleph* visualizations, Sister Margaret uses *samekhs* and a piece of wooden molding to work through the disturbing paradox of God's beneficent and demonic qualities (fig. 1.14).

Workshop Samples

Calligraphy is one of my primary art forms. I appreciate the high contrast of the white and black when placed together. . . . Those areas that have a higher concentration of seemingly random black, such as the base of the vav, *represent the more explored areas in striving to learn more of my true self and thereby more of God. The varying densities of lines show that my efforts are not always of equal intensity. Vav . . . reaches an arching pinnacle in the heavens and is firmly grounded on the earth. Its curve is feminine and joyful with a*

DENISE:
Aleph: Toward Intimacy
(fig. 1.8)

fig. 1.7. Carl, *Aleph: God and Man Are Parallel Creations.*

fig. 1.8. Denise, *Aleph: Toward Intimacy.*

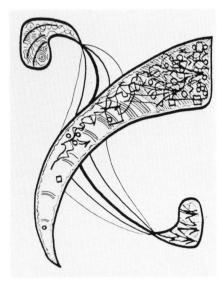

hook ready to reach down again if necessary. The yods are attached with several lines in attempts to unify in some form of intimacy.

Within the figure are the symbols that I formed as I drew line representations of the eight words (analog drawings). The lower yod is filled with energy and excitement in striving to reach up toward the yod that touches God. The upper yod has a strong sense of joy about it, but it also contains peace, femininity, and excitement. The vav is made up of all the symbols. There is nothing that I experience that is incapable of leading me toward God. Peace flows around the entire edge as a unifying characteristic that is always of God and that signals to me when I am "on track." A great deal of the understanding at the base, which shows the "black fire on white fire," is created out of my joy symbol because as aspects of God are discovered, my joy increases.

When Denise deliberately reverses the direction of the *yods*, amusement becomes surprise. Instead of God reaching down to her, she exercises the initiative, striving first to reach up and touch God. The visual result is a "backwards" *aleph* but with a forward-looking feminist assertiveness. Her *vav* in the form of a shofar transmits God's voice, ironically within the silent *aleph*. Again, the reversal of form catches us unawares. We would expect the shofar to emanate from below, its bell reaching upward. Instead, God sounds the horn from above, its staccato calls reaching down to become the vehicle of our connection.

Denise has objectified subjective feeling, making inner thought visible in the language of lines. This kind of visual training makes the forms and lines of abstract art accessible to the untrained in art, who may turn away from nonobjective forms in puzzlement and irritation.

ALICE:

Sanctity in Small Things

I completed the Aleph by pressing into it all manner of things that compose my understanding of who God is, who I am, and what happens between us. My yod has a jaded heart, a vessel waiting to be filled. The divine yod has a ring for promise, a key to many mysteries, a jewel of perfection, and a spiral inviting me to come closer. Between us are elements of the natural world; all of what exists on the axis mundi can either draw me closer to an awareness of the Divine or divert me from it. All of the activities have made me aware of the enormous significance implicit in even the most common thing. Or to put it another way, what an enormous lack of meaning is generally invested in much of what we do.

I feel renewed in my commitment to the aleph to looking for God in the almost invisible events of my days. I want to turn too, inward and outward, to extend myself and my awareness beyond God-and-me to God-and-us. I want it to be a dynamic relationship, full of color and mystery. And yet respectful of the distances. There is a whole world of difference between the human and the Divine, after all.

The supple movement possible in clay became symbolic of the flexible relation between Alice and her Maker. She chose blue for mystical serenity of the Divine, red for "my life, my very blood," and green for the axis mundi, for growth and the cycles of seasons and possibilities. Her forms are grounded, simple, and clear; their message is the dignity, worth, and power of revelation implicit in even the most common things.

It suddenly occurred to me that the structure of the Golden Gate was a kind of aleph. *I wanted to emphasize the conjunction of tower and span. . . . The amazing thing to me is that as I stood there under the bridge, my time, light, and film gone, with no tangible result, I became exhilarated instead of discouraged. I was happily obsessed with the idea of getting this picture. I felt like a real artist in the sense that I had a message to convey about this bridge, and I became committed to trying to convey it.*

For me the Golden Gate has always meant more than a way to get across the mouth of the bay. It is more gate than bridge. To the east, it represents all that is safe, solid, and known. To the west . . . lay the Pacific bordered only by the horizon. Here is everything deep, mysterious, unknown, and dangerous. The bridge is the thin line that separates the two worlds. . . . It speaks to me of a spirituality that is rooted in the depths of the soul and reaches up to the heights of heaven—which somehow spans the gate of my person separating the familiar and safe from the deep, mysterious, unknown.

JEFF:
The Golden Gate Aleph
(fig. 1.9)

fig. 1.9. Jeff, The Golden Gate Aleph.

The bottom line for me is that it makes me aware of God's pull on me to move at times from the safe to the risky, from the mundane to the mysterious, from the horizontal to the vertical, from the fragmented to the whole.

Jeff thought of himself as a nonartist, incapable of artistic interpretation—"But the frustrating thing is I know I have it in me." He began his paper with a quote from *Will and Spirit* by G. G. May, in which the writer admits to never doing anything that will make him feel too good because he is frightened of life's beauty and fragility, afraid that if he touches it he will spoil it. Jeff's paper witnesses the surprise and joy of his artistry and the transforming power of spiritual insight. He also grasps and integrates the concept of the sacred portal as the archetypal "fall" (into time) and "rise" from static Eden to a conscious and fuller life experience.[13]

FRANZ:
Looking for an Aleph in Nature

(see fig. 1.10, Color Section 1)

The slide of the thicker, stronger roots is the best of all in my eyes. That slide is my Aleph. Roots are a fine material for the Aleph because they connect with the earth, with the inside, and also lead to the tree, which aspires to heaven. Here, roots are a mystical symbol. They are the axis mundi, leading up to God and even down to the underworld.

These roots show strength, power, and naturalness. Yet they move so slowly and their lines are unsure; they are blind: they must grope toward God. This comes close to my own relationship to God. Like a root, I am bound to the earth, blind, twisted. Yet it may be said I too am part of the axis mundi, the Tree of Life. If there is a Godhead I know that I aspire to it. I think if I can become as a root to the Tree I will be fulfilled.

At first, Franz thought of expressing the Aleph through gesture and movement of his body, but he found that familiarity interfered with transcendent expression. Then he rejected meditation and calligraphy because they required greater stillness of mind than he could muster. Finally, camera in hand, he turned to the hills "with the intention of finding a form that by my action would be consecrated as a sacred image." Significantly, the image alone could not be sacred, without the interaction, the process of the seeker. Franz was saying that a segment of nature has also to be reenvisioned by the artist if it is to constitute an aspect of the sacred.

HELEN: *A Third World Aleph Made of Rice*
(fig. 1.11)

Helen's Aleph came in a small picture frame, about three by five inches. Delicate grains of dark and light rice and leaves shaping the Aleph were held in precarious stability only by the pressure of the glass.

fig. 1.11 Helen, *A Third World Aleph Made of Rice.*

I have used rice grains for the picture—black and white for black light and white light (revelation). Rice is important in Asia—it is our staple. Especially for those who suffer in hunger and poverty, G-d [sic] can only be experienced in food. This to me is the acid test for the experience of G-d in our lives. The experience must make sense, it must have to do with our needs—body, mind, spirit, soul, wholesomely within the whole of Creation.

This experience—perhaps even as small and seemingly insignificant as a grain of rice—can "open up" the whole Heaven's worth of openness to God's revelation [visually analogous to the tiny *yod* particle].

Helen's practical *aleph* theology, grown in Vietnam, is in stark pragmatic contrast to the visionary, armchair musings of her middle-class American colleagues, most of whom are blissfully distant from any daily life-threatening need. Her anguish for a theophany in the rice field is not far from the talmudic plea in *Ethics of the Fathers,* which reads, *Im eyn kemah eyn Torah:* "If there is no flour there is no Torah."

Relating to the *vav* stroke, Amy cited the following passages:

1   *And God said, "Let there be light"* (Gen. 1:3).
2   *And a flaming torch passed between the pieces* (Gen. 15).
3   *And the angel of the Lord appeared to him in a blazing bush* (Exod. 4).
4   *And there appeared to them tongues of fire . . . and they were filled with the holy spirit* (Acts 2).

Amy associated light and fire with a succession of God's appearances: first in the creation of original light and then its revelation to persons of heightened consciousness—Abraham, Moses, and the apostles.

For the *yod*/hand particles, she wrote:

1   *"In the image of God He created him; male and female He created them* (Gen. 1:27).
2   *Mother Teresa has said, "We are Christ's hands."*

Amy tore out a flaming torch of yellow light for the diagonal *vav* stroke. The *yod* particles are two green hands, the upper somewhat larger than the lower. Underlying the center of the torch is a thin green archway, which, besides providing a delicate compositional element, relates the hands to each other and identifies them as a focal support for the torch. In addition, the green archway makes the *vav* into a passage. Both the center of the torch and the area above it have been torn away, exposing space so that the *aleph* can take flight.

Amy is a former Jew for Jesus, who currently holds a master's degree in theology and the arts. Amy's Aleph is also a cross as she struggles to integrate two traditions and to find her identity in their resolution. After a subsequent course with me, she wrote of the "affirmation of visualization, an experience of inner and outer alignment," climaxed by a *sefirot* assemblage of seven hubcaps that marked her personal journey from the Exodus to the receiving of the Torah (Passover to Shavuot). In her words, "Traditional symbol and ritual became points of departure . . . and personal symbol, empowering Jewish worship and mitzvot."

The outcome speaks of my current relationship to Judaism. Three colors—stripes in the center—convey the range of feelings that pulsate within me. Black conveys the bitterness and resentment left over from my Jewish upbringing. Red is the passion I tasted when I re-explored Judaism about ten years ago through the writings of

Martin Buber. Yellow is the sunshine of hope that through my willingness to once again explore Judaism, I may grow into a new and more receptive relationship with the treasury of Jewish wisdom.

The cross in the lower right corner is in some ways a cornerstone of the image. Equally important is the Star of David inside the cross. Both the Jewish and Christian perspectives are integral and foundational elements of our Western religious context. I stand on a theological ground that embraces the essential truths of both traditions.

The flamelike design in the upper left is the fiery anger that I experienced when I attended the Rosh Hashanah service at the International House. The other designs are kinetic in their effect; that is, they convey motion/movement/change. I see myself beginning a transformational process that is exciting, unsettling, and vitally alive. I'm glad for the opportunity.

Some of David's words lean optimistically toward a reintegration within the Jewish community. Others candidly profess dual loyalty. David explained that the anger he felt at the Rosh Hashanah service was toward the indifference he saw among those attending. I reminded him that people who sit on the periphery of the congregation are often those with peripheral affiliation. Considering the black stripe of residual childhood bitterness, one need not wonder at the eruption of projected anger.

David clearly sees the cross as "in some ways a cornerstone." All the emotions are attached to it. The Star of David occupies a minimal space inside. (Similarly, Marc Chagall, bridging two worlds in *I and the Village* [1911], wears a necklace with a cross and a ring with a Star of David.)

The block print is an art form I have used before, and the only one in which I consider myself to be at all accomplished artistically. So I was sure I would use it when I initially thought about this assignment. Black is the commonly used color in this kind of printing, so it lent itself well to the image of black fire on white fire, with its sharp contrast.

The idea behind the two yods is that, when the larger one is in the upper right, I feel very small in the face of a huge God. God is so huge, in fact, that God extends to the walls of the creation and encompasses all that is. The print may be turned upside down, and then I am the large encompassing body, in which God is a small piece. God is within me.

When I thought about the vav, I wanted to express what it is that separates me from God. I imagine blinders to seeing and accepting God in both the context of me being in God and of God being in me. The blinders vary in their thickness and strength and the amount they

ANDY:

Aleph, Separation from God

(fig. 1.13)

fig. 1.13. Andy, *Aleph, Separation from God.*

obscure my perception of God, so the line is narrower at one end. The length of the "blinder" makes it look from the small yod as if it could be part of a wall all around me, surrounding me, cutting me off from God, in a time of deep depression and despair. But the surrounding walls are actually God, and the "blinder" only masquerades as being part of God. I suppose then that the "blinder" is evil or the demoniac, which is present both within and without myself, trying to pass itself off as part of God, but really being a hindrance to getting to God.

After I had cut the block, I realized there was a strong resemblance between the large yod and a wave and the small yod and a drop of water. This is quite appropriate. I see myself as being a drop in the "waters" of creation, the waters of life. A song I know has the chorus: "We are drops of water in a mighty ocean, we are sons and daughters of one life." Alternately, human bodies are something like 98 percent water, so God can be a drop in the water of my being, a drop indistinguishable from all the other drops.

SISTER MARGARET:
Seven Samekhs and the Presence of God

Shortly after beginning the course I awakened one night and perceived myself suspended in the hollow of a large letter samekh, which filled most of the room. It did not fade away as dream images do but became more present the more awake I became. It had an air of independent reality, as if it had been waiting in the dark for some time, glowing with no one to be aware of it. Next day I looked up the letter samekh in Kushner's and Shahn's books on the alphabet[14] and there found it associated with God's support and shelter, and with God who upholds those who fall.

With these words, Margaret introduced her culminating project. Her Aleph, not included here, was only a warm-up. The full integration of the course and her healing came about as a result of the *samekh* vision and its artistic unfolding. Her materials came from the ragbag and rummage: some beads, cardboard, scrap-lumber molding, a Styrofoam container. Her concepts came from the ambiguous and paradoxic nature of both the Jewish and the Christian God.

I wanted to use ordinary things because one of the wonders of God's presence is that He lives in the ordinary, which now and then becomes transparent with grace and weighty with a reality denser than itself. Black and white are the predominant colors, because of what they call forth in each other and because of their connotations in the culture in which I live. The black cloth is the sort used for our habits. It stands for turning away from what is unnecessary. The spareness of life that it symbolizes gives a space in which the mystery of God can be experienced.

Margaret said she worked on all seven *samekhs* more or less simultaneously—moving from one to another as ideas and needs occurred to her. In fact, she actually started with No. 6, "God's Threatening Presence," climaxing the project with No. 7, "God's Presence in All Life's Seasons." Thus the two ever-present and paradoxic characteristics of God frame her work: God's benevolence and His or Her terrifying demonic opposite.

The Seven Samekhs, summarized here, proceed from spare simplicity to visual complexity, with greater detail on the most difficult aspects of God in numbers 5 and 6:

Thus *No. 1*, "God in Himself," consists only of the black *samekh* with a flawed fragment of pale rose quartz, "making a motionless gesture like the mute realization with which we stand before God unable to grasp Him in any way."

No. 2, "God and the Earth," is a black *samekh*, "which stands for the cold emptiness of space, with spare hints of earth and galaxy. A single ray of white light protects the earth."

No. 3, "God and the Questions," is a wooden molding into which cup hooks, representing question marks, have been screwed. "God is the greatest question of them all. The questions create reality and war against it, for they draw forth significance without explanation. A few years ago, when my mother and sister died within a month of each other, I realized that faith does not give answers. It only enables me to live with the questions."

No. 4, "A Day with You Is Worth a Thousand," is Psalm 84, a statement of God's fullness and nourishment of heart, shaped like a *samekh* in a simple pseudomicrography inspired by calligrapher Jay Greenspan, who writes: "What is important in a *sofer's* work is a principle called *kavvanah,* intention." As a *sofer,* you must take aim at a certain center within you and see each letter with your inner eye and inner hand, with the pure dedication that must accompany a spiritual activity.[15]

No. 5, "God's Respectful Presence," is an ominous, black, buckled Styrofoam "gift" box opening onto the glitter, dazzle, and danger of God's overt and covert presence. "The case and its fastenings are black to signify secrecy, concealment, and darkness in which nothing is seen. I chose a matte black because it is negative black, as opposed to the elegant shiny black. The case resembles a coffin because what is hidden or unknown in a relationship drains some of its life. When the case is opened, it reveals not only what was hidden (the fragments of broken colored glass) but also God's presence to what was hidden. I chose glass for its ambiguity: the light reveals its beauty and its danger. When the hidden is made known, it becomes another thread in the fabric of presence."

No. 6, "God's Threatening Presence," is a cat/snake face form, a *samekh* with its "wheel full of eyes" in the corner (fig. 1.14). "The presence of God is not always comforting. Sometimes my dreams are filled with the presence of an enemy, powerful and dangerous, who is always near and whom I never see. The letter is in Yerushalmi script, a triangular shape that suggests a cat face or snake face to go with the three inhuman eyes in the upper left-hand corner. I elevated the letter slightly so that it would be outlined by its own shadow in the threatening darkness in which it moves. When I finished, it reminded me of the Christian symbol of the triangle denoting the trinity, with an eye in it, denoting God all-present and all-knowing. This symbol was quite common when I was a child and always filled me with a dread of its cold surveillance. The model also brings to mind the 'wheel full of eyes' in Ezekiel 1:18, a figure frightening in its alienness."

Finally, *No. 7,* "God's Presence in All Life's Seasons." Four grand *samekhs* form a tree of life. The open face of each *samekh* admits the light of God in each season, stained glass in cardboard, tissue, and needlework. The six preceding Samekhs are each a single or conflicted image of God: mysterious, distant yet caring, the endless question, the language of nourishment, ambiguous Presence, frightening One. No. 7 in its mandala-quaternity integrates all opposites. It lightens the spare dignity of black and bursts into color with passionate restraint. It was Margaret's new self-portrait. It was also a witness to her transformation in presenting to the class—flushed, animated with understated wit, powerful in the sanctity of her revelation.

HOW THE SAMEKH PROJECT AROSE FROM THE CLASS ON JEWISH SPIRITUALITY

Recalling her initial unease as a Catholic nun in an experiential course on Jewish spirituality, Margaret later wrote (referring to Roger von Oech's book, *A Whack on the Side of the Head*)[16] how contact with the

fig. 1.14. *Sister Margaret, Wheel Full of Eyes.*

unfamiliar jars us into new ways of seeing what we already know. The Samekh arose from such a whack on the side of the head, an immediate experiencing of Jewish spirituality through symbols and symbolic actions connected with the Hebrew alphabet and the Jewish celebration of history and identity through the liturgical year.

The vitality and foreignness of the symbols and actions jolted my own experience into new dimensions and new integration. In another class I might have accumulated more facts about Judaism, but facts would not have given me the experience of Jewish spirituality that so electrified what I had lived as a Christian.

The tangibility of the three-dimensional models affected me physically in a different way from the effect of words. My body spoke in these models, and in the making of them, it juxtaposed in my awareness the different modes in which I have experienced God's presence: mystery, delight in Him, awe, dread and aversion, trust, desire for His company. Contrary to my usual way of learning, my body taught my mind in this project, and has brought a new integration to the way I experience God's presence to me and my presence to Him.

Three Alephs in Contemporary Art

One of the benefits of involvement art, the playful manipulation of common materials by the untrained, is the creation of greater awareness of and deeper access to the larger world of the visual arts, particularly in its abstract forms. Three examples of the continuing presence of the *aleph* in Jewish art suggest to participants that their own work is part of a tradition that has flourished from medieval manuscript sources, to the modern revival of the Hebrew manuscript, and into the galleries of contemporary art.

These three examples, though not strictly abstract, make accessible to the student both the artistic process and the commonality of theological and conceptual concerns. They are significant also because they merge the concerns and skills of mainstream contemporary art with the transcendent issues of religious art.

The first example, Beth Ames Swartz's *Aleph as the Shekhina* (see fig. 1.15, Color Section 1), was born of her personal quest for rootedness in the spiritual past of Israel. During her two years in Israel, Swartz created ten ritual-based sculptures, each associated with a particular site. At each site she echoed Divine Creation by combatting chaos and creating anew from the ravaged handmade papers she had originally produced. Only then could she re-form the fragments into the dappled, layered, gilded sculptures associated with each of the ten sites. If *aleph* is associated with God, her Aleph—created in the Kabbalistic hills of Safed—honors the Shekhina, the feminine aspect of the Divine. It is a configuration of four major sections composed of many smaller parts that open to expose its *aleph* within the negative space of its womb—black fire on white fire again.[17]

The second example is part of a larger work called *The Tent of Meeting*, conceived by Michele Zackheim during her pilgrimage to Jebel Musa, popularly known as Mt. Sinai. *The Tent* recalls the biblical tent of Moses, where "whoever sought the Lord would go out to the tent of meeting. . . . And the Lord would speak to Moses face to face, as one man speaks to another" (Exod. 33:7, 11). Incorporating Jewish, Christian, and Islamic imagery, *The Tent of Meeting* expresses the hope that all who trace their origins to Abraham may see and understand in a new way.

There are some 250 narrative vignettes on the Tent's walls, and each one is an assemblage of images drawn from a variety of sources and focusing on a particular biblical theme. The vignettes are executed on canvas panels measuring twenty-six feet by twelve feet. The panels are supported by a fiberglass frame and unified by a handsome mahogany center pole resembling the tree of life, which, like an axis mundi, unifies heaven and earth. Thus *The Tent* becomes a portable, sacred space.[18]

Relevant to our Aleph Exercise is Zackheim's panel on the receiving of the Torah on Mt. Sinai (see fig. 1.16, Color Section 1). Moses and the tablets are dwarfed by the awesome mountains of the Sinai wilderness supported by the wings of the cherubim, which extend the length of the Judaic wall. Hovering over him is the Divine Presence, represented as the pillar of cloud in the form of an *aleph*. Thus the voiceless first letter of the first word of the First Commandment is given visual articulation. Through her sophisticated use of hi-tech xerography, Zackheim combines two age-old characteristics of Jewish art — narrative and symbol.

One third, and final, example is the folk art Aleph of Michoel Muchnik, mentioned previously.

Muchnik divides the *aleph* into three parts. First is the upper right-hand *yod* stroke which is like an apostrophe; it can make visible some aspect of God's presence. The lower left *yod,* also like an apostrophe, can make visible some human quality, perhaps a reflection of the Divine image. The diagonal *vav* stroke demonstrates the way the human being and God are connected. In a charming down-to-earth interpretation by Muchnik, the family seated at the Sabbath table becomes the human reflection of the Divine sphere; the Jewish practice of God's commandments — the mitzvot (attendance at *shul,* meaning "synagogue"; the lit Sabbath candles; the mezuzzah affixed to the doorpost) — is the way these traditional Jews make the Divine–human connection.

Conclusion

Probably the most significant achievement of the Aleph Workshop has been the discovery of the participants that they can articulate a connection with the Divine Presence, however they define that illusory Being, through a simple process that requires neither talent, nor wisdom, nor saintliness. Not only is the connection achievable, but it is usually honest. The art of making an Aleph gives autonomy to our hands and our bodies — hence, direct access to feelings. The result is that for the moment we can sidestep the rational, cleverly manipulative, and defensive processes of our minds. The Alephs disclose our tension, fear, yearning, and awe, our quarrels with and our love for the Divine connection. Once these thoughts are made visible, all our academic theological training can be brought forward to engage in further dialogue, unifying mind and body, rational and feeling modes, verbal and nonverbal, linear and imaginal thinking.

Additional benefits are an understanding of the role of language as the means for the Divine connection in Jewish thought, a grasp of the mystical and rational modes in the transmission of Torah, and an entrée into the thought of Mircea Eliade about sacred space.

Finally, the workshop can create a community out of disparate individuals who discover how much they have in common as human beings. In an ecumenical atmosphere emphasizing common theological concerns that underlie diverse expression, the workshop also gives articulate voice to the Jewish roots of Christianity.

Even though handmade midrash has no aesthetic goals, the activity begins to access to those untutored in art a growing appreciation of the problems of abstraction, composition, and the role of spiritual concerns in the creative process. Thus the inclusion of the *aleph* in art from the medieval to the modern period is meaningful, terminating in the three recent Alephs of Beth Ames Swartz, Michele Zackheim, and Michoel Muchnik.

The Aleph Workshop: Summary

OBJECTIVES

To appreciate the role of language in connecting with God; to understand the symbol set of the *aleph* in its graphic, phonic, and numerologic *(gematria)* functions; to appreciate both the rational and mystical roles of the *aleph-bet* in Jewish thought; to explore the concept of sacred space in comparative religion; to experience the Divine–human connection by creating one's own personal Aleph; to create a community out of disparate individuals.

PRIMARY TEXTS

Ben Shahn, *The Alphabet of Creation.*

RECOMMENDED READINGS

Betty Edwards, *Drawing on the Artist Within.*

Mircea Eliade, *The Sacred and the Profane.*

Jo Milgrom, "Some Consequences of the Image Prohibition in Jewish Art," in *Religion and Law.*

Gershom Scholem, *On the Kabbalah and Its Symbolism.*

See chapter Notes for additional related readings.

MATERIALS REQUIRED

1 For the *aleph* in the language of lines: plain white paper, pencils, and erasers.

2 For the *aleph* collage done in class: colored construction paper and glue.

3 For the *aleph* done outside of class: Imagination is the limit.

PROCEDURE

1 Presentation of *aleph* symbolism and texts as done in this chapter.

2 Presentation of *aleph* in the visual arts.

3 Explanation of the language of lines and preliminary signature exercise.

4 Preliminary exercise in analog drawings.

5 Options for creating a sensory *aleph:*
   a. an *aleph* in the language of lines, and/or
   b. an *aleph* collage
   c. an *aleph* by other methods, achieved out of class.

6 Participants discuss their work in small groups.

7 Participants write about their personal Alephs.

8 Discussion of *alephs* in contemporary art.

9 Feedback; ideas for exploration and application.

Notes

1. Gershom Scholem, *On the Kabbalah and Its Symbolism* (New York: Schocken, 1974), 167–168.

2. Ibid., 38.

3. Ben Shahn, *The Alphabet of Creation* (New York: Pantheon, 1954) (cover illustration).

4. Mark Podwal, *A Book of Hebrew Letters* (Philadelphia: The Jewish Publication Society, 1978), page *nun.*

5. Scholem, *On the Kabbalah and Its Symbolism,* 29–30.

6. Gershom Scholem, "The Names of God and the Linguistic Theory of the Kabbalah," *Diogenes* 79 (1972):59–70.

7. Gershom Scholem, *Mada'e Ha-Yahadut II* (Jerusalem: 1927) 201–19 (Heb.). See also Jo Milgrom, "Some Consequences of the Image Prohibition in Jewish Art," in *Religion and Law,* E. Firmage, B. Weiss, and J. W. Welch (eds.) (Winona Lake, Wis.: Eisenbrauns, 1990), 263–299.

8. Mircea Eliade, *The Sacred and the Profane* (New York: Harcourt, Brace and World, 1959), 26.

9. Elie Wiesel, *The Golem* (New York: Summit, 1983), 101.

10. The Aleph of Michoel Muchnik can be seen in *Hadassah Magazine,* vol. 64, no. 5 (January 1983):15.

11. Betty Edwards, quoting George Orwell in *Drawing on the Artist Within* (New York: Simon & Schuster, 1986), 50–51.

12. Ibid., 56–70.

13. Edward Edinger, *Ego and Archetype* (New York: Penguin, 1974), 3–36.

14. Lawrence Kushner, *The Book of Letters* (New York: Harper & Row, 1975), 44–45; Shahn, *The Alphabet of Creation,* page *samekh.*

15. Jay Seth Greenspan, *Hebrew Calligraphy* (New York: Schocken, 1981), xix.

16. Roger von Oech, *A Whack on the Side of the Head* (New York: Warner, 1988).

17. Beth Ames Swartz, *Israel Revisited* exhibition catalog (Scottsdale, Ariz.: B. Swartz, 1981); see introduction by Harry Rand, 3–18.

18. Anna Walton, ed., *Tent of Meeting* exhibition catalog and guide (Santa Fe, N.Mex: The Tent of Meeting, 1985), 7.

Workshop 2

Creation Through Analogy:
An Introduction to Synectics

This chapter describes three separate exercises that involve close readings of Genesis 1, the story of Creation. The first exercise confronts the challenge of creating light as a personal experience without diminishing its cosmic grandeur. The normal order of the Handmade Midrash Workshop—textual study followed by an art exercise—is reversed; instead, the visual results of the exercise become the organic context out of which the leader may draw attention to issues in the text as well as to a number of Creation myths and theories that are evoked by the work of the participants.

The second exercise also involves the creation of light, but here it is based on the study of the structure of Genesis 1 and its relationship to Exodus 19 and 34. Light is an important part of the Sinai experience; we recall that Moses was transfigured by light, unaware when he came off the mountain "that the skin of his face beamed." Through our encounter with these three texts from the Torah (Gen. 1, Exod. 19, and Exod. 34) participants learn that light is the image of God. When they themselves "create light," it is with the idea that creation also signals God's revelation.

The third exercise on the creation theme focuses on the Biblical Narrator's use of purposeful repetition and artful omission to disclose other fascinating and bewildering facets of Creation, such as the irregular use of the formula "and He saw that this was good." This discussion is prelude to the exercise itself, in which creative visual analogies call attention to what is good and what is deficient in Creation and what this tells us about the human condition. These discoveries can be applied effectively to the process of turning things around as a new year approaches or working for *tikkun olam,* the repair of the world, all the year round.

My own preoccupation with beginnings and endings received affirmation from *The Common Expositor* by Arnold Williams,[1] a volume that I came across as a graduate student some years ago. In my reading of this history of Bible commentaries during the English Renaissance, a curious fact surfaced: No less than forty commentaries on Genesis alone and thirteen on the Pentateuch rolled from the presses of continental Europe between 1527 and 1633. Why those dates, and why Genesis? I wondered. Who lived during those years? I asked. In the visual arts, there was Michelangelo, Titian, Rubens, El Greco, and Rembrandt; in literature, Shakespeare, Spenser, Cervantes, Donne, and Milton; in science and theology, Copernicus, Galileo, and Luther. During this period of great intellectual and artistic enlightenment, it still seemed that Genesis was essential to understanding the development of human history. Addressing themselves to Genesis, scholars centered their theories of philosophy, science, politics, and religion on a divinely inspired account of cosmic beginnings.

Alan Watts personalizes our obsession with beginnings and endings in an introduction to a series on myth and experience:

> Nothing is more provocative than the idea of death. It is because men know that they will die that they have created the arts, sciences, the philosophies and religions. For nothing is more thought-provoking than the thought which seems to put an end to thought: "What will it be like to go to sleep and never wake up?" Irresistibly this seems to suggest a corollary: "Where and who was I before my father and mother conceived me?" For the unthinkable-after-death appears to be the same as the unthinkable-before-birth, so that if once I came out of nothing, the odds are that I can come again and again. . . . Nothing seems to create something by implication just as low implies high. This is why the cycle of birth, death, and rebirth is about the most basic theme of myth and religion.[2]

Every culture—ancient and recent, primitive and sophisticated— has its own accounts of beginnings and endings. In the mid-seventies, an intense popular interest in ethnic origins was seen, for example, in the explorations of Armenian, Jewish, and Black heritages in, respectively, Michael Arlen's *Passage to Ararat* (1975), Irving Howe's *World of Our Fathers* (1976), and Alex Haley's *Roots* (1976). Test-tube conceptions and space voyages are yet other aspects of the indefatigable human quest for origins. As for the creation accounts in Genesis, the perpetually recurrent furor over the literal truth of Scripture and the truths of science is again a reflex of our concern with origins and purpose.

I have included the preceding excerpts to place my own sustained fascination with creation into a larger context. But my concerns are less with ultimate beginnings and endings than with a grounded response to personal reality and the development of skills with which to promote change in human relationships. Therefore, our concerns with creation and other biblical narratives are directed to that purpose.

Exercise 1: Experiencing the Creation of Light

The purpose of the first meditation is less an appreciation of creation than an attempt to experience the nothingness that precedes it. This, of course, we cannot do; but how close can we come? Only if we approach nothingness can we experience the words "Let there be Light; and there was Light."

I begin by having the participants read the biblical account of Creation together, pausing after each day's increment. I ask the participants to listen, to hear, and to personalize. Whatever is created that day should not be an intellectual abstraction but a personal association with the process of creation. At the cry of "*Yehi Or*, Let there be Light," participants are called upon to dip into their memories, as recent as yesterday or light years ago, and open up to a private experience of Light.

Next is the process of addition, which is usually pleasant, mounting the increments of each day. In the addition meditation, I encourage individuals to smell the sea; marvel at the heavens; puzzle about the light from those heavenly bodies; imagine the earth giving birth to animals.

The subtraction exercise is much harder for it is harder to subtract from Creation, counting backwards from Day Seven. It can be shocking to realize that you are starting out without civilization; without house or car; without city streets; without underwear and socks; without animals and birds; and then, with a shudder, without all the people you know and love. We are back to Day One and the five primeval elements of Creation: the deep, darkness, water, formlessness, and the wind/spirit of God. These are the very conditions associated with birth.

When we cry out, "Let there be Light," it is with the joy of emergent consciousness. In other words, it is really the cry of birth. Something new has emerged into light from deep, dark, watery formlessness. No wonder the word *Bereshit* ("In the beginning") finds its root in *rosh* ("head"), which calls to mind the crowning of the head as it emerges from the darkness of the birth canal. Even the Old English root of *beginning*, namely *ginn*, has to do with a gap, an abyss, or an opening.

Now the scene is set for the first exercise on the creation of Light. The assignment is to "create" Light out of darkness by freely tearing and pasting black and white shapes. I distribute black and white construction paper and no tools. Accidents happen more easily in tearing without tools. There is less control and therefore greater opportunity to honor the role of chance in the creative act. I remind participants of the pleasure in loosely directed play. I repeat the caveat against judgment and intimidation. I hand out a reading on light, providing several literary associations that students find helpful in freeing images (see Appendix 1). I encourage participants to let themselves float, to daydream to no immediate benefit, to be like children at play. The kinship between art and play has long been recognized, but the kinship between play and all forms of creative adult activity has been overlooked. The pleasure of play generates creative energy; it is therefore an end in itself.

Participants have twenty minutes in which to complete the exercise. Their torn forms will be coarse but vital. Unintended movement will play its inevitable role as their souls bring forth images that the rational mind may at first consider worthless but, once evoked, may become symbols that mediate the opposing forces in our lives. The forms, in their own time, will reveal their own meaning.

What is happening here is actually a form of synectics. The term, which is of Greek derivation, refers to a type of metaphor that joins different and apparently irrelevent elements, often giving them new meaning. It is a theory that recognizes the role of pre-conscious psychological mechanisms in human creativity. Initially used to enhance problem solving in science and technology, synectics is being explored by William J. J. Gordon and others for its potential usefulness in education.[3]

When I first began to use techniques such as the exercise in the creation of light, I expected that the synectic process would produce new and deep personal meanings for the participants. What I did not anticipate was that major theological and artistic issues would surface from the collective unconscious into the torn black and white forms. The crude collages of torn paper illustrated Eliade's theory of sacred space; they embodied mythological and mystical creation theories; they represented various concepts of Light—Light as transformation, as divine succor, as consciousness of duality, and more. One collage even presented revelation as an audible, not visible, experience, expressing the fear of making a visible Divine image. All subjects for academic research and theory making came from the organic situation created by art play and personal interaction. This was by no means an arbitrary imposition of a syllabus, which has only chance relevance to anyone's life issues.

This handmade midrash experience develops in three stages—the tearing and pasting, then the verbal reflections, and finally the writing. At each stage, something additional is revealed. For some, text and personal experience achieve a new synthesis. Often, motifs appear that enable the leader to move organically from the art work to deeper levels of textual meaning and artistic exploration. Sometimes the responses are deeply personal, generating further insight and even healing. (Whatever "therapy" takes place results from the interaction among the participants and the insight achieved by an individual in a given moment. The workshop is not led by a professional therapist and makes no such claims, nor should the leader attempt to go further into psychotherapy.)

My dark page is all windows, seven windows waiting for me to open. Help me say, "Let there be Light." "Behind me and before me You hem me in" (Psalm 139).

MARTHA ANN:
*Darkness
Means Loss*

Martha Ann identifies darkness with recent losses in her family; her work is a prayer for rescue from sorrow. The passage from Psalms is not so much an expression of protection as of being trapped in the darkness, pleading for release into light. She asks for help but knows she must take the initiative and tear open the windows to tear away the darkness. It is only the first meeting, yet the class is supportive. The art play has the unforeseen effect of releasing tension and making a group out of disparate individuals in an atmosphere of unexpected friendship.

In synectic terms, Martha Ann's visual midrash is a symbolic analogy, what Gordon calls "viewing the problem qualitatively with the condensed suddenness of a poetic phrase." Light is a window. Not just one window but seven, the Light of the primeval week. Martha Ann's metaphoric use of window for Light is also kinesthetic. Once a passage for Light is created it is able to reach her. Light thus becomes synonymous with the vehicle of its passage, the window. The art play enables her to release metaphors within herself that might otherwise have been blocked.

The mercurial metaphor is the foundation for the Bible–midrash relationship. Thus the Light of Day One and the window acquire each other's features. As a result, Martha Ann now has a deeply personal association with Genesis 1:3 through symbolic preconscious play, where something commonplace (a window) is used as a metaphor to make the remote (Divine Light) familiar. Her symbolic analogy also has personal repercussions: In the process of synectics, she is "enlightened," thus becoming her own source of Light.

Gordon asserts that whereas literary metaphor is usually after the fact, namely decorative or descriptive, synectic or creative metaphor is generative or inductive, before the fact. It is a leap in the process of discovery. Gordon also turns to the physical sciences, affirming that the metaphoric nature of language is grounded in neurophysiology—that the nervous system returns not direct impressions of the external world but indirect symbolic representations. The roots of language, therefore, are in metaphor, not in utilitarian principle. Gordon reminds us that Helen Keller learned her first word, *water*, when her hand was plunged into a cold moving stream; her initial awareness of words was kinesthetic and relational. Thus in a rudimentary sense, it was a metaphoric, not a utilitarian, association.[4]

I take the synectic method one step further by putting a device in the hands of participants to enhance the workings of their imaginations. The simple tearing of paper forms is a catalyst that generates images, which then give birth to metaphors. Since forms are the voice of the individual psyche, an unmediated bond is created between the individual and the biblical text, which is the first and last objective of the search for meaning.

CLIFF:
The Birth Imagery of Bereshit

I tear the black paper leaving a jagged area of white underneath. The rip spreads outward like light exploding, an egg cracking, the light expanding in those cracks. I want to show the cracking of the cosmic egg. Fertile feminine darkness is pierced and fertilized by light. The darkness is passive yet full; the light is active. They are not in conflict but are explosively creative together.

Cliff is aware of his association with the primordial point and the *sefirot* ("emanations") of Kabbalistic creation. His art play stimulated a discussion of the Lurianic theory of creation: While God is contracting Himself to make space for the less than perfect world, something unforeseen happens. There is an unaccountable shattering of those mysterious vessels of light (the "fall"). Adam, representing all humanity, then gets the assignment of *tikkun olam*, to repair the evil and restore divine harmony to the world. Interestingly, the "fall" is a no-fault case, and Adam gets a lifetime commission out of it.[5]

KAY:
The Three-tiered Universe

Kay folds her white paper into an M shape in which ancients visualized the three-tiered universe, with the two peaks being the pillars of the sky. The central point of the M is the navel of the earth, and the dark, crumpled, disordered paper below can be seen as Sheol, the limbo station of souls after death (the biblical image of the three-tiered universe).[6]

The black sheet is chaos, darkness, the waters of the deep, echoing Tiamat, the goddess of the deep who is sliced up by Marduk, who then creates the world from her material, in Enuma Elish, *a prebiblical Babylonian creation epic. Since gods are regularly demoted in the Bible, Tiamat sneaks in as "tehom," "deep," a personalized noun, but without divine identity.*

By negating Tiamat's mythic fertility, Kay affirms the biblical view of asexual creation by God's will alone.

The white sheet is order, the breath of God, a nesting bird [the spirit of God hovering]. Since the white is above the black, order is being imposed on chaos. No adhesive has been used. The powerful shape of order itself does this. The act of creation is ongoing, and only the power of the spirit keeps chaos at bay.

Nancy focuses sharply on one of the more hidden concepts of Genesis 1: the true inseparability of Light and darkness. God separates Light and darkness and names them "day" and "night." Yet we hear the recurring refrain at the end of each of six days' labor, ". . . and it was evening and it was morning."

NANCY:
The Inseparability of Light and Dark

My immediate impression was that of the paper folded back on itself, closely adhered, with no space between it. The relationality of Lght and dark—the inseparability of the concepts. Then the two sheets are wrenched apart, seen as distinct in a false way. If I come to know the terms that way, I must backtrack to the relationality. It has struck me again and again in life how my first encounter defines what something "is." To know something is to first separate it off, and then the relationality must be perceived. The separateness, the naming, can only be a tool for discerning connections.

Separateness comes from the process of individuation that characterizes Genesis 1. The verb *l'havdil,* "to distinguish," appears repeatedly in Days One, Two, and Four, as does the phrase *l'mino,* "of its own kind," like a refrain in Days Three, Five, and Six. Everything is individuated in Chapter 1, in order for opposites to come together in a new relationship, except the earthling, *ha-adam,* whose sexual distinctions are completed in Chapter 2.

Mircea Eliade's comments are particularly helpful here:

Out of the chaos of undifferentiated matter, God brings order by distinguishing and separating the elements: Light and dark; sea, land, and sky; solid, liquid, and gaseous; animal from plant; then in all their details, each form of life in its own kind; and man and woman. Only when everything is distinct and separated from everything else can a new order be established; the opposites can come together in a new relationship: man with woman; human with animal and plant. It is as if spirit and soil had to be separated from one another in order, after their "divorce," to become "married" again. A law of creation seems to appear: The substances must be sorted out, separated and opposed, in order to connect again in a new way; as with the individual human being, the differentiation of sex becomes more and more precise before the opposite poles can unite for a new generation.[7]

Where, then, do evening and morning suddenly come from? They are not created; they are tossed in like a bonus. For there can be no absolute separation of Light and dark. Rather, there are infinite gradations between black and white, between morning and night. What a gift! Robert Sacks writes that inherent ambiguity was created with evening and morning.[8] Two other "unlimiteds" are named in Genesis 1, the heavens and the seas. In each case, separation, or naming, results in a shadowy area of ambiguity, of transition. Where heaven meets land, horizon comes into being; where sea meets land, the seashore emerges.

Consider now the handmade midrash by Rochelle, who tore open the darkness so that light could be born and in so doing allowed a shadow of transition to appear. Again, Hebrew is insightful. The root for *morning* is *b-q-r*, "to slit," "split," "scrutinize," or "break through"; hence, "to *become* morning." The root for *evening* is *e-r-v*, "to enter" (referring to the sun), "to go down"; hence, "to *become* evening" (a blending of the light?).[9]

NIKI:

Binary Opposites

Niki produced a black horn spewing white streamers of light as sound, reflecting the biblical concept that revelation was heard, not seen: "You heard the voice of the words but saw no likeness" (Deut. 4:12). For the written follow-up, she produced a list of words that contains the tension between opposites:

first	last		speak	listen
front	back		create	kill
light	dark		white	black
form	empty		hungry	full
good	bad		slow	fast

stop
start
stop
start

Through these contrasts of color, form, and movement, Niki expressed Light as the consciousness of all the dualities of life and death. This is the central preoccupation of religion everywhere. As anthropologist Edmund Leach puts it:

Human thinking requires binary opposites, what something is, and is not. But religion seeks to deny the link between the dual pair, life and death. It does this by creating a mystical "other" perfect world where the dead are perpetually alive. Ironically because this other world is perfect, God comes to be associated there, not here. Thus the eternal quest of humanity is to bridge the gap between man and God.[10]

The Zohar calls the Divine Light of Day One, *ohr ganuz,* "hidden Light." The presence of evil, its dark opposite in the world, causes its concealment. *Ohr ganuz* thus becomes the binary opposite of solar light. It is therefore kept in reserve for the benefit of the just in the world to come.

Sandy tore a small triangular shaft of light, whose tiny sharp point emanated from the corner of the black page. She wrote:

SANDY:
Wherever God Is, Is Center

Wherever God is, is Center. Darkness and Light, dynamic, impacting on each other. At the moment of Light—perhaps as dramatic as a beam piercing the darkness, or as subtle as the infinitely quiet approach of dawn—blackness fades and yields to the radiance that comes from the God-Center.

Thus Light is God's presence, God's space. Did Sandy know that the root of *deity* and *divine* is the Sanskrit root, *div,* meaning "light"? She found a way to distinguish between ordinary space and sacred space and a way to connect with sacred space. Her shaft of light operates as an axis mundi. Eliade reminds us that all space is not homogeneous and that the religious person strives to transcend secular space because she or he cannot live without the Divine connection. The same concept, a point become a triangular shaft of light, is illustrated by sculpture that is architecture, in Richard Lippold's dramatic baldachin, a canopy of Light suspended over the altar in St. Mary's Cathedral in San Francisco. Whether latent in the lay person or active in the artist, the images all originate in the same collective reservoir.

Jayson's drawing shows, in his own words,

JAYSON:
Light Is Associated with Growth

radiance, the creation of pattern, order, symmetry . . . a skeleton of rays, the fuzzy paper-torn flesh growing from these rays contained within the frame, yet expanding toward these limits; or is it the frame that expands and draws the Light to its ever-widening edge.

Jayson's association of Light with growth is basic to the Hebrew text. The verbs *to look* and *to sprout* share the Hebrew root *n-v-t; to peek* and *to blossom* share another root, *h-ts-ts.* Certain figures of speech do likewise: One might say, for example, "It is beginning to grow on me," to indicate that perception (i.e., vision) of something is increasing. The relation of growth to light and fire occurs in the well-known vision of the Burning Bush. Finally, it should be recalled that the menorah is a tree of light, originally patterned after the almond tree (Exod. 37:17–24)[11] associated with the Tree of Life.

HOPE:

The Butterfly of Transformation

Hope wanted to express the idea that darkness must be crushed in order for light to emerge. In her drawing, the butterfly became the symbol of light penetrating and emerging from darkness, a symbol of transformation. Intention notwithstanding, her autonomous hands delivered a different message, namely, of the transforming character of enlightenment. The victory turns out to be not in the simplistic triumph of white over black or light over darkness but in the gradual, healthy growth of consciousness.

In Hope's handmade midrash, the butterfly appears as the soul being breathed into the resurrected bodies in the vision of dry bones from Ezekiel 37 and in the wall paintings of the Dura-Europos Synagogue of third-century Syria. The same image of soul as butterfly appears centuries earlier on a Roman sarcophagus in which the original man is formed (enlivened) by Prometheus but given his soul-butterfly by Athena. The theme migrates through time and appears again a thousand years later in the mosaics of San Marco.

Exercise 2: Structure Conveys Meaning in the Encounter with God

One can read the six days of Creation as a sequential development of our physical universe, with humanity the final creation. Generally, the sequence makes good sense. It gives one theological pause, however, to note in the second Creation narrative that Adam is created first. The careful reader may also observe that although the sequence of the first Creation narrative seems fairly orderly, there is something strange about the creation of Light. Light is created on Day One, but the sun and its heavenly hosts do not appear until Day Four.

If we divide the six days of Creation into two pairs of three days each, we see a parallel structure that is more informative:

Day One: Light   Day Four: Sun, moon, and stars
Day Two: Sky and seas   Day Five: Fish and birds
Day Three: Dry land and vegetation Day Six: Animals and earthling

Whereas the first three days are concerned with the stable elements of Creation, the second group is concerned with the users of the elements. Thus Day Three and Day Six are a pair because animals and human beings need dry land and vegetation; Day Two and Day Five are another pair because fish and birds are users of sea and sky. The most curious pair, however, is Day One and Day Four: What are the implications if we say that the sun, moon, and stars are the users of the Light that is created on Day One?[12]

Most significant is that our text seems to be denying the automony of the sun, moon, and stars, which elsewhere in the ancient Near East are independent deities. In the Genesis cosmology, they are not even named but are called only the greater and lesser lights. To name the sun *Shemesh* would be to utter the name of a sun god. Far from being an autonomous deity, the sun is subservient to the One and only God who is the source of the Divine Light of Day One. In fact, Light is the image of God. We open our eyes each morning to Light, which is sunlight only secondarily; primarily, it is the daily reaffirmation of God's presence in Creation.

From outside circles of traditional Jewish learning, yet strangely resembling Jewish mysticism, comes support from psychologist Gerald Epstein for a view of Divine revelation as not *verbal* (linear, sequential, rational, logical, intellectual) but *imaginal* (experiential, acausal, nonrational, intuitive, and associative). In his book *Waking Dream Therapy*, Epstein synthesizes traditional psychotherapeutic methods with the insights of Eastern theology:

> It is well known that many religious and spiritual experiences which convey knowledge to the individual such as Moses at Mt. Sinai are not describable in words and frequently are attainable only when the content of linear thought is slowed, stopped, emptied. . . . It is only when such non-linear thinking is embraced that a holistic (incorporating the concept holy, healthy) experience can happen. It is here, then, that a possibility of healing asserts itself through an experience which abrogates the activity of linear thought.[13]

Psychology is no stranger to visual imagery. Both Jung and Freud evoked active imagination and visual scenes from their patients. However, Epstein's method is particularly welcome because he counsels that "restoration of health is a process that includes the holy, a concept that has generally been avoided or ignored by most Western therapies. If therapy tries to invalidate man's relationship to God, it does so at the expense of dissipating our fundamental wholeness. If this is the case then the whole picture of a man's potentials cannot be addressed." Just as Epstein restores the healing perspectives of religion within psychology, my approach affirms the neglected functions of psychology in the study of religious texts and experience.

Divine Light, then, is the link between Creation in Genesis 1 and revelation in Exodus 19–34, the Sinai experience. One could say that Genesis 1 is the universal experience of God, whereas Exodus is the Jewish experience. We continue to work with black and white construction paper for these final examples. Preparation for this part of the activity includes discussion of the nonverbal aspects of revelation (refer to "Black Fire on White Fire," Chapter 1). In reading Exodus 19:16–18, we emphasize the word *va-yeherad*, the fear and trembling of both the people and the mountain; in Exodus 34:29–35, we stress the encounter with God in which Moses' appearance is transformed by radiance.

The desired effect of this handmade midrash is to lift participants out of the restraints of historical sequence, to free the imaginal life from the familiar, overrationalized view of a problem. The resulting images make one's emotions visible to the individual, to the intelligence of the heart. Imaginal seeing allows one to get outside and to view one's self from a nonhabitual vantage point. It is like bending over and looking at something familiar from between your legs. What is thus seen brings with it the power to change one's fixed-in-concrete relationships.[14]

Recalling the Light of Genesis 1 and of Exodus 19 and 34, the assignment was to tear black and white construction paper showing how it might feel to encounter the Divine. Two of the participants are in striking contrast to one another. The first merely tears the shape of a crown. She says simply that the exalted experience leaves her feeling every inch royalty. The second person, using white paper as the background for the Divine, places himself in the corner, a tiny frightened owlish face around pinpoint eyeballs, wreathed in black hair and beard. He says that confronting the Divine reduces him to a nothing (even though he is high in the upper right corner). Both achieve a personal analogy in a blurt of association—integrated, compressed, and completely opposite.

Remarkably, the specific yet universal responses of these two, in their polarity, explicitly echo the Psalmist. Grandeur and humility meet under the sky in Psalm 8:

> When I behold Your heavens, the work of Your fingers,
> the moon and stars that You set in place,
> what is man that You have been mindful of him,
> mortal man, that You have taken note of him,
> that You have made him little less than divine,
> and adorned him with glory and majesty. . . .

The responses of these two persons enable us to view Psalm 8 in a midrashic relationship to Genesis 1. Psalm 8 is the affective response of awe and appreciation to the discursive, understated account of Creation in Genesis 1. These diverse passages are brought into a direct relationship by the creative analogy of handmade midrash; the result: a personal connection with a sacred text is bonded, in which the cognitive and experiential modes successfully complement one another.

Israel is terrorized by the Sinai event, but Moses is transfigured by the Light. He returns to his people radiant with the second set of commandments. Unknown to him, the skin of his face shines (or beams).

Varya is touched by the notion that both the mountain and the people tremble. In answer to the questions, What does it feel like to confront the Divine? and What is my image of God in form?, she works with black and white art paper and comes up with a "before" and an "after." She writes:

VARYA:
Encounter with God, Before and After
(fig. 2.1)

It feels like a first-time experience filling me with excitement and a feeling of intimacy within myself—trying to make contact with a real feeling lying dormant yet yearning to be brought to light. I think of God as an encompassing radiance. I take the whole sheet of white paper (the "before") and then add the black square of mankind's ignorance and separation from the Divine, due to his lack of insight and understanding. Within the darkness I place the white square of man. He is closed off from God.

Moving to Moses' confrontation (the "after"), I feel that his direct contact with God leaves his usual "self" shattered, as physically represented by the trembling of the earth. Within him, then, God appears through the revelation on Mt. Sinai, as the Divine is within all of us; through the shattering of his earthly self (the torn black paper), the Divine appears as described by the Light shining from him. The experience is very strong and moving.

Between the pride of the first participant and the humility of the second is the introspective sensitivity of Varya. In each case the human being is blocked off from God by his or her ego. The liturgy of the High

fig. 2.1. Varya, *Encounter with God, Before and After.*

Holy Days is helpful, echoing Psalm 34:19, "God is near to those who are broken-hearted," the tearing that makes it possible for one to experience *t'shuva*—a turning around, a reversal of orientation, healing, in the vocabulary of Epstein. Is it the cracking, the trembling of the ego that invites God's Light, the real "Self," to enter? When the imagination confronts vital human issues, "the exalted state . . . adheres to holiness," says Rabbi Abraham I. Kook.[15]

JIM:

God Within, God Without

(fig. 2.2)

Jim uses the black as background and places upon it a large eye and eyebrow. The pupil of this eye is the figure of a person. Rays emanate from the figure in four directions. I asked two questions: How does the art play connect you to the text? How does the text dialog with your own self-perception? Jim wrote:

I am Moses. I am glorified and made radiant in the presence of God. I am God. I am the source of light and channel to people broken and hiding in the shadows.

Jim then analyzed his process, which began as a play on words. His mind moved from *ohr*, a homonym meaning either "light" or "skin," to *ayin*, meaning both "eye" and "source/spring." Jim continued:

In putting together the picture of the eye, I am struck by a hesitation to make the figure in the eye Moses or God. I become comfortable with the ambiguity of the God-man tension in experience; that glorification is to be found only in this tension."

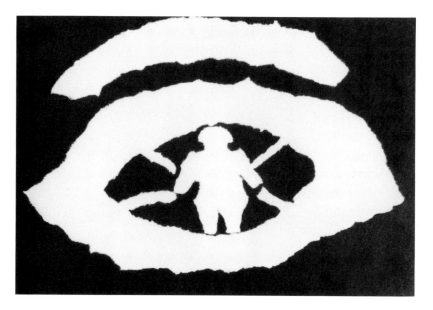

fig. 2.2. Jim, *God Within, God Without.*

In the interplay of human and Divine, black and white, Jim confronted the synectic category of personal analogy: "I am Moses, I am God," the paradox of God's being at once at our center and our circumference; God within and God without.

Some time later I came across a verbal and a visual text I wish I could have shared that day with Jim and the class, to show how "on target" he was; how an ancient midrash had anticipated his intuition and a famous contemporary artist had mirrored his imagination. The verbal text is Targum Jonathan on Exodus 19:17, "Moses led the people out of the camp toward God, and they took their places at the foot of the mountain." The Targum, relishing word play, reads "foot of the mountain" as "under the mountain," an acceptable translation of *taḥtit*. The Targum continues: The mountain became transparent, like an *aspaklaria,* meaning "window/mirror." Thus Israel's vision of God through the mountain was through a window which was also a mirror; God within and God without.

The visual text was a painting by Salvador Dali, *Moses After Michelangelo.* Dali copied Michelangelo's famous sculpture of the horned Moses, placing Moses' head within an eye. I am certain Jim knew neither source; again, the reservoir of the collective unconscious surfaced in his collage.[16]

Exercise 3: Purposeful Repetition and Artful Omission

Let us focus on the clever repetition and omission of two recurring sentences in the Genesis cosmology: "God saw that this was good" and "And it was so." Can the very presence or absence of those phrases tell us in greater depth what they mean? Here, too, textual study culminates in an art activity: a "self-portrait" of the student reflected in images of "good" and "so."

The first step is to take an inventory of the appearances of the sentence "And God saw that this was good": once on Day One, twice on Day Three, once each on Days Four and Five; twice on Day Six (but not regarding man and woman); including, finally, a "very good" with regard to the totality of God's Creation. Why the absence of "good" on Day Two and on Day Six, with regard to Adam? Is there a connection between the two omissions?

Looking back to Day One, we see that a naming process is associated with coming into being. It is possible to "see" light once it is set against darkness. And so light and darkness, having been distinguished, can be named "day" and "night."

If we look at the details of what happens on Day Two, we see that God, in the manner of a metal worker, makes a firmament, which is like a lid on a pot. It is the lid on the earth that separates the upper waters from the lower waters. The image is the biblical portrayal of the three-tiered universe. Firmament and upper waters are now distinguishable, so the firmament is named, and sky comes into being. But the waters are not named because they are not yet distinct; they still cover everything.

Day Three opens with the gathering together of the waters under the sky, enabling the dry land to appear. At last the waters and the dry land have been separated from each other. Once distinguished as separate and complete entities, they can be named "oceans" and "land." Only then do we have the formula, "And God saw that this was good." From this we may conclude that the waters could not be named on Day Two because they were not yet finished and thus not yet ready for God's stamp of approval. If we apply this idea to Day Six, we perceive immediately that even as God put man and woman on earth He recognized the incompleteness of the human being.

There is still the matter of "And it was so." We learn that "so" (*khen*) comes from the Hebrew root *koon,* meaning "to be fixed," that is, to have a fixed place and function. If we follow the same sleuthing procedure through Genesis 1, our findings are equally intriguing. The light of Day One is not "so" ("fixed"), nor are fish and fowl or human beings. The light of Day One stands in a class by itself. Its place and role are part of the mystery of God's immanence. In the instances of fish and fowl and the human being, we understand that unfixedness means freedom, and the class is invited again to scour the text for the compensation provided against the danger of being unfixed and incomplete. "Blessing" is that compensation: "God blessed them" (Gen. 1:22, 28).

Blessing addressed to the fish and fowl means fruitfulness. Blessing addressed to Adam is more complex, for it includes the exercise of power over the rest of Creation and, by implication, over one's self. Unfixed (free) is no less complex. It means that Adam is the least programmed of all Creation and therefore maximally free to learn. (I believe that the unfixed attribute to fish and fowl applies to their apparent visible freedom of motion and not to what the ancients must surely have known, namely, the actual fixed nature of their seasonal migrations.)

From this analysis of Genesis 1 a pattern emerges in which it is better for one species to be free, incomplete, and blessed than for everything to be finished, unmysterious, and predictable. At this point, the group leaves the written word and turns to making images through paper play. The instructions are to show oneself, in three forms freely torn and pasted in a relationship, as free, incomplete, and blessed.

Colleen chose a red background for what she identifies as her awareness, growing, hope, and experience. She writes:

COLLEEN:
The Tree of All

(see fig. 2.3,
Color Section 1)

I started with my incompleteness—shaped like a pit whose bottom is ragged, mysterious, and extended beyond the edges of my awareness. Overlaid on my incompleteness is blessing—shaped like a tree, a life-giving, growing tree; its roots extend even further beyond my knowing and grow beyond my hopes, extending beyond the edge of my experience. Supported by the tree of blessing, a small three-dimensional winged "freedom" poises partly within my range of experience, partly extending beyond what I have known.

Colleen's self-portrait is a tree. The three required elements— incompleteness, freedom, and blessing—overlap and are therefore part of the tree. Incompleteness is part of the root system. In the text we saw it exactly that way—the "absence" of *tov* (good) is "ever-present," fundamental to the structure of Genesis 1. The blessing of unfathomable proportion exceeds her consciousness, yet it allows the incompleteness its space. Though she describes the incompleteness as a rough pit, it is also a well that nourishes the root system, which in turn is balanced (upper left) by the three-dimensional butterfly-shaped fruit of the blessing tree, her transformative freedom.

It is noteworthy that the image of the Cosmic Tree belongs to a coherent body of myths, rites, images, and symbols that compose what historian of religions Mircea Eliade calls "symbolism of the Center." It is an image that structures one's experience of the physical world and the world of the imagination. Like the Tree, imagination connects heaven and earth; it is rooted below and unites the luminous world of consciousness to the dark underworld of the unconscious. Like the Tree, the individual draws nourishment from the "heavenly" immaterial world of the intellect and the "earthly" material world of the senses. Like the Tree, the individual experiences periodic autumn and again regeneration and fruitfulness. Thus the Tree is an archetypal axis mundi (an axis of the world linking heaven and earth), and like the Tree, the centered individual needs to see himself or herself as a discrete vertical link between heaven and earth. In sum, the arborescent motif is one of the primary visual images, employed as early as the fourth millennium B.C.E., reflecting the human need to grasp the essential reality of the world.[17]

Because the arborescent motif is part of the shared treasury of human images, it is fitting for the reader to place Colleen's work into the iconographic context that the doer herself achieved intuitively. To supplement that treasury of tree images is a work unknown to the group, done twenty-five years ago by the gifted young artist Charles Knowles. His original woodcuts and senior project at the Putney School in Vermont, *The Psalm Book of Charles Knowles*,[18] can be seen

fig. 2.5. *Goddess as a Tree Nursing the Infant Pharaoh.* (*From* Othmar Keel, *Symbolism of the Biblical World.* New York: Crossroads, 1978, p. 186. Reprinted with permission.)

fig. 2.4. Charles Knowles, *Psalm 1.* (*From* Charles Knowles, *The Psalm Book of Charles Knowles.* New York: Viking & Pinnacle Press, 1959, p. 19. Reprinted with permission.)

at both the Museum of Modern Art in New York and at the Israel Museum in Jerusalem.

As a visual response to Psalm 1, the text of which he printed on a handpress and placed on the page facing the woodcut, Knowles did his self-portrait as a tree (fig. 2.4). He saw himself as the "happy/ fortunate man" of Psalm 1:

Like a tree planted beside streams of water
that yields its fruit in season,
whose foliage never fades
and whatever it produces, thrives.

His tree/self is sturdy, deep-rooted, and abundantly fruitful in his season, wholly successful, but there is a strange scattering of something to the left of the tree and close to its roots. Contrasting with the happy/fortunate man are the "ungodly who are like the chaff which the wind drives away." The chaff is the "ungodly" part of Charles Knowles, the chaotic, disorderly, even demonic; the incomplete part of the person, close to the roots; the hidden part of us; the mysterious shadow source that nourishes the creative freedom/fruit.

Like the contemporary aware individual who perceives the human self in arborescent forms, the ancients saw the original Divine Self also as a tree, nourishing humanity. An Egyptian illustration from the second millennium B.C.E. (fig. 2.5) shows the breast of the goddess emerging from the sycamore tree to suckle the young Pharaoh. The image gives clear expression to the Divine Presence therein.[19]

As the tree is a primary symbol in the human imagination, so are the seed and the spiral/serpent, evident in the work of Liz, who wrote:

LIZ:
The Blessing Spirals Like a Serpent

Surrounding, enfolding, and grounding me is God's blessing, the blue circle; it gives me life and God's love. Springing forth from the blessing is my freedom, spiraling up and sometimes confining as it folds in on itself, making me two-dimensional. I have the freedom to confine myself. In the center is the seed, the egg. It is potential, not complete. It is also secure in the blessing and touched by the freedom. There is freedom and choice in my incompleteness.

The spiral emerging from the egg has at least two powerful meanings. First, it recalls the serpent of the ancient Near East, which is associated with feminine regenerative power. Since the feminine is in turn associated with the earth (bringer of new life and receiver of the dead), the ambiguous serpent has come to represent both life and death, the marriage of opposites and their synthesis into a higher form.[20]

Second, the spiral suggests a labyrinth representing the long and difficult initiatory journey of the hero and of all the demons, battles, and fears to be conquered en route to the sacred center and one's final reward. This motif, too, has traveled through time, from hoary beginnings to the present.[21]

Womb and tree formations recur in our handmade midrash samples. The protean arborescent form that Susan describes in the womb recalls the description of the placenta as prenatal and perinatal psychologists study its symbolism.

SUSAN:
Womb and Tree
(see fig. 2.6, Color Section 1)

The pink womblike form represents incompleteness. Freedom is the shape above it in blue, a vital, pulsating, fully alive shape that partially fills out the incomplete form, emerges from it, reaches up, and yet is equally capable of contracting and expanding—like a cell, like breath in one's lungs, like the movement of all organic energy. The purple shape is human blessedness. It serves as the foundation for all experience; it is threaded through the other forms, serves as a base and an anchor, unifying all aspects of human experience. There are risks associated with the freedom, especially as it expands beyond the blessedness.

MIRIAM:

Recovering Losses

(see fig. 2.7, Color Section 1)

Miriam, a child of Holocaust survivors, is challenged by the world to perceive life in terms of recovery from loss. The broken heart is the loss of a partner:

A sense of incompleteness I will change. The bars are the restraints, the bondage and torment of my parents' experience. They have in the subtlest ways transmitted these concepts from which I must struggle free. Finally, the Star of David (on the edge of the paper), a rediscovering of my Jewish identity, which I now realize is an inextricable part of my being. This awareness and certainty bring great joy to my life. I feel a sense of direction in my life, a sense of positivism that has been missing for a long time.

EDWINA:

Rhythmic Filling and Emptying of the Tomb

The blessing started with the color blue, which has always had significance in my life, and as I tore, it became an empty tomb with a spiraling "stone"—always coming into place yet always being removed. Later I had to tear out the background center of the tomb to make it both "completely" empty and completely filled. My life has been such a series of experiences of moving into darkness/death/tomb and yet such a series of resurrection/renewal/new birth/light. The blessing is that no matter how deep the darkness/death/burial comes now, I have experienced so much of resurrection that I know it will always come again.

Edwina understands the caveat, the powerful thrust of creativity that is like electricity to be harnessed, that doesn't always know its own structure and goal (flying off the edge of the paper). It is the arbitrary "curse of the blessing." But that erratic force is balanced by the rhythmic filling and emptying of the tomb, expressed by the ebb and flow, the serpentine movement of the spiral. As we have seen, the serpent is an image of periodic renewal, particularly associated with the feminine. In this instance, Edwina uses her deep faith to harness the rhythms so that filling can surpass emptying, so that she can keep a watchful eye on the incomplete freedom flashing up on the left.

The recognition of one's openness to freedom (i.e., unfixedness) is nurtured by blessing, which strives toward completeness and brings into focus the power of the individual to turn and to change, the "bottom line" of this exercise. It is thus particularly appropriate in connection with the new year.

PAM:

T'shuva
(Turning)
(fig. 2.8)

Pam provides the final example. The red blessing flows out of the dark spiral, which combines incompleteness and freedom. Pam writes:

No matter which way I look at this form, it looks right. Each way suggests new ideas to me, which may say something about the act of turning itself—that sometimes the turning must come first and the meaning of the turning follows. As I compose it, with the dark spiral in the upper lefthand corner, there is something elementally female about the form, with a rich red life emerging from a dark and mysterious interior. There seems to be a pun involved. The form needs to illustrate the act of turning from a "stuck place"; yet in this visualization it is the "stuck place" that turns (i.e., incompleteness is the freedom). It turns in on itself, which links me back to the Buber material we read in class:

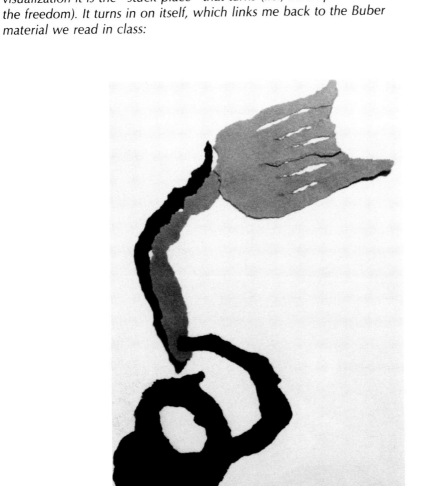

fig. 2.8. Pam, *T'shuva* (Turning).

It is known that turning (t'shuva) stands in the center of the Jewish conception of the way of man. Turning is capable of renewing a man from within and changing his position in God's world, so that he who turns is seen standing above the perfect zaddik who does not know the abyss of sin. But turning means something much greater than repentance and acts of penance; it means that by a reversal of his whole being, a man who had been lost in the maze of selfishness, where he had always set himself as his goal, finds a way to God, that is, a way to the fulfillment of the particular task for which he, this particular man, has been destined by God. Repentance can only be an incentive to such active reversal.[22]

Addressing the possibility that missing the mark (Hebrew for sin) contains its own stimulus for correction, Pam concluded:

Is the momentum for turning and changing, for becoming unstuck, contained in the stuck spot itself? Can the force that spirals us in on ourselves become so great that we are eventually flung outward by it?

Achieving Closure

Each of the handmade midrashim in the preceding exercises is a self-portrait of a person involved in a symbolic search for a missing part. We have sought Light to identify the suprapersonal source of our being; we have examined ourselves as unprogrammed, and therefore freer, than all other creatures; we have seen ourselves as imperfect and therefore forever in search of wholeness; and we have recognized ourselves as blessed, though perhaps uncertain exactly what that means. Giving form to these aspects of our nature and condition has sharpened our understanding of the symbolic quest.

Our efforts may be further enhanced by Edward Edinger's discussion of the word *symbol* as derived from two Greek words: *sym,* meaning "together," and *bolon,* meaning "that which has been thrown." In Greek antiquity, the word meant "coin," and a transaction was sealed by breaking a coin, the buyer and seller each retaining his half. The halves brought together gave proof of the transaction. Thus, according to Edinger, the "symbol" was

the missing piece of an object which, when restored to or thrown together with its partner, recreated the original whole object. . . . The symbol thus leads us to the missing part of the whole person . . . relates us to our original totality, heals our split, our alienation from life . . . relates us to the suprapersonal forces which are the source of our being and our meaning. This is the reason for honoring subjectivity and cultivating the symbolic life.[23]

In Jewish terminology, the symbolic quest that we have been pursuing is a process of *t'shuva* Liturgically, *t'shuva* means "repentance"; theologically, it means "turning," or "returning." Grammatically, it can mean "an answer," which is of course a form of returning. The opposite of t'shuva is "missing the mark," which is the essential meaning of sin. Het (sin) is actually an archer's term for the physical experience of missing the mark; you can only repair your shot by turning to correct your aim. Physical turning is antecedent to emotional turning. It may be turning away from or turning toward something or someone; whatever the application, the basic meaning is return—first physical, then attitudinal.

Our basic recipe for a handmade midrash specifies doing, talking, and writing, in that order. In this case, it seems that the sequence should be expanded: doing, talking, writing, and then really doing.

The Creation Workshop: Summary

OBJECTIVES

1 To introduce synectics—problem solving through creative play; to apply synectics to understanding personal creation in Genesis 1.

2 To experience Light as the presence of God by learning how the structure of Genesis 1 conveys its meanings.

3 To experience God as internal (our center) and external (our circumference) through metaphoric uses of Light in Genesis 1 and Exodus 19 and 34, and handmade midrash activity.

4 To experience the implications of human nature as unfinished, free and blessed through a study of purposeful repetition and artful omission in Genesis 1.

5 To examine the possibility of t'shuva, personal change, as a climax to Objective 4 and its concluding handmade midrash activity.

PRIMARY TEXTS

Genesis 1.

Exodus 19:16–18; 34:29–35.

Auxiliary texts: Psalms 1 and 8.

RECOMMENDED READINGS

Roger Cook, The Tree of Life.

William Gordon, Synectics.

Jo Milgrom, "The Tree of Life Springs from the Threshold."

ART WORKS FOR DISCUSSION IN EXERCISE 1

1 The Three-Tiered Universe, in "Cosmogony," Interpreter's Dictionary of the Bible, vol. 1 (Nashville: Abingdon, 1962), 703, fig. 50.

2 *Primordial Point,* as Genesis 1:1 in "Kabbalah," *Encyclopedia Judaica,* vol. 10 (Jerusalem: Keter, 1971), 574, fig. 8.

3 *Primordial Man in the Womb of the Ein Sof,* in "Kabbalah," *Encyclopedia Judaica,* vol. 10, (Jerusalem: Keter, 1971), 647, fig. 14.

These works are useful to show iconography related to the participants' collages.

MATERIALS REQUIRED

Exercises 1 and 2: black and white construction paper and glue.

Exercise 3: all colors of construction paper and glue.

PROCEDURE

Exercise 1: Imagine God as Light. Allow Divine Light to come into being as whiteness out of blackness in a concrete and physical, rather than philosophical, manner by tearing white and black shapes and pasting them into a relationship.

Exercise 2: Add a sensory step to Exercise 1 in order to personalize your encounter with the Divine. When you want to imagine a distant God coming closer, put thinking aside and use your senses. In addition to seeing it, imagine what such an experience might sound and feel like. If you could touch it, what are its texture and temperature? Does the experience have taste or aroma? Where is it in your body? Does it move? When you tear and paste the forms, show in detail (also tell and write) what has happened in this encounter. You may choose one color in addition to black and white.

Exercise 3: Tear three forms that show yourself as (1) incomplete, (2) free—unfixed, relatively unprogrammed—and (3) blessed. Paste them in a relationship, on a fourth paper, flat or three-dimensionally. As in Exercise 2, use other than the visual sense to help you visualize. Pay particular attention to how these three elements interact. Refer to the basic recipe for a handmade midrash in the introduction to facilitate both the discussion and the writing.

FOLLOW-UP

Although three exercises are given in this chapter, each one is a separate event. Each one is processed on three levels: doing, talking in small groups, and writing, followed by group feedback with the leader.

1. Arnold Williams, *The Common Expositor* (Chapel Hill, N.C.: University of North Carolina, 1948), 6–25.

2. Joseph Henderson and Maud Oakes, *The Wisdom of the Serpent* (New York: Brazilier, 1963), xi.

3. William J. J. Gordon, *Synectics* (New York: Harper & Row, 1961), 3–5. A. Kaunfer, "Synectics: An Approach to Teaching Midrash," *Melton Research Center Newsletter* 11 (Fall 1980):2–5. Jo Milgrom, "Handmade Midrash," *Melton Journal* 17 (Winter 1984): 16–18.

4. Gordon, *Synectics,* 111.

5. For illustrations of the primordial point as Genesis 1:1 and primordial man in the womb of the Ein Sof, the Infinite One, see Figures 8 and 14 in "Kabbalah," *Encyclopaedia Judaica,* vol. 10 (Jerusalem: Keter, 1971), 574, 647.

6. See "Cosmogony," *Interpreter's Dictionary of the Bible,* vol. 1 (Nashville: Abingdon, 1976), 703, for diagram and interpretation of the three-tiered universe.

7. Mircea Eliade, "The Myth of Alchemy," *Parabola* III, no. 3 (1978):28.

8. Robert Sacks, *The Lion and the Ass* (Santa Fe, N.Mex.: St. John's College, 1976), 1–28.

9. In addition to the concept of ambiguity and transition but different from shadow, artists call our attention to "hialation," the visual effect of greater light that appears as a kind of prism-halo around a silhouetted dark object. Whether it is conceptual or visual, we observe a margin of transition between opposites. (Conversation with artists Jim Rosen and Claudia Breese, Graduate Theological Union, Berkeley, Calif., March 1988).

10. Edmund Leach, *Genesis as Myth* (London: Jonathan Cape, 1960), 7–10.

11. Jo Milgrom, "The Tree of Life Springs from the Threshold," in *Art as Religious Studies,* Doug Adams and Diane Apostolos-Cappadona (eds.) (New York: Crossroads, 1987), 58–70.

12. Nahum Sarna, *The JPS Torah Commentary, Genesis* (Philadelphia: The Jewish Publication Society, 1988), 4.

13. Gerald Epstein, *Waking Dream Therapy* (New York: Human Sciences Press, 1981), 51.

14. Ibid., 18.

15. Ibid., 163.

16. Ever since the eleventh century Moses' beams of radiance have been visually translated as horns. This is not a result of mistranslation, contrary to the popular notion. It is simply the literal translation of a metaphor in order to assure the ambiguity that invites levels of meaning. Horns and beams of light are the same word in Latin, *cornu,* and in Hebrew, *karan.* See Ruth Mellinkoff, *The Horned Moses in Medieval Art and Thought* (Berkeley, Los Angeles: University of California, 1970), 13–17.

17. Roger Cook, *The Tree of Life* (London: Thames & Hudson, 1974), 7–29.

18. Charles Knowles, *The Psalm Book of Charles Knowles* (New York: Viking & Pinnacle Press, 1959), 18–19.

19. Othmar Keel, *Symbolism of the Biblical World* (New York: Crossroads, 1978), 186.

20. See a Mithraic image of time wrapped in a serpent, surrounded by the zodiac and emerging from an egg, in E. R. Goodenough, *Jewish Symbols in the Greco-Roman Period,* vol. 8 (Princeton, N.J.: Bollingen, 1965), 184.

21. Seonid M. Robertson, *Rosegarden and Labyrinth* (Dallas: Spring Publications, 1982), 109–135.

22. Martin Buber, *Hasidism and Modern Man,* Maurice Friedman (tr. and ed.) (New York: Horizon, 1957), 164.

23. Edward Edinger, *Ego and Archetype* (New York: Penguin, 1974), 130.

fig. 1.10. Franz, *Looking for an Aleph in Nature* (p. 30).

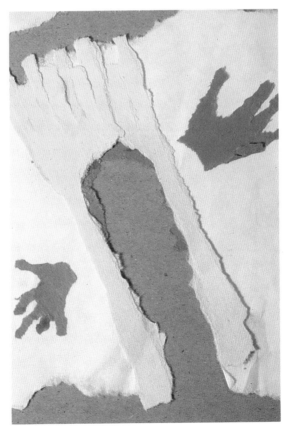

fig. 1.12. Amy, *A Divided Jew's Aleph* (p. 32).

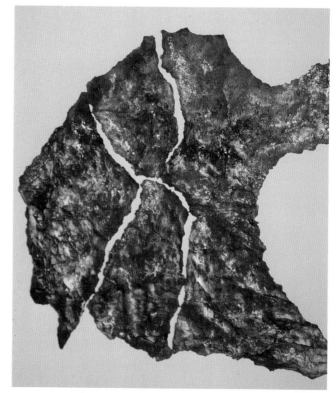

fig. 1.15. Beth Ames Swartz, *Aleph as the Shekhina, Safed Series #1* (mixed media on layered paper; p. 38). (*From* Beth Ames Swartz, *Israel Revisited,* Scottsdale, Ariz., 1981. Reprinted with permission.)

fig. 1.16. Michele Zackheim, *Aleph* in "Moses on Sinai" (p. 38). (*From The Tent of Meeting,* Santa Fe, N.Mex., 1985. Permanently installed in the Cathedral of St. John the Divine, New York City. Reprinted with permission.)

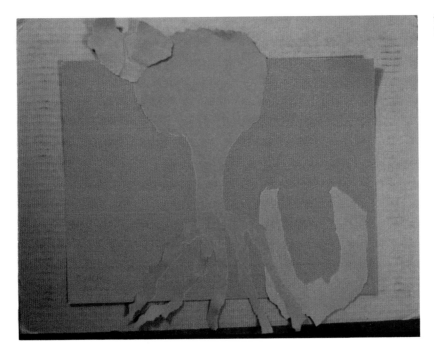

fig. 2.3. Colleen, *The Tree of All* (p. 59).

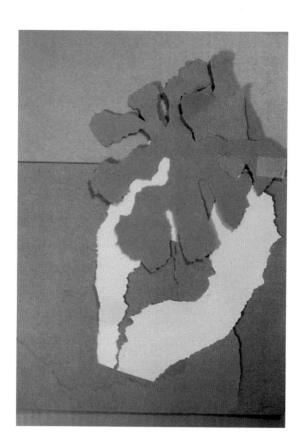

fig. 2.6. Susan, *Womb and Tree* (p. 61).

fig. 2.7. Miriam, *Recovering Losses* (p. 62).

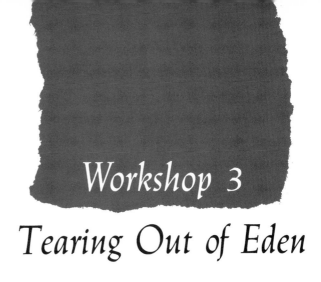

Workshop 3

Tearing Out of Eden

The first chapter of the Book of Genesis is characterized by a determined process of individuation. The verb *to distinguish* appears repeatedly in the accounts of Days One, Two, and Four of Creation; similarly, the phrase *of its own kind* recurs, like a refrain, in the descriptions of Days Three, Five, and Six. It isn't clear, however, whether Adam is also individuated[1] as Day Six of Creation comes to a close. On this matter, the text seems deliberately ambiguous: "And God created man in His image, in the image of God He created him; male and female He created them (Gen. 1:27).

Did God create male and female humanity simultaneously? Is Adam a generic "earthling"? Did God create a single male and a single female, or a single androgynous being? Perhaps all of the above. Can the text really be saying that we start out as androgynous beings before we individuate into separate male and female?

The climax of Workshop 3 is an individuation activity in which participants repeatedly tear out of paradise. This is accomplished through torn fabric sculpture and ceramic sculpture. It follows a close reading of Genesis 2 and 3, which constitute a "day" in the life of Adam: his birth, adolescence, betrothal, marriage, parenthood, and mature age. The dramatic shift in relationships between Adam and the animals, Adam and his wife, Adam and the earth, Adam and God provides the pattern for our own individuation and life passages.

The procedure for this workshop incorporates a psychological view of Eden as well as a study of two famous works of art, four hundred years apart, by Michelangelo and Chagall. Because of their respective Christian and Jewish approaches to our theme, their powerful visual symbols, and their midrashic lure, these works make an important contribution to the experience of workshop participants.

A Close Reading of the Text

The Individuation of Adam

During a close reading of Genesis 1 in Workshop 2 (p. 49), Mircea Eliade's comments on creation and distinctions focused us on the separations that must take place within the mineral, vegetable, and animal species before a new order could be established and opposites could come together in new relationships. Eliade's principles can now help us understand Adam's process of differentiation as the first human being prepares to unite with his opposite to generate history.

Naming, Sex, and Sexuality

From this perspective, let us attempt to clarify the perplexing ambiguity of Genesis 1:27 in the subsequent unfolding of Adam's nature. In Genesis 2:7 God sculpts Adam out of a combination of masculine dust (*afar*) and feminine earth (*adama*). His resultant bisexuality is further emphasized when he and God search for his mate, "corresponding to him." God now creates the animals and Adam, modeling God's power, uses language to name them. In the naming process it seems that Adam identifies the masculine and feminine of the various species but cannot locate among them the feminine of his own species. This is the beginning of Adam's separation from his animal nature. Later, he tests his connection with the Divine to see if he can affiliate with that league (". . . as soon as you eat . . . your eyes will be opened and you will be like divine beings who know good and evil" [Gen. 3:5]). Eventually Adam learns that in reality he hovers somewhere in the unique human and oxymoronic no man's land between the two; he is both and he is neither.

The infamous rib story, in which Adam "mothers" his own wife, so to speak, is actually the removal of the feminine side (*tsela* in Hebrew means both "rib" and "side") of this androgynous being. Awareness of one's sexuality is thus mythically presented as the removal from the inside (unconscious) of one's otherness so as to relate to it externally, consciously, in a new way.

The most striking proof text of the androgynous nature of the first human being, however, is in Genesis 5:1–2. Here Adam's origins are reviewed before the listing of his genealogy: "This is the record of Adam's line. When God created man, He made him in the likeness of God; male and female He created them. And when they were created, He blessed them and called *their* name Adam."

Now that God has brought woman around to the front so that Adam can see her, his enthusiasm knows no bounds. He waxes poetic in praise of *zot* (Hebrew, feminine, "this one"). Adam can name her now; later he will change her name when they take another giant step toward individuation.

> *This (zot) one* at last
> Is bone of my bones
> And flesh of my flesh.
> *This (zot) one* shall be called Woman,
> For from man was taken *this (zot) one* (Gen. 2:23)[2]

The Biblical Narrator announces: "Hence a man leaves his father and mother and clings to his wife, so that they become one flesh" (Gen. 2:24). At the height of their physical powers and mobility, they leave the parental home. New relationships begin in their present stage of individuation. For now, their relationship with the animals is close, though no longer intimate. After all, she and the serpent have serious talks. Their dominion over the beasts is complete, however, when God dresses them in animal skins before evicting them from the Garden. Their removal from the parental home prefigures their own stage of parenting and the complex child and parent relationships that will characterize intergenerational bonds forever after.

Before the curtain falls on Chapter 3, God confronts the new couple with the realities of human life. His first question to them is *Ayeka*, "Where are you?" (Gen. 3:9), which really means, Do *you* know where you are? Do you know there is no hiding from me or from responsibility for your own acts? God then informs them that there will be pain both in their physical labor and in the labor of birth. This is sometimes understood as punishment for their disobedience. In fact, it is an etiological statement, explaining the origins of the human condition.

What appears to be male domination is more likely male braggadocio in the face of male submission to the human condition. Immediately after the statement "dust you are, And to dust you shall return," Adam changes woman's name (Gen. 3:20). He calls her Eve, "the mother of all living." With full consciousness of his own mortality, the mature adult, no longer the idyllic bridegroom, realizes that the continuity of the species depends on the woman, the mother. We have come full circle. The "day" in the life of Adam takes us out of Eden, soberly into the real world. Extended knowledge of sexuality gives profound meaning to the act of sex. Sex produces new life. Cradling new life in one's arms gives us a poignant grasp of our own mortality. Thus the knowledge of good and evil gained in the Garden is the knowledge of the duality of life and death, that is, the rise into awareness of time. In the Garden we knew immortality. Out of the Garden we are confronted with mortality. Once out of the Garden we fall into history and morality, how to live our time. Therefore, the very next story, Chapter 4, is the unfolding of the life of the first family, the first children, Cain and Abel, and the first crime.[3]

A Psychological View of the Garden Narrative

According to Edward Edinger's interpretation of the Garden narrative,[4] eating the forbidden fruit marks "the transition from the eternal state of unconscious oneness . . . to a real, conscious life of the ego in space and time." Since consciousness alienates one from his or her original wholeness and brings awareness of the opposites, one thus moves into a world of suffering, conflicting choices, and uncertainty. Hence comes the theological doctrine that consciousness is the original sin, the original hubris, and the root cause of all evil in human nature. *Heresy* is the Greek word for "choice." *Sin* comes from the Sanskrit root "to be."

Another point of view, expressed by a second-century Gnostic sect, the Ophites, objects to the one-sided view that Adam and Eve are shameless orchard thieves. Their action could just as well be described as heroic, for they sacrifice the passive comfort of obedience for greater consciousness. The serpent thus proves to be a benefactor in the long run if we grant consciousness a greater value than comfort. One cannot reach a new stage of psychological development without daring to challenge the code of the old one. Thus every new step is experienced as a crime accompanied by guilt.

Paradise is thus the secure, known, and sometimes confining place of one's immediate past or present, characterized by a series of passages away from original security as the individual grows in freedom and choices. Each exodus is courageous, frightening, and perhaps exhilarating. Each passage is growth from which there is no retreat. Once our eyes have seen, they cannot unsee. The Bible conveys this consciousness by means of the metaphor of sexual knowledge. Sex produces the baby, the next generation. When new parents embrace the new life, they see their own mortality in a profoundly fundamental way. Paradise and the knowledge of time are therefore mutually exclusive. Expulsion from the Garden is the shock of instant, irreversible recognition that one has tasted the fruit of the Tree of Knowledge, of good and evil, of life and death.

From Words to Pictures

Human beings think in images. In fact, the visual record of humanity is thousands of years older than the verbal. The study of a picture brings us into contact with the pre-verbal associations on a subject. A parallel verbal text thus acquires a richness of texture not otherwise accessible.

In the Eden Workshop, visual art is a catalyst for the creation of midrash. When Michelangelo shows Adam also reaching for the fruit, which is contrary to the text, and when he shows the primeval couple initially more interested in each other than in the serpent, he is expanding a laconic text by means of his personal experience of human nature, rendered in visual images. Clearly, the word is not enough.

Just as the word is not enough in any humanistic study, so the cognitive mode is also insufficient. Hence we use handmade midrash to free us, at least momentarily, from linear, rational thinking into an imaginal mode, to access unexpressed feelings, our affective nature that underlies and motivates all our behaviors.

In keeping with the principle that words are not enough, I have chosen to discuss two works of art that follow the text study and lead us into the handmade midrash exercise: Tearing Out of Eden. The earlier painting is Michelangelo's famous *Temptation and Fall*. It is figural and therefore more immediately understood. It is also Christian, yet bravely untraditional. The later painting, created exactly four hundred years later, is an early Chagall of distinct Jewish content, yet less accessible because of its cubist style. Traditional shapes are broken up and reassembled like a puzzle, with a fault line encouraging us to seek new understanding by making the familiar strange.

The first chapters of Genesis are the material that constitute the basis of Michelangelo's immense cycle of paintings, three hundred figures in an area of more than five hundred square feet on the ceiling of the Sistine Chapel, c. 1512. The subject of the "Temptation and Fall," as it is traditionally known in Christian art, appears in every major period and style of art. The usual interpretation is the single scene known as early as the third century: Adam and Eve stand frontally before us, separated by the Tree of Knowledge, around which the serpent is entwined.

But Michelangelo is an innovator and has given us two great moments of drama. The Tree of Knowledge stands between the two moments that give the work its theme: temptation and expulsion, or sin and punishment, or still another, consciousness and the cost. On the left, Eve's body forms a sensuous question mark. Both reach for the fruit, he more aggressively (a midrashic digression from the biblical text in which Adam is the passive recipient). In fact, both seem more interested in the fruit and the fruit-giver than in each other, at least for the moment (fig. 3.1).[5]

Michelangelo
Temptation
and Fall
(fig. 3.1)

fig. 3.1. Michelangelo, *Temptation and Fall.* (*From* the Sistine Chapel, Rome; c. 1512. Alinari/Art Resource, New York. Reprinted with permission.)

THE BIFURCATED SERPENT

Whereas the couple is the erotic focus, the serpent is surely the exotic focus, with its python-like extremities coiled about each other and the tree. One of those extremities terminates in a nude female with long flowing red hair—the fruit-giver. A look of profound recognition passes between the two women (Eve and the serpent), and Adam is not partner to this exchange. He knows much less. His face is in the shadow, and although he reaches aggressively, it is not clear that he gets anything.

If one follows the corkscrew motion of the other coil up and around the tree, the coil seems, amazingly, to terminate in the right arm of the sword-brandishing cherub, moving us visually to the parallel scene on the right: the exile from paradise. What is the curious and fascinating relatedness of the serpent to the cherub? "In formal linear terms the symbol of evil, the serpent, and the symbol of good, the cherubim, seem to spring from one source. Is Michelangelo expressing an insight into the ambiguity of good and evil," the image of God?[6]

WHO IS SHE?

Both religious traditions, Christianity and Judaism, credit Eve with bringing death to the world. A small desiccated tree behind Eve and parallel to her arm might represent the lost potential of the Tree of Life. Dillenberger (see n. 5, p. 91) suggests that it may also be an allusion to a messianic passage in Isaiah, "But a shoot shall grow out of the stump of Jesse, A twig shall sprout from his stock. The spirit of the Lord shall alight upon him. . . ." (Isa. 11:1–2). In the Bible, the tree is often a figure of continuity of self as well as of Israel, Torah, and Messiah.

The association of woman with death is mythic and therefore illuminating psychologically. Woman is fundamentally associated with the earth, which produces new life and receives the dead back into her. Michelangelo's knowledge of Greek myth would have led him to the Sirens, whose seductive music was mortally dangerous to Odysseus's sailors. As we have already learned, death is the ultimate "consequence" of sex, because sex brings new life and therefore full awareness of the life cycle. Since the man's role in human reproduction was not fully understood, credit was given to the woman.

ENTER LILITH AND SAMAEL

The famed Medici salon was Michelangelo's school of higher learning, and his mentor was Giovanni Pico della Mirandola, the most influential Christian scholar of mysticism of his time. It was here that Michelangelo learned about Lilith, Adam's first wife in Kabbalist tradition, who left him for reasons of sexual inequality.[7] In her appearance in medieval art Lilith bears an astonishing resemblance to Eve. The real curiosity about Lilith, however, is that she has a male counterpart, Samael (meaning "Satan," and also meaning "left").[8] They are a sexually associated couple. They are the "other" (shadow) aspects of Adam and Eve. Another careful look at the bifurcated Sistine serpent reveals that the serpent is also bisexual. The fruit of the Tree of Knowledge of Good and Evil is indeed sexual knowledge, and Eve is the catalyst.

But what is the serpent's connection with God? In the ancient Near East the characteristics of the serpent were often attributes of the gods. Swift and sly, mysterious bringer of death, sloughing its skin to achieve new life, the serpent was a living analog of ultimate power and immortality—the two exclusive attributes of God.

The cherubim were also Divine associates. In the Bible they were part of God's throne and his means of transport. Extrabiblical imagery portrays them as hybrid beasts who guarded the temple portals and controlled access to the gods.

Thus the Sistine ceiling tells us visually that the serpent is the sexuality of man and woman leading to a critical experience of human time; and the serpent is also the shadow side of God, who enigmatically sets up the forbidden in order to guarantee that it will be done, deliciously tempting us to experience what we were designed to experience, irrespective of the price tag, the offer we could not refuse. The narrative, like an oracle, is uncanny and baffling, but the artist is clairvoyant in making visible the tantalizing ambiguity and contrary nature of symbols.

Marc Chagall, who died in 1985 as he neared the age of ninety-eight, is the Jewish artist whose presence dominated the twentieth century. His large-scale works are seen in the major capitals of the world: New York, Chicago, Paris, Rheims, Zurich, and Jerusalem. He worked in many mediums—oils, fiber, clay, glass, and stone—and produced works that range from drawings, etchings, and paintings to murals, tapestries, and stained glass. His metaphoric imagination thrived within the cubist style, fracturing the figural images of the early years of our century. He translated the wry Yiddish shtetl wit into visual idioms such as levitating violinists, cows, Torahs, and rabbis. He was good for the Jews. He expressed the ambivalence of many—intoxicated by the Enlightenment for the first time in a millennium, seduced by the dazzle of secular urbanity, and yet still smitten with nostalgia for the celebratory intensity of a close Hasidic community.

When Chagall painted *Homage à Apollinaire* in 1911–12, it was his most important work to date. Its subject is the same as Michelangelo's *Temptation and Fall* of the Sistine Chapel: what happened when they disobeyed. Every vestige of earthly paradise has disappeared. The androgynous pair is fused up to the hips in a single body. The lines of a great X intersect at the sacrum, where life begins and where the serpent appears ambiguously as both Adam's hand and his phallus. The couple is surrounded by a cosmic wheel of time but is not enclosed by it. The sides curve upward and out, creating freedom of movement. A diagonal of cool moonlight silver unexpectedly marks the masculine side, while hot golden red lies adjacent to the feminine, thus indicating that each sex shares characteristics of the other.

The most curious aspect of this painting is the clock numbers on the outer rim: 9, 10, 11. Once the couple has eaten the mythic fruit, the cosmic wheel becomes a human clock. Adam and Eve stand within the clock almost as if they were its giant hands. This clock is a visual adaptation of a midrash probably known to Chagall from his childhood shtetl learning. The midrash tells how God made frantic haste to start and finish the creation of Adam and allow him to transgress and be forgiven all in a single liturgical day, Rosh Hashanah, the new year, and the anniversary of Creation:

> The first hour He generated the idea of creating Adam. The second hour He consulted with a committee of angels. The third hour He assembled the dust; the fourth He kneaded the dough; in the fifth He shaped his complex insides; in the sixth He gave form to the golem (the amorphous mass); in the seventh He breathed his soul into him; in the eighth He brought him into the Garden; in the ninth He commanded him regarding the fruit of the trees; in the tenth Adam transgressed; in the eleventh, Adam was judged; in the twelfth, Adam went free. This, said the Holy One blessed be He, to Adam, will be a sign to your children. Just as you stood in judgment before Me this day and came out in amnesty, so will your children in the future stand in judgment before Me on this day and will come out from My presence in amnesty. When will that be? On the seventh month, the first day of the month.[9]

The Chagall painting emphasizes the hours when Adam exercises his will (ten o'clock) and experiences accountability (eleven o'clock): He hears the command, rebels, and is judged. Pardon comes at the "twelfth hour."

This midrash reflects a distinctly Jewish solution to the alienation of exile from paradise. The laconic text elaborated elsewhere tells us that Adam does *t'shuva*. He repents, changes his ways, and is thus worthy of forgiveness. His pattern on the first Rosh Hashanah must be ours on every succeeding Rosh Hashanah. We must turn, change our ways, and be worthy of forgiveness. Thus "original forgiveness" in an early rabbinic text offers a powerful alternative to the oppressive guilt of original sin, and a modern master provides us with an unforgettable visual midrashic interpretation.

fig. 3.2. Marc Chagall, *Homage à Apollinaire*. (*From* the Stedelijk Museum, Amsterdam; c. 1912. Copyright © ARS NY/ADAGP, 1991. Reprinted with permission.)

Experiencing Separation: The Handmade Midrash

The exile from Eden provides a paradigm, an archetypal structure of meaning. It evokes a metaphor that "fits" the universal and the particular simultaneously. It is the tearing and re-forming of fabric that make the full metaverbal experience of the passages from Eden possible.

In his writing about Jung and the "active imagination," Wayne Rollins describes how Jung invited patients to draw out their unconscious life through the exercise of the imagination in concrete form, such as a drawing, a painting, clay modeling, dance, free writing, storytelling, or spontaneous fantasies. By means of this strategy, the conscious side of the self was enlisted to coax the unconscious side into expressing some of its undisclosed content, so that it might be brought into the daylight of consciousness and used as a resource in coping with the problems of the day. As Jung observed, "Often the hands know how to solve a riddle with which the intellect has wrestled in vain."[10]

Tearing has a biblical background. Confronted with real or imminent loss, biblical persons tore their garments. When the stolen cup was found in Benjamin's sack, the brothers, not knowing what would become of him and them, rent their clothes (Gen. 44:13). Jacob, presented with Joseph's bloody tunic, assumed the death of the "son of his old age," rent his clothes, and refused comfort (Gen. 37:34). Another example comes from common Hebrew speech, in which the most difficult task imaginable is compared favorably with the splitting of the Red Sea. The literal Hebrew idiom is *kashe k'kriat yam suf,* "as hard as the tearing of the Red Sea." Spiritual loss may also be expressed by *kriah* (tearing). Ezra the scribe (Ezra 9:3), lamenting intermarriage and loss of faith among the returning exiles, rent his garments and tore his hair and beard. Contemporary Jews are most familiar with *kriah* as the tearing of their own garments by the mourners before the burial of a loved one.

It seems appropriate for this workshop, then, to confront loss by performing *kriah* and, at the same time, calling out the loss or the feeling; I note that *kriah,* spelled with an *aleph,* means "to read" or "call out." This activity need not necessarily be the literal traumatic separation of life from death, as a recall of other kinds of passages that are part of growth and consciousness.

I demonstrate by tearing muslin slowly, pausing every several inches to hear the tearing and to call out—or cry out—a sigh, a word, a feeling and to write a word or fragment that would help later in the fuller writing. After all the tearing and calling out are done, each would be left with a pile of ragged muslin strips and holes. These are now to be built, rebuilt. As the tearing is a separation-away-from, the new sculpture made from the old fragments would honor the past while also showing insight, movement into the future.

When I first implemented this exercise, I provided half a yard of plain, unbleached muslin for each participant. Foolishly, I even nicked the places for easy tearing. Then I demonstrated tearing, pausing, thinking, or grieving over a separation, calling out the name or the event of the loss. For the traditional Jew, the sound of *kriah* is immediately associated with the separation of the living from the dead, which takes place at graveside. The lapel of a jacket or the collar of a dress is wrenched and torn. There is no other sound like it. Just imagine the raw, cruel force it takes for someone standing before you to tear your clothing! It is not the polite, pre-torn little piece of black ribbon provided for your collar or lapel by present-day funeral parlors—like a badge worn for the duration.

It didn't take me long to realize that I was inhibiting instead of liberating my students. Beginning with Rose (fig. 3.3), there was a qualitative difference in the expression. From that time I had participants tear material of their own choice, from the context of their own lives, not the sterile, odorless, story-less new rags that I provided. Only the first time was the *kriah* done in class.

Each participant selects the material or garment for tearing. Natural fibers tear most easily. Allow time and privacy at home. Prepare paper and pencil for writing between tearings. If you like, gather some of your favorite readings for comfort. Tear, call out, read, write—altering the order according to your own needs, again and again, until you feel you can stop. When the *kriah* is done, the rebuilding can begin. Loss is a prelude to a new beginning; the past cannot be discarded or erased, but it can be understood in a new way and can even give direction to the future. Form a sculpture from *all* the torn remnants. You are free to use any additional scraps on hand—wood, paint, buttons, glass, ribbons, to satisfy your requirements. Write about your process and passage from a safe but confining "Eden" to another level of consciousness. Is there someone you need to call or write immediately to share this with?

Doing this project involves a very personal issue for me. During the last few weeks I have had something on my mind that happened to me a year ago. I was attacked one morning while walking to work. This affected my life in some big ways. To deal with it at that time I decided to put the pain into my hair (which was down to my waist) and cut it off. I kept my braid as a reminder. Since this occurrence is very much on my mind again, I am using this assignment to tear out any leftover fear.

I braid the strips like my hair. It pleases me that the muslin is such a light color. My own hair is dark. The muslin braid is like hair that has turned white with age. When I look at it I think of the wisdom and strength that I have gained during the past year. I think about how I now have all the things that I wanted so badly at that time (to go to school, have some time for my artwork, and a boyfriend who treats me well) and I feel very blessed.

Mary has experienced a passage beyond fear for her own physical safety. The attack against her "aged" her; it literally thrust her out of the paradise of idyllic, protected innocence. The art exercise enabled Mary to confront the old pain, resolve it on a higher plane, and affirm her growing maturity and wisdom.

DON:

Greater Pause

I tear my cloth. I think of six items that have become real to me recently. I have lost (am losing) youth, my sons as babies, the less complicated past, early marriage, certain focuses of my ministry, and some of my ministerial reputation. I tear it very slowly and try to experience the emotional upheaval that this might avail me. . . . I guess I am just not capable of it.

The resolution of the tearing actually gives me greater pause. I tie all the loose ends at one end and tie the rest at the other. As I do this, I think of the promise of the Scripture that the Lord will restore to His people that which they have lost . . . (Joel 1:3–4 and Joel 2:25–26). That concept is very precious to me, and for the moments that I spent in thinking again of the promise, I am grateful for the project.

The knots that Don tied are beginnings and ends. The first knot is the secure binding of the preconscious state of perfection. Then the tearings, the six ways that security is becoming undone by the complexities of life, evoking the destruction wrought by the plague of locusts (Joel 1:3–4). The final knot is Don's faith in the restoration of his wholeness and status: "I will repay you for the years consumed by swarming locusts . . . you shall eat your fill and praise the name of the Lord your God who has dealt so wondrously with you, and my people shall be shamed no more" (Joel 2:25–26).

As I tear the cloth, I feel a tearing in the center of myself, as one arm stretches one way; the other, the other way. Yet I also feel the effort tearing takes; there is a sense of choice, of deliberateness in the effort. I become aware of the strength in my arms, of my own power to choose and to act. I experience the strength as channeled by action. I also hesitate a few times. Yet there is none of the panic that goes along with victimization in the pain I feel. Occasionally I feel exhilarated.

I am helped over the inertia of contemplating to rebuild. I seek the comfort of pattern and lay out the strands for weaving. Weaving and braiding also provide simple, repetitive movement, which is an aid to concentration. Concentration while creating is a "high" for me. This is a way to "gather" myself and my emotions even as the strands are gathered. I reflect on the Kabbalistic task of regathering the scattered sparks of creation. I also remember how much repetition is in the text of Genesis 1.

Images that flash as I work: tefillin, tsitsit, windows, bandages. What I end up with suggests for me a mask, or cap (a wedding veil?). I am pleased with how textured the piece is.

I am grateful to discover that it's okay to be "conventional" when beginning. I feel disappointed at first with how "unoriginal" weaving and braiding are as my initial impulses. But I follow through, and the form I had wanted to "innovate" emerges.

Amy experiences a release from inertia and fear of being dull and conventional. Her passage is from a "paradise" of constricting intimidation from the success patterns of a family of gifted parents and older siblings.

1 *To feel the material rip. To hear it tear. To counter the resistance of the fabric.*

2 *Tearing myself from myself. Like a butterfly from a chrysalis.*

3 *Definite and determined tear from my father's influence, dominance, expectations.*

4 *No feeling. Just ripping. Maybe some anger I can't pinpoint.*

5 *Gentle tear from some of my mother's teachings. I no longer believe them. No black and white.*

6 *From dead relationships, especially the one where I tried so hard and it was getting too close to the line of being taken advantage of.*

7 *From my loss of self, depression, deadness.*

8 *From my loss of self, depression, deadness.*

9 *From my loss of self, depression, deadness. Gotta get it out of my system.*

I tore from both sides of the cloth to make sure I got it all. The rest of the material, I don't need to tear from end to end. I love the threads. They're the ties, the unexpected chance reminder of where I came from. I also like the pinching of the material, like flesh seeking to heal.

First I lay the strips out across the table. Some strips can be tied together because the issues are related. Some are tied so the secrets don't fall out. Then I bunch and gather them straight down the middle. After all, it's all me. And I brush the strips, break some threads, stroke them a bit, and tie them together. In a love knot. Now I attach it to the piece of cloth. All tears need to heal and become part of a whole, and wholes tend to tear at one time or another. A reminder that I've torn and I'll heal.

The whole thing looks better than I thought it would. Just needs a little bamboo stick across the top to hang it up with. To think that a piece of cloth would become infused with meaning! A wonderful experience.

ROSE:

Re-turn

(see fig. 3.3, Color Section 2)

The tearing sound and feel are satisfying because they represent to me the years I spent trying to fulfill the traditional female role and not being stimulated and challenged by it. I did try very hard; it just never worked really well. . . .

I tear up an old yellowed and very plain pillowcase. I tear up the "shoulds" and "oughts" of that traditional role to make me free to see myself for who I am and can be as a person, not a role. I couldn't have done that two years ago with children still home and the nurturing role still part of my life.

When the sculpture forms, it is a rough and convoluted base like the twisted intricacies of balancing a job I hated, with my home and family and the work in the church, both of which I live for and love. The base opens into a black hole. The opening is not without pain and bleeding. The hole I fear is empty, but it is not emptiness, only unknown to me. What was in it? The forms that emerge are leaflike and growing. There are two of them, and they shelter and nourish a yellow bud that starts to unfold. I am startled by the two forms because I see my husband and myself as both being engaged in nourishing this new self that emerges. It is not yet distinguishable in its full shape but gives promise of beauty and health. It has the potential for growing, but as yet it does not stretch above the level of the torn past.

P.S.: When I painted this, I discovered that each form flows into the other without a boundary. The past is part of the dark hole, the dark hole is part of the leaf, the leaf cannot be separated from the bloom.

Rose is a mature woman who has returned to seminary for a master of divinity degree. Her husband, a pastor of reputation and long service, has left his post to be with her. When she is ordained, they will seek a joint position for two pastors.

At some level, many of the sins I had written down (for an al het *Yom Kippur* exercise) have to do with my need to overstate my own self-worth. With this idea of pride haunting me, I turn now to the kriah. What concerns me most is what to tear. It appears to me in the readings that many folks feel it important to tear an article of clothing that is meaningful rather than a substitute. After much thought I decide on a T-shirt (T-shirts are the mainstay of my wardrobe), which is very old and one of my favorites. I bought it in support of an emergency shelter for street people in New Haven, where I was in school at the time.

Soon after this time, I myself would leave seminary to work in street ministry. This shirt has always represented this transition to me. I have always worn it (with pride) about the work that I do, yet something always haunts me about it as well.

I begin to realize that within my "activism" is a confused passion that I am totally responsible for changing God's Creation. As can be expected, this idea has led to many dangerous conclusions. In any event, I hope this kriah might tear away at some of my pride and offer some rebirth to a better relationship with God. The preparation for this act is the most climactic moment for me. As I hold the shirt for tearing, I recall all that it means to me. For a time, I am almost too afraid to begin tearing. However, once that process begins, I feel a releasing of all that is inside me. I concluded the activity with some good time in silence.

STEVE:

Emergency Night Shelter

(fig. 3.4)

fig. 3.4. Steve,
Emergency Night Shelter.

FRANZ:

Letting Him Go

(fig. 3.5)

Even before I begin the tearing I am thinking of my grandfather. His life is ending. Soon will come the parting of our ways. So when I think to tear the cloth, I think it symbolizes my tearing myself away from him. This makes the act very deliberate and slow.

It comes to me in my tearing that I am freeing him. I am not tearing me away from him. I am tearing him away from his body, his earthliness, from me and everything here. When I rip a hole in the fabric, I rip a hole in the universe, through which he can escape.

And I look at the fabric I am ripping, a shirt I bought in India, as his body. I am tearing holes in his body to release him, not with anger. This earthly shirt is his old and no longer useful form. The holes are like the yods in the aleph, the holes in the universe that lead to God. As I make more holes, I am making more passageways up to God for him. All over the shirt I open them, that all his body's spirit should be liberated. He is bound and I loosen him. At least in my mind.

This whole chain of thoughts is my letting him go from my life. I was binding him to me, and I still am, but this helps me let him go. He must die, and now I feel more able to let that happen. I hope it will be later rather than sooner, but I feel that more for his sake than mine now. This exercise makes me a little less selfish.

After this, my sculpture is very simple to make. I want to show his empty form unadorned, uncorrupted. The shell of his body, as formed by the shirt, full of space, of light, of freedom, that is what we now have, where before was only a dying man.

fig. 3.5. Franz, *Letting Him Go.*

Franz's *kriah* is actually a ritual preparation for the final *kriah*, the actual death of his grandfather. His act of separation, a mourning in advance, represents a reconciliation with the inevitable and actually seems to facilitate a peaceful appreciation of his grandfather's final days.

The final sample of "Tearing from Eden" is that of a young woman whose group did not experience a tearing exercise. Just as clay had been used for the forming of Eve and Adam, Caroline, a potter, continued with clay for the Eden assignment. She achieved a powerful synthesis, integrating her own psychic growth with the biblical and midrashic texts. The process and result of this integration is a series of porcelain plates that constitute a visual midrash (fig. 3.6, A and B), accompanied by her own verbal midrashic commentary. The plates emerged step by step, giving visual form to her emotional development and strengthening belief in her self-worth. They demonstrate yet another migration of the protean symbols of the Garden: the center, sacred space; the tree; the serpent; human consciousness; and the miracle that is Creation.

CAROLINE:
Creation and Individuation
(see fig. 3.6A,B, Color Section 2)

This project was a synthesis of my personal experience and my study. During my first semester of graduate study and especially during this course, I came to an understanding of the past two years in my life that is new and encouraging. Two years that seemed filled with pain I now perceive as periods of great personal growth and maturation. After nearly losing track of myself and my self-confidence, I have found a more positive interpretation of my past and present. Our study of Genesis—of the creation of Adam as "imperfect, unfixed, but blessed" and of the Fall as fortunate and necessary—has been particularly helpful in this light. Creating this project allowed my pain, grief, and subsequent joy to be expressed as they never had.

MIDRASH ON THE CREATION OF THE BEN-ADAM (HUMAN BEING) AS ARTIST

After my creation, I opt for rest, but too soon my Creator is upon me with an ultimatum: You have two choices: You may have seven days to finish your creation or you may choose to do nothing at all (i.e., once begun, the irresistible force to bring to birth, baby or art).

A strange ultimatum I think, and with no consequences. But wanting to please, I choose the first and pray for seven short days. The first day is sunny and warm, with me at the very center of warmth. It's perfect. I'm perfect. Why would I change it? Yet how much nicer if I were a bigger center of that warmth—if I could just possess more to feel it. Yes, that surely will be better. And night falls.

The second day I wake to more of me than before. I feel enveloped by warmth. Oh what an improvement! How amusing, how simple to create—to make more and better. But wait, something's missing. I feel warm only on top; I want rather to be surrounded by it. Night falls.

The third day I rise. I'm emerging from my surroundings and feel an intense heat all around. What painful, beautiful heat! Oh how wonderful to create—to make full, brimful. But what's this unexpected pressure pushing me from each direction? With each push I feel heat increase. The pressing continues; it's hot now, and I'm choked by both. What's gone wrong? What interrupts my process of creation? I'm incensed—getting hotter—I must know what's pressing. Night brings dark. In it, I dream of a fight—there's a struggle—and then pain. Sheer pain.

I waken the fourth day to realize my dream was no dream. I am broken, still hurt. All that I created is spilling from me. I can't look. I'm ugly—how beautiful I seemed before. I see the culprit that surrounded me and presses me still, and I blame my Creator for sending it. "I've lost everything," I yell. "You've made a joke of me, a mockery of my creating. Nothing is left of what I was." I am glad for the dark that night brings.

On the fifth day I instinctively gather together my broken parts, piecing them together—to give them a semblance of order. I'm not the same! But I stand back, look myself over, and wonder if I'm still creating. Night comes too soon.

The sixth day, I've changed, am newer than in my beginning. I now have dimension whose center is what I had lost, whose outer limits are my gain. I carefully plant seeds inside of me and wait for their growth. Night comes briefly.

The seventh and final day arrives. That, I perceive, is the joke. I lie, relax, and admire what has grown and imagine what will grow. Every leaf, every petal stretches higher than even I can see. My roots extend and penetrate beneath. I give each a message to take with it, telling my God that I've begun.

REFLECTIONS ON THE UROBOROS

The reading that was most influential in terms of this project was Ego and Archetype by Edinger. I created the plates first, then read Edinger, and then wrote the story/midrash above. It was uncanny to me how many of the images I chose were ones that Edinger described as typical and universal. He began by discussing Jung, who described one's process of psychological development as a gradual separation but [one that] retained connection of the collective Self (or God) and the ego. My plate series can be seen as a development from total unconscious unity with God and my surroundings to a conscious awareness of my relationship with God.

Jung finds a characteristic image in the uroboros, which is a circle circumferenced by a tail-eating snake. I had read of this image before I used it in the plates but had not known of its typical connection with the uroboros. Edinger proceeds to discuss maturation as a continuous process of movement from inflation to alienation to individuation. He cites the circle as an "inflated" shape, assuming a complete or Godlike form. It is interesting to find that I chose a circular shape to describe myself in the first plates. Of this, Edinger would say that I existed solely for myself and interpreted creation as intended for me (see fig. 3.7, Color Section 2).

Edinger then speaks of the "inflated act" that leads to alienation and loss. One example he uses is the eating of the fruit in Paradise. Similarly, my "inflated act" occurs between the third and fourth plates, when I choose to discover what is surrounding and squeezing me. The images for the third and fourth plates I conceived and held in my imagination during my past two years, which I described above. The fourth plate represents Edinger's state of alienation. My boundaries have burst open, and my sense of self is shattered. The last three plates can take shape only as a result of the fourth and can represent Edinger's process of individuation, in which I encounter the Self, or God, and establish a conscious relationship with Him/Her.

Finally, I was struck in almost all of the readings with the emphasis on the center of existence, the central point of creation, and the process of centering oneself. One emerges centered as a created being, as I am in the first three plates. In the fourth plate I suddenly become aware of "profane space" as opposed to the "sacred space" of my previous existence. It is as if the chaos of profane space has thrown me off center. By ordering what's broken in the fifth plate I re-establish my center; thus I become aware of the sacred space that I had previously ignored.

THE SERPENT AS CATALYST

My plates are really a midrash on the biblical Fall, hinging on the snake as agent for the discovery of consciousness and of God's grace. However, the snake is not the only agent. Adam and Eve play their roles as well, as they choose to gain knowledge. In this sense, they are fulfilling what was set up in Genesis 1, where Adam is created, but incompletely. By choosing to know, Adam and Eve continue their process of being created—now created into time, space, and awareness. It is only then in their disobedience, their sin, and with open eyes that they can perceive God's grace. And so alienation or the Fall followed by self-realization or forgiveness, as Edinger suggests, becomes a cyclical development that recurs throughout one's life. Because of this cyclical quality in psychological and religious experience, I chose to create images alluding to movement and to growth. In that respect, my art and the process of its creation exemplified the act of creating. It is not only in psychological or religious experience that we experience pain and suffering that lead to joy and discovery, but also in the primary act of creation itself are the pain and the joy of birth.

The Self as Tree

At the end of her midrash, on the seventh day, Caroline relaxes and lies back to admire what has grown and what will grow. She finds her image is not the external object of her creation—the series of seven dinner plates—but rather her internal, self-created portrait, which, not so curiously, is a tree. "Every leaf and every petal stretches higher than even I can see. My roots extend and penetrate beneath." She has become a conscious, centered, arborescent axis mundi, retaining her developing connection with God. "I give each [leaf and petal] a message to take with it, telling my God that I've begun."

Is there a connection between this personal tree/self-image and the mythic trees of the Garden of Eden? Let us briefly review those baffling Garden symbols. Let us say that both trees are a kind of projection of our own self-image. Let us say that Caroline's Tree of Knowledge was a nothing-tree till she "ate of the fruit of consciousness," till her "inflated act" occurred and she chose to discover what was surrounding and squeezing her. Only then did it begin to flourish and blossom. And only then did she develop a conscious relationship with the other tree, which was at once part of her and at the same time a much greater and unknown entity. Thus God is at once part of us and extends far beyond our wisest grasp. Nor can we realize that God is part of us till we separate from God. The infant "knows" it is one with the breast.

The Bible has little to say about Eden once real life and history begin with the family of Eve and Adam in Chapter 4. But the midrash appreciates our appetite to know the God–Tree of Life that is part of us and beyond us. In fact, the midrash even tells us how to reach and embrace the longed-for Tree of Life, our immortal aspect:

> In Paradise stands the Tree of Life and Tree of Knowledge, the latter forming a hedge about the former. Only one who has cleared a path for her/himself through the Tree of Knowledge can come close to the Tree of Life, which is so huge that it takes five hundred years to traverse a distance equal to the diameter of the trunk, and no less vast is the space shaded by its crown of branches. From beneath flows forth the water that irrigates the whole earth, parting thence into four streams.[11]

The midrash presents the Tree of Life as an omphalos or world navel. It is likely that Adam and Eve, before they ate the fruit of knowledge, had access to this tree whose fruit gave immortality. So they were immortal, which is the bad news. The good news is that they didn't know it because they were not time-conscious. After they attained knowledge (which means power), God was unwilling for them to be immortal. That would make them God, having both knowledge (power) and eternal life. The postbiblical legend gives us a clue to how mortal humanity outside the Garden can achieve eternal life:

One must clear a path through the hedge-like tree of knowledge. In other words one must continually accept the temptation of the serpent and repeatedly eat the fruit of knowledge, and that way eat one's way through to the tree of life. In other words, the recovery of our lost wholeness can only be achieved by tasting and assimilating the fruits of consciousness to the full.[12]

The Bible, however, has no illusions about physical immortality. Already in Proverbs (3:18), the Tree of Life is defined as a life of Torah. This is Judaism's grasp of achievable, metaphoric immortality.

THE PAIN AND JOY OF BIRTH

Finally Caroline writes of the urgency and power "in the primary act of creation itself [which] is the pain and the joy of birth," the birth of her consciousness through her art. Her statement is further illumined by Isaiah Berlin's observation that art is the human creativity that is closest to Divine Creation:

> The only activity that rises not from man's imperfections, but from a sheer wish and need to express and create, is art. That is why every vision of paradise, in which men are finally liberated from all their earthly needs, contains some kind of artistic activity: the angels are represented as playing musical instruments, in the Indian world of the blessed gods there is dancing; there are, I am told, among them divine beings who paint and sculpt. Art is thus the only activity that is not, in Plato's words, a *plerosis*—the filling of some void. It is the only activity that can fitly be called divine—the nearest that mortals can attain to pure creation.[13]

Conclusion

The combined Creation narratives of Genesis 1–3 reflect a birth experience. The first one (1:1–3) is the birth of the universe, and the appearance of light in verse 3 heralds the actual birth. According to verse 2, it is preceded by the conditions associated with birth: darkness, deep, water, formlessness, and breath.

The second account, concluding with Chapter 3, reflects the psychological experience of birth. Here, the exodus from the womb is viewed as the coming to consciousness of mortality, a basic grasp of which unceremoniously boots one out of paradise. The knowledge of good and evil (the dualities, the opposing conditions of human life and death) is conveyed through the experience of sex, which results in the birth of a new generation. Ironically, it is in embracing the new baby that one profoundly recognizes the shortness of life.

The goal of the Eden Workshop is to experience psychological rebirth by separating again and again from the Edens that are warm and secure but also confining. Participants accomplish this through the tearing of fabric to approximate the Jewish experience of life's separation from death by *kriah*. The torn fabric is then revisioned or rebuilt both to honor its initial form and its destruction through memory and to clearly illustrate personal growth into the future. The last example, Caroline's creation plates, also affirms through the rupture that takes place midpoint what creation myths faithfully recount: that breakdown and apparent loss are integral to the creation process.

The recurring motifs of tree and serpent (as spiral, labyrinth, or uroboros), in this workshop and the previous one, invite an additional comment. Nothing in the biblical Eden narrative indicates that the serpent is wrapped around the Tree of Knowledge, yet we find infinite numbers of that visual interpretation. Psychologist Terence Dowling recently noted that the human fetus of seven months has vision and, until its birth, continually perceives the placenta, shaped like a tree, with the umbilical cord attached to it. It is no wonder that the tree is our self-portrait, and the serpent, in its various guises, the catalyst of our life forces.[14]

The Tearing Out of Eden Workshop: Summary

OBJECTIVES
To understand the Garden narrative as the individuation of the human being from his or her original androgynous state; to experience the expulsion from paradise as the archetypal rite of passage, the rebirth that we continually experience whenever we are forced out of the secure past or present into the unknown future.

PRIMARY TEXTS
Genesis, Chapters 1–3 and 4:1–2.

Midrash, "On the Seventh Month, the First Day of the Month" (see note 9).

RECOMMENDED READINGS
Edward Edinger, "Adam and Prometheus."

Jo Milgrom, "Some Second Thoughts About Adam's First Wife."

MATERIALS REQUIRED
Fabric or old clothing to be torn.

Glue, paint, thread, any notions that might be used in the re-forming of the torn pieces.

PROCEDURE

1 Do a close reading of Genesis 1:27 through 4:2.

2 Present and analyze the two works of art:

Michelangelo, *The Temptation and Fall,* c. 1512

Marc Chagall, *Homage à Apollinaire,* c. 1912

3 Integrate the secondary readings and the midrash into the discussion of the art works.

4 Introduce the concept of *kriah.*

5 Explain and assign the *kriah* exercise, to be done at home.

6 Participants present their *kriah* projects, with written material, at next meeting.

7 Closure, feedback.

Notes

1. See "My Own Journey," Introduction, p. 9.

2. The Hebrew word *zot* appears three times in Adam's three-line poem; it is the first word of the first line, the last word of the last line, and the linchpin in her naming line.

3. Joel W. Rosenberg, "The Garden Story Forward and Backward," *Prooftexts,* vol. 1, no. 1 (Jan. 1981): 1–27.

4. Edward Edinger, "Adam and Prometheus," in *Ego and Archetype* (New York: Penguin, 1974), 16–26.

5. Jane Dillenberger, *Style and Content in Christian Art* (Nashville: Abingdon, 1963), 120–125.

6. Ibid., p. 125.

7. Jo Milgrom, "Some Second Thoughts About Adam's First Wife," in *Genesis 1–3 in the History of Exegesis,* Gregory A. Robbins (ed.) (Lewiston, N.Y.: Mellen, 1988), 225–255; see also Jane Schuyler, "Michelangelo's Serpent with Two Tails," *Source,* vol. ix, no. 2 (Winter 1990):23–29.

8. Joseph Dan, "Samael, Lilith and the Concept of Evil," *Association of Jewish Studies Review* 5 (1980):17–40.

9. The midrash is entitled "On the Seventh Month, the First Day of the Month," which, oddly, is Rosh Hashanah, the first of Tishri, the new year, reflecting the liturgical fall calendar of the Bible. Passover marks the new year of the agricultural spring calendar, when Nisan is the first month. H. Freedman and M. Simon (eds.), *Leviticus,* in *Midrash Rabbah,* vol. 4 (London: Soncino, 1939), 369–370.

10. Wayne G. Rollins, *Jung and the Bible* (Atlanta: John Knox, 1983), 103.

11. Louis Ginzberg, *Legends of the Jews,* vol. 1 (Philadelphia: The Jewish Publication Society, 1909), 70.

12. Edinger, *Ego and Archetype,* 21.

13. Isaiah Berlin, President of the British Academy; quoted from the forward to *Album International* I, by Fred Picard (Geneva: Editions Alpic, 1975).

14. Terence Dowling, "The Psychological Significance of the Placenta," presented at the Third International Congress on Pre- and Perinatal Psychology: Nurturing the Possible Human, San Francisco, July 9–12, 1987.

fig. 3.3. Rose, *Re-turn*
(p. 82).

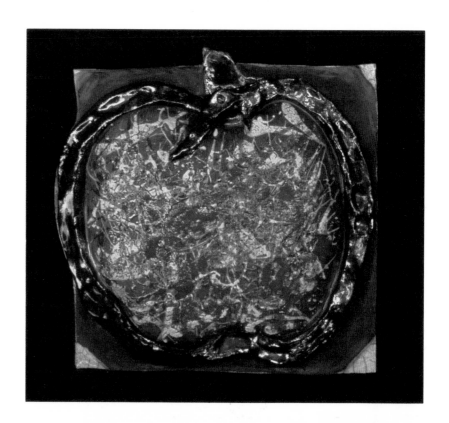

fig. 3.6, A and B.
Caroline, *Creation and Individuation* (p. 85).

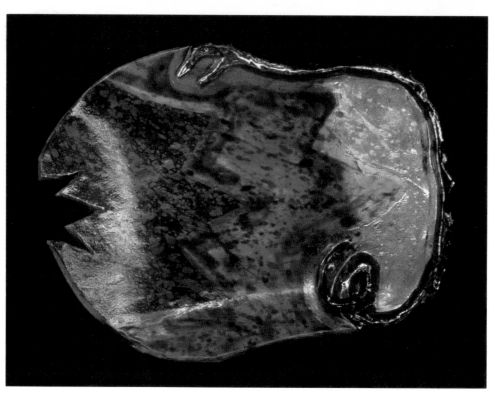

fig. 3.7. Hannah Rivkah Hermann, *The Whale* (embroidery on silk; Shabbat cloth, 19th c.; p. 87). (*From* the Israel Museum, Jerusalem. Reprinted with permission.)

fig. 4.2. Siong, *The Three-Day Journey* (p. 102).

fig. 4.5. Megan, *The Triangle Trial* (p. 105).

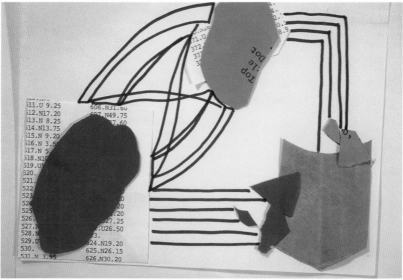

Workshop 4

Lech-Lecha: *Go Forth*

The third chapter of the Book of Genesis ends with the expulsion from Eden. Adam and Eve are out. The cherubim flash their fiery swords, barring any chance of return. The primeval couple has been given the *lech-lecha* order: Go forth. Literally, go to yourself. Go for your own sake. Of course, the literal *lech-lecha* order does not occur until Genesis 12. There, Abraham, living in the safe but confining Eden of Ur and Haran, becomes conscious of the Divine call: *Lech-lecha*. Go forth.

This workshop draws on several aspects of the *lech-lecha* experience: select passages from the biblical text of Genesis 12–22, brief references to midrashic material, and psychological writings on the stages of Abraham's adult development. In the last category are a psychobiography of Abraham by Henry Abramovitch and Erik Erikson's treatment of the emotional and social growth of Abraham as developed in his seminal work, *Childhood and Society*. According to Erikson, the last four stages of adult life correspond to the biblical narrative of Abraham's mature years: identity versus role confusion; intimacy versus isolation; generativity versus stagnation; and integration versus despair. We also consider a mystical approach, in the manner of Jung, whereby each element of the story is interpreted as an integral part of the "whole" truth that the psyche is presenting, independent of the history and tradition of text analysis. It becomes evident that Abraham's stages of development are our own and that they constitute an indispensable prelude to the last trial, namely, the binding of Isaac.[1]

"Testing" is a recurring biblical motif. God and Israel are constantly trying one another. At one point, God says in exasperation that Israel in

Jubilees 17:7; 19:9

1 Leaving his country

2 Famine in Canaan

3 The wealth of the kings

4 Sara and Pharaoh

5 Sara and Abimelech

6 Circumcision

7 Hagar's expulsion

8 Ishmael's expulsion

9 The binding of Isaac

10 The death of Sara

Avot de Rabbi Nathan 33:2

1, 2 Twice when ordered to move on: 12:1, go forth; 12:10, to Egypt

3, 4 Twice regarding his sons: Ishmael, 21:10, and Isaac, 22:1

5, 6 Twice in connection with his wives: 12:11 and 21:10

7 Once regarding the covenant of the pieces, Chapter 15

8 Once, the war with the kings, 14:13

9 Once in Ur

10 Once in circumcision

Pirke de Rabbi Eliezer 26

1 Infancy in Ur

2 In prison and in fire

3 Go forth

4 Famine

5 Sara with Pharaoh and Abimelech

6 Lot (rescue or separation, unspecified)

7 The covenant between the pieces

8 Circumcision

9 Ishmael's expulsion

10 The binding of Isaac

Midrash Tehillim 18:25

1 In the fiery furnace

2 Go forth

3, 4 Two with Sara

5 Hagar

6 Ishmael

7 The kings

8 Circumcision

9 The covenant between the pieces

10 The binding of Isaac

the desert "has tried me ten times over" and surely will not see the Promised Land. There is even an old and persistent motif that the trials of Abraham are used as "credit" with God against the debit of the later suffering of Israel.

What do the traditional midrashim say about the trials? There are four lists of ten trials spanning about a thousand years. The earliest is found in *Jubilees,* dating from the second century B.C.E. Others are *Avot de Rabbi Nathan, Pirke de Rabbi Eliezer,* and *Midrash Tehillim* (on Psalms), dating from about the ninth century. *Pirke Avot (The Ethics of the Fathers),* Chapter 5, is a sketchy fifth source that notes ten trials but does not specify them. The credit motif occurs in *Pirke Avot* and in *Avot de Rabbi Nathan,* in which ten miracles occur during the Red Sea crossing to balance Abraham's trials. This is a preview of the maximum merit that will accrue to Israel because of the last trial of Abraham and Isaac.

Most striking is the absence from all the lists of Abraham's arbitration on behalf of Sodom and Gomorrah, in which Abraham voices the ultimate chutzpah that the Judge of all the earth might be guilty of injustice in condemning the just together with the wicked. Social ethics are inescapable, allowing no hesitant weighing of alternatives. This was no personal test. Yet we will puzzle elsewhere in the Abraham narratives, where the complexities of family relationships seem to obscure the clarity of ethical vision and behavior. In the case of the dismissal of Hagar, p. 105, the laws of Nuzi and Hammurabi shed light on Sara's behavior. In the case of the wife/sister motif, pp. 97 and 104, in which Abraham passes off Sara as his sister, scholars have yet to sleuth the data that will clear Abraham's compromising maneuver.

The full accounting of the four lists of trials appears in the table, "The Ten Trials of Abraham, According to the Midrash." They are quoted exactly, with their almost monosyllabic rabbinic economy and without comment, except for a later illuminating note by Maimonides.[2] The reader will observe that all the biblical topics are accounted for; yet it took the insights of theology and behavioral sciences to flesh out the archetypes.

To shake the reader out of any fixed mindset, I include another short list of trials. Based on the first nine verses of the opening chapter, Genesis 12, this list was designed by a participant named John, whose view is both larger and smaller than that of the traditional midrashic lists. It focuses on unique mystical relationships—with one's self, one's tent, one's blessing and curse, one's environment, one's shadow:

1   Being blessed and cursed. Any time a person is favored, the jealous rage of his or her neighbors is aroused.

2   Going with Lot. Learning to live with the "shadow" of our past, the circumstances of one's life.

3   Passing through Canaanite land. Going through hostile territory, breaking down old barriers, walking with a desire for peace with your environment.

4   Building an altar. Attempting to find expression for the religious and transcendent without cutting one's self off from this world and its concerns.

5   Pitching a tent. Learning how to live off the land, being responsible, setting down historical roots.

6   Journeying by stages. Being patient with self and others, learning to take small steps toward the ultimate goal.

Actually, John is very much in harmony with Jung, who would take each element of a client's dream or fantasy as an integral part of the "whole" truth that the psyche is presenting. With this approach to interpreting a biblical passage, the text is taken as it stands. All historical critical analysis and source criticism are set aside. This is not to devalue these tools of biblical analysis but rather to trust that the form in which the text comes to us today is sufficient, just as a dream should be approached without preconceived ideas. Thus all the symbols in the story are open to individual interpretation in the context of our lives, and all of these will change with age and circumstance.

It is instructive to examine the English word *test*, which initially was not associated with human behavior but with an earthen vessel and a process for assaying metals. In a test, or *cupel*, precious metals were separated from lead (that which weighs down?). This actually recalls Malachi 3:3, in which the purification of metals is directly associated with human behavior, so that priests are to be purified like gold and silver in a crucible of fire and lye in order to present offerings justly. We are encouraged therefore to experience the ten tests with a Jungian perspective, as vehicles of psychic transformation and, in the language of Bible and midrash, as complex conflicts and challenges that confront a spiritual leader.

The first test (Gen. 11:26–12:4). This trial motif is in the command "Lech-lecha," go forth. But the forward action of "go forth" is deeply affected by a backward look. The nuclear family leaves Ur for Canaan and stops halfway at Haran. One brother has already died. Abraham continues on with an even smaller nucleus, his wife and nephew, Lot, the son of the deceased brother. The father remains in Haran. Who will care for him? The second brother, Nahor, is no longer in the record.

Covert tension between Abraham and his father, Terah, is subtly revealed in the genealogy (Gen. 11:26–32) and in the casual aside (Gen. 12:4b) that Abraham was seventy-five when he left Haran. In the genealogy we learn that Terah was seventy when Abraham was born and that Terah died in Haran at the age of 205. When we lift the veil from these mythic numbers we learn what was concealed in the arithmetic: Abraham left his father at Haran at age seventy-five; Terah, who died at age 205, at that time was 145. Terah therefore apparently remained alone for sixty years, since his other son, Nahor, is no longer mentioned. Abramovitch suggests that we cut these figures in half to achieve human proportion. Accordingly, Abraham would have left home in his mid-thirties, which we recognize as a mid-life transition. But the moral question is not resolved by dividing the figures. By their juxtaposition we recognize that the Bible itself was uncomfortable with the fact that the father was apparently abandoned in his old age.

Thus we are given to wonder how Abraham's earlier family life may have influenced his subsequent ambivalent relationships with his wives, nephew, and sons during his perilous path, the hero's journey to maturation, along which surprising barriers spring up again and again.

The second test (Gen. 12:1). Within the alienation, childlessness, and marginality of the old life, Abraham discerns the Voice that permits him the clean break with his past in his exceptional need to find meaning, which is the central theme of biblical history. *Lech-Lecha* means "go forth," "go to yours," or "go for your own sake." The only other biblical occurrence of this phrase is the beginning of the Akedah (Gen. 22), the risk of separation from his future. The full implications of this motif are developed in Workshop 5.

The third test (Gen. 12:6–13:18). Abraham wanders in isolation, despair, and hunger. The promise of land gives way to exile from the just-promised land and by a threatened separation from Sara, "his sister" (?), in a survival stunt that no scholarship known to me is able to decipher or justify.

The fourth test (Gen. 13:14ff.). Abraham forces a separation from his nephew, Lot, but is compensated by God's renewal of the promise of land. "Look . . . to the north, south, east and west, for I give all the land that you see to you and your offspring forever."

The fifth test (Gen. 14–16). Abraham grows in military prowess and argues confidently with God that just persons should not suffer along with the evil. He refuses booty, accepting material loss. His manhood is affirmed by the birth of Ishmael. Yet his public morality does not penetrate the private domain, as he condones Sara's abuse of the pregnant Hagar. Abraham has, in effect, separated from her and the child, which constitutes *the sixth and seventh tests,* beginning with Chapter 16 and ending with Chapter 21.

The eighth test. Chapter 15, a crisis of faith: Despite his military victory in Chapter 14, his sensitive refusal to take booty, and his honored encounter with Melchizedek, Abraham falls into post-victory depression. He laments to God that he is childless and that his steward Eliezer will be his heir. Finally God takes him outdoors to count the stars, confirming that his seed will be that many and that his merit is deserved. In part two of Chapter 15 Abraham envisions God's promise as a fiery treaty between kings. At last he can separate from the old context of Ur. God says (15:7), "I am YHWH, who took you out of Ur." This declaration anticipates the exact formula of another exhilarating turning point in Israel's history at Sinai, "I am YHWH, who took you out of Egypt, out of the house of bondage" (Exod. 20:1).

The ninth test (Gen. 17:1–18:15). Abraham's circumcision is a rebirth. It marks separation from an old name (Abram to Abraham, Sarai to Sara, each name acquiring a *heh* particle, the presence of God's name) and an old physical and spiritual state. The effect of the circumcision, together with the prophecy of the Divine visitors, renews the marriage of Abraham and Sara, who now conceive Isaac.

The tenth test. (Gen. 22). The near sacrifice of Isaac. Elie Wiesel claims that every conflict that ever arose in Judaism carries echoes of this trial: the terror of Divine confrontation; the quest for purity of purpose; the dilemmas of rebellion versus obedience, morality versus religion, faith versus justice; the yearning for both freedom and commitment.

Jung's definition of trial as psychic transformation and the Bible's articulation of ultimate values in a spiritual journey merge in an adjunct meaning of "test" (Hebrew n-s-h, "test-try-experience") in Exodus 20:20.[3] Israel has just received the Ten Commandments and stands in terror before the smoking mountain, begging Moses to mediate the Divine Presence. Moses answers, Don't be afraid because God is giving you this experience/test so that the fear of Him will be on your faces and you won't sin. In other words, don't be afraid to be afraid of coming to consciousness of this greater experience. A trial, therefore, is also an experience. Try it. Test it. Experience it despite the fear. The idea of test/trial in the Bible is a matter of experiencing God, not only when crossing the Red Sea or on a smoking mountain, but even in the ordinary daily acts of living and human encounter.

A spiritual person is vulnerable to experiencing psychic transformation that the Divine encounter can evoke. It is the psychic transformation that, in turn, engenders changes in one's interaction with the world.

These several trials, however one chooses to count them, acquire a structure within Genesis 12–22 that is visible within a giant pair of verbal brackets. These brackets refer to the only two biblical occurrences of *lech-lecha*, which roughly frame the beginning and end of the Abraham narratives (Gen. 12:1; 22:2). A close reading of those two passages shows how structure conveys meaning. In each case, *lech-lecha* is accompanied by a short three-part phrase of narrowing focus and increasing intensity.

Thus God tells Abraham in Genesis 12, to "*lech-lecha,*" go forth, from your land, your next of kin, your father's house. If you internalize that imagery, you can see yourself leaving your familiar physical neighborhood, then more intensely, your extended family, and finally —the greatest wrench—the intimacy of your childhood, those scenes and smells in the kitchen and the family room. That everyone leaves one's past is a given. That we leave our past many times and in many ways is an archetypal experience that lies behind the specific biography of Abraham. The threat appears, however, when *lech-lecha* turns up again in Genesis 22 and an old man is asked by God, with increasing specificity, to give up his future. We are forced to ask: Is this too an archetypal experience, a human crisis we must anticipate?

What actually do the words *lech-lecha* mean? Go to yourself. Go for your own sake. Go to yours. Get thee. All these suggest the internal, introspective journey, the great journey of personal destiny, the urgent change of one's focus and direction.

The structure of the beginning verses of Genesis 12 and 22 conveys both the trauma of departure, with its attendant promise of blessing, and the total reversal.

Genesis 12:1–2		Genesis 22:2
"To the land that I will show you"	parallels	"the land of Moriah" (which means "land of vision")
"I will make you a great nation"	is undone by	"and offer him there as a burnt offering"

What is meant by archetype? An archetype is a key to psychological and spiritual truths that are essential to the process of individuation, of becoming fully an individual. When we hear an archetypal story such as the Akedah, our psyches dimly recall that this is something of meaning to us, which is unknown and yet known, and it makes us want to explore our inner world.

Edward Edinger suggests that Abraham's call by God in Genesis 12 initiated his individuation process. Abraham is the father of the Jewish people, and if Jews are a chosen people, then all Jews who are chosen choose to make the journey with him. He is the representative of the "inner person" who psychologically begets us all. We too are repeatedly called forth by God from where we are to wholeness, to move into a new stage. Will we respond as Abraham did or not?[4]

Following the study of the text, we are ready to introduce the exercise in handmade midrash.

The Personal Lech-Lecha

Betty Edwards, in *Drawing on the Artist Within,* sets up two insightful exercises in which the reader or participant learns that a line can express a personal emotion. For example, you can draw energy or joy or depression without drawing a representational figure. This discovery is a great relief to those of us untrained in art who see ourselves as nonartists.[5] Workshop 1, the Sensory Aleph, uses the first two exercises of Edwards to show how simple lines can convey personal feelings.

Edwards's exercises have been applied there to the making of the Aleph.

A third exercise illustrates how one's complex relationship with another person can also be expressed through lines without figural forms. Thus Edwards has her class illustrate "good and bad marriage" with the language of lines. The meandering lines of the good marriage are mainly parallel, occasionally intersecting. The author writes, "A good marriage is two people together but as individuals. They both recognize each other as separate from each other but also involved with each other." The bad marriage shows lines that are heavily entangled with one another. The author writes, "A bad marriage is one where two people support each other and are absorbed into each other. When a conflict occurs, they cannot help each other." Thus do lines become visual analogs of feelings. It has been my experience, confirming Edwards's, that once the requirement to picture objects is removed, participants enter into the activity with resourcefulness and enjoyment.

Participants in the Lech-Lecha Workshop are instructed to choose an experience of *lech-lecha* in their own lives and draw it in the "language of lines." The drawings are to be in pencil, and erasers may be used freely. The lines may be dark or light, thick or thin, dense or sparse, many or few, strong or weak, fast or slow. They may go in any direction. They may take any shape. The only restriction is that they may not be pictures of anything recognizable, such as hearts or arrows, figures or faces. Somehow, though, the lines will represent the people and the actions involved, without looking like the people (no figures or faces). They will most likely make visible the participants' feelings about particular people and events. Those who wish may add collage elements of found materials—a fragment of color from a magazine, a piece of string, and so on.

When the analog drawings are finished, participants are asked to "read" the lines and identify the feelings and thoughts that they express. Finally, they interpret and translate the analog drawings into the verbal mode. Thus the personal Lech-Lecha is written twice: first as an analog drawing, which tries to gain access to thought that is outside of verbal awareness; second, as its verbal translation. The result is often new awareness and perspective on both the text itself and the parallel experiences that we all have as we make our way through the stages of adult life—in biblical language, the trials of adult life.

SIONG:

Too Far from Singapore (fig. 4.1)

I am a Chinese born in a moderate, well-doing, but conservative family. During my childhood my family was large, consisting of my grandparents, nine from my side, and nine from my only uncle's side. And I am the second eldest among all my brothers, sisters, and cousins. As in rigid Chinese tradition, the parents' attitude of hoping

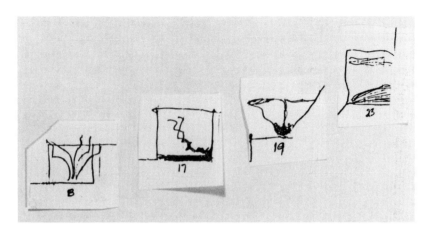

fig. 4.1. Siong, *Too Far from Singapore.*

*children doing well in the future predominated, they were concerned
about their children's education.*

*Indeed, I was doing very well in my school work, all the while
among the top. This might mainly have come from my lure of
knowledge, self-discipline, and fulfillment of my parents'
hope. . . . However, a turning point of my life came when I faced a
mass of never-thought-of problems during the period of my father's
death. I was left alone to think of all these because my mother and
close relatives were illiterate. Yet I had to, first time, think of family
income stability, my handicap in English (Mandarin was my first
language). First time I learnt that I had constraints and weaknesses
when I wanted to do something.*

Siong's self-portrait at age eight is one of vigorous flourishing,
branching out in unprecedented success in school. Later, images of
hope, despair, and conflict follow. The scraggly twigs when he is
seventeen show grief and disorientation when his young father died at
forty-five; at nineteen, his split and hopelessness in the army; at
twenty-three, his conflict over design work; at twenty-five, "when I
entered alone into the departure room in the airport leaving for the
U.S., I cried in my heart as I knew I could not afford a failure again."

The logical next step is for each participant to apply the personal
Lech-Lecha to Abraham. I ask students to identify a series of trials
culminating with the Akedah. I explain that the biblical text does not
speak of Abraham's experiences between Genesis 12 and 22 as trials.
Nor do I disclose the midrashic list of trials, not wishing to influence or
simplify their choices. I ask participants for analog drawings that
explicate the trials on a deeper level. Finally, they are to translate back
into words the meaning of the lines.

In the following examples, the reader sees a range of feeling

The First Trial: Go Forth

responses to the awesome prospect of leaving home for the unknown and to the complex love and hate ambivalences in Abraham's home and family and in his religious orientation.

The first example is another work by Siong, which links his own traumatic *Lech-Lecha* to the journeys of Abraham's *Lech-Lecha.*

SIONG:

The Three-Day Journey

(see fig. 4.2, Color Section 2)

Abraham knows he has one of two choices. The first choice is hard but shows his loyalty to God because to kill his only loved son is like terminating the hope that touches his deepest prudence and soul. The second choice seems to be easy because it satisfies his immediate need. Three days is the time allowance to decide to obey God or fulfill his self-interest.

My collage shows the conflict during the journey. First, the unordered overlapping black-and-white lines at the bottom with flamelike red form symbolize Abraham's heart burning helplessly in the choices. It also reminds him of the possible scene of burning his son at the top of the mountain. He steps on the journey toward God but is surrounded by the conflict of giving up all hope.

On the upper lefthand space the form of three different colors symbolizes the image of God viewed by Abraham. The shining radiating red and skinlike colors symbolize the perceptive image of an all-present, all-powerful, and benevolent God with humane and personal qualities. Yet God's unquestionable authority presents a black spot in Abraham's mind.

On the right Isaac is presented in the form of two wings. Abraham's life is limited, and Isaac is the one who will carry his blood and heritage to the unknown future. Hence Isaac is his hope. The soft and delightful color shows Isaac is pure, innocent, and the colorful dream of Abraham. All three figures, Abraham, Isaac, and God, are equally important in forming the composition. The distances between the forms of God and Isaac to Abraham show it is impossible for Abraham to gain both together. He can choose only one.

Siong started out conceptually with simple triangles on the right that illustrate Abraham's route and his impossible choices. He then added fragments from the glossy pages of a magazine, as design elements conveying texture and color appropriate to his language of lines and the dilemma of feeling.

JOANNA:

Go Forth (fig. 4.3)

This is the moment of hearing "Go forth." It shows an ear with a spring to the left that compels the ear to follow. The three "fingers" to the right are the part that tries to cling to what it knows.

Joanna responds to the intensity of revelation as a sensory experience. It is not yet the journey that concerns her, or faith or doubt, but

fig. 4.3. Joanna, *Go Forth.*

fig. 4.4. Joanna, *Abraham's Own Path.*

the unsettling internal effect on the individual who has heard something that cannot be put aside.

Joanna has a second Lech-Lecha drawing in an unexpected place. She attaches it to Genesis 18:33 (fig. 4.4). Abraham and God have just completed their bargaining session over the possibility that the presence of ten just persons might avert the destruction of Sodom and Gomorrah. She asks, "By stopping at ten does Abraham realize that he has reached the limits of God's intention? Does he intuit that God has finished speaking to him?" The text reads, "God went his way when he finished speaking with Abraham, and Abraham returned to his place."

In translating her lines later, Joanna writes:

The drawing shows Abraham quietly carrying out his own path amid the unknown fury of God. He pushes into the morass, as far as he dares, stops, and asks his question. He is relieved and moves a little further to the left before he pushes forward again. Each time he pushes further in, there is a risk he won't get what he wants because God is so powerful. He is concealing his intention.

Although I have drawn the path opening out beyond this immediate issue, I can't help feeling Abraham does have to tread warily with God, and more such encounters are to come. I also think that Abraham has been equipped to deal with God and is special in this respect. No one else can walk through the outer lines. Abraham has forged his own path. (This exercise felt wonderful—I see the power of the drawings—wow!)

Joanna has made an additional Lech-Lecha out of the Sodom and Gomorrah confrontation. This meeting with God is really a pathfinder. What chutzpah. God's image gets tarnished as Abraham comes out looking a whole lot more just and compassionate than the Creator of the universe. No wonder he must tread warily, uncertain of the sharp turn the next *lech-lecha* may require. Perhaps this is the real *lech-lecha:* not just obeying the word of God without question but challenging it as you go.

The Sodom and Gomorrah narrative is a trendsetter. Jews always argue with God; here's where it started.

Two of Sara's Trials

Three times, in Genesis 12, 20, and 26, Abraham and then Isaac respond to personal danger by ranking their wives as sisters and placing them in the harem of an enemy king for their own protection. Ephraim Speiser explains that in Hurrian society, whose customs were intimately known by the patriarchs, a marriage was strongest when the wife attained the simultaneous legal status of sister regardless of blood ties. Therefore, a man might marry a woman and at the same time adopt her as his sister in two separate documents. This gave him greater authority, and also granted her greater protection and higher social status. This background would also in some way guarantee the purity of the wife's descendants.[6] This is the good news: We now understand something of an ancient exotic practice. The bad news is that it does not shed light on the mysterious conditions of the patriarchal marriages.

VIJI:
Power, No Power; but Faith, Sometimes

A soft-spoken Indian convert to Christianity, Viji has the least experience with art education and the technology and materials of American affluence. Sara's wife/sister traumas are delivered with visual understatement and eloquence. Sara and Pharaoh are represented by the conditions of their relationship. Repeated short strokes are her helplessness engulfed by the wavy lines that are his power. The entire yellow filled-in area of the rectangle stands for God's protection. Both figures are enclosed in the rectangle and are subservient to the solid color of God's protection.

In the *Sara/Abimelech/Abraham* triangle, Abimelech and Abraham are V and inverted V (Λ) respectively, placed over each other. Their points impinge on Sara, who is caught between them, a horizontal slab, an altar. Again the area is filled in with solid Divine projection, although this time, significantly, Viji doesn't comment verbally on God's presence. I remembered accounts of Indian widows who were slain and cremated on funeral pyres in order to accompany their deceased husbands to the afterlife. I wondered what picture floated in Viji's memory behind her analog drawings.

Abraham is diminished by the presence of Hagar in the household. His vulnerability is illustrated by his damaged form. The shapes of Sara and Hagar are torn from out of his shape. His torment is only exacerbated by his conscience—the broken lines leading to Hagar's dismissal.

LAURA:
Abraham's Vulnerability

Megan emphasizes the overt and covert communications of the problematic household of Sara, Hagar, and Abraham. Abraham's being is augmented by parts of Sara (red) and Hagar (green) that are now part of him. Sara has his ear directly: Straight lines travel loud and clear from her to him. Hagar has to go around corners to reach Abraham, perhaps looking back stealthily as she moves about. As for the two women, tangle, cross-purpose, and circumlocution characterize their language. Each has her own agenda of intrigue, illustrated by the patches of mysterious mathematical calculations that lie beneath each figure. Only Abraham seems free from covert operations. Is it because he is wholly manipulated by external forces and unaware of his own unconscious motives?

MEGAN:
The Triangle Trial
(see fig. 4.5, Color Section 2)

Sara's damaged image in the scene of her abuse of Hagar (Gen. 16) acquires new perspective in light of the Code of Hammurabi, paragraph 146, and a text from Nuzi (Hurrian) family law, both known to the patriarchs. In the former, a ranking priestess who does not conceive gives her husband a slave girl to provide him with a son. If the concubine tries to arrogate to herself a position of equality with her mistress, the wife shall demote her to her former status of slave, but may not sell her to others. In the Nuzi family law a childless wife is required to provide a concubine but would have all the legal rights to the offspring. Thus Sara did what she did not out of rash impulse but in accord with the well-known customary law of the Hurrians. The laws thus provide the framework of action, but nothing can dictate the feelings with which the laws are acted out.[7]

Here Ishmael is the focus of attention. He is represented as the middle gray figure connected by lines to his real mother (Hagar, pink) and his real father (Abraham, blue). The blue lines represent God's promise to make Ishmael a great man. There is a bond between Abraham and his son, and between him and his wife Sara (the purple and orange figure on the right), but no bond between him and Hagar.

DIANA:
Triangles (fig. 4.6)

fig. 4.6. Diana, *Triangles.*

There are two curiosities in Diana's interpretation. The first is her failure to see that she does in fact show a bond between Abraham and Hagar. It is the line of relationship that goes from Abraham to Ishmael, which goes through Hagar. True, Abraham's relationship with Hagar is for the purpose of creating an heir. There is apparently no conscious development of a relationship. But it happens. The surrogate mother is a reality in the heart. Diana knows instinctively that it can and does happen.

The second is a Freudian slip. This version is her second. In the original version there was no connection between Abraham and Sara. Sara simply stood alone on the right—another intuitive "right" insight. Sara was in fact totally alienated by the birth of Ishmael and the inevitable growing relationship between Abraham and Hagar. Only in her second "improved" version does Diana render the establishment position.

It is most illuminating to compare Diana's midrash with four versions (fig. 4.7, A to D) of Hagar's dismissal by Rembrandt.[8] Rembrandt's preoccupation with the dismissal of Hagar may be related to the troubled circumstances of his own life. After the death of his wife, Saskia, Rembrandt hired a nurse, Geertghe Dircx, to care for his young son, Titus. She stayed with the artist until 1649, ending up in a madhouse in Gouda. It is not certain when exactly or under what circumstances she left. But in 1645 or 1649 Hendrickje Stoffels became Rembrandt's common-law wife. Art has an uncensored, disconcerting way of cloaking convention with undisguised, raw emotion.

fig. 4.7, A to D.
Rembrandt, *Dismissal of
Hagar*. (*From* the
Metropolitan Museum
of Art, New York City; c.
1645. Reprinted with
permission.)

fig. 4.8. Laura, *The Trial of Circumcision.*

LAURA:

The Trial of Circumcision: The Mini-Sacrifice

(fig. 4.8)

The two cut-out circles represent the covenant made between God, the top circle, and Abraham and his people, the bottom circle. The red flower on the right represents the flowering of a nation that has resulted from Abraham's tribes' acceptance of the covenant. The pencil lines drawn around the picture show the radiance and far-reaching magnitude of the covenant.

This picture illustrates to me a joyous occasion. It is a significant period in history, for Abraham's people are becoming more closely bonded to God, as they circumcise their males to physically consummate the covenant.

Laura's example, like many others in this book, illustrates how the language of lines creates the analog drawing; in other words, how the language of lines helps to unlock creativity by releasing a surprising metaphor. In this instance, Laura's analog drawing, richly augmented by collage, is a visual analog for circumcision and the subsequent flowering of generativity, not only of the old couple, but of their descendants.

JOANNA:

The Trial of Laughter as the Promise

(fig. 4.9)

Finally, Joanna has another comment about God's promise to Sara. Her analog drawing reflects Genesis 18:10–15:

I will return to you when life is due, and your wife Sara shall have a son. Now Sara had stopped having her period. She laughed to herself saying, Now that I am dried up, am I to have enjoyment—with my husband so old? Then the Lord said to Abraham, Why did Sara laugh saying, Shall I really bear a child, old as I am? Is anything too wondrous for the Lord? I will

fig. 4.9. Joanna, *The Trial of Laughter as the Promise.*

return to you when life is due and Sara shall have a child. Sara dissembled, saying I did not laugh, for she was frightened. He replied, Yes, you did laugh.

Is God's promise laughable? Is this in fact proof of the divine path? The lotus-looking thing is God's promise. It has organized shape and form. It is sound, it sits solidly. The lines to the right are laughter. I have the feeling that the laughter lines come together to form the promise. The promise has discipline and is not arrived at easily, although it looks simple enough. The energy of the laughter lines has to be organized willingly.

JOANNA
The Trial of Ambivalence: Genesis 15:1–3, 8

Here are Sara (the left rectangle) and Abraham in their own home or enclosed space. They are quite happy together, and if it weren't for the disruptiveness of the promise hanging over them, they could be happy. I see Abraham angry with God, shaking his fist, as he hears once more about the so-called heir. When I drew this originally, I was probably showing the ambivalence of Abraham. Yes, surrounded by God's shield, but angry nevertheless.

In her recent psychoanalytic study *Psychoanalysis and the Bible*, Dorothy Zeligs raises the question of Abraham's ambivalence toward an heir who would displace him. There are recurring clues.

Lot, Abraham's nephew and closest descendent, goes his way as the result of a confrontation initiated by Abraham. In the passage Joanna cites for this analog drawing, Genesis 15:1–3, Abraham repeats his automatic childless lament but seems almost relieved to announce that, as a result, his chief steward, Eliezer, will inherit him. A few short chapters down the road, Ishmael, whose birth was engineered at great cost to domestic peace, is sent off with his mother, albeit by Sara, but with God's approval. Perhaps God is fronting for Abraham's unconscious motive, at least with regard to the son.

Finally, we arrive at the tenth trial, which Zeligs calls "the culmination of Abraham's lifetime of ambivalence toward a son." Zeligs continues:

> As the time drew near for the son to displace the father, a powerful struggle of conflicting feelings within Abraham must have brought about the crisis which reached its peak in the near sacrifice of Isaac. The call from God to sacrifice the ambivalently loved and hated son must also have involved repressed feelings of hostility toward the Father who ostensibly made this demand upon him. Such a deed would unconsciously have been an act of aggression toward God himself by frustrating the entire grand design for which Abraham had been called in the first place. The man who, according to rabbinic tradition, had been the first to comprehend God as the Creator of the universe, was now about to commit him to an act of annihilation.
>
> The biblical narratives about Abraham can be understood as a kind of psychological documentary of his life. They deal with his struggles to grow in emotional and spiritual maturity. His problems mainly involve the basic relationships of family life where man's most intense emotions are rooted. By overcoming the inner conflicts of jealousy and competitiveness, with their accompanying aggression and fear, the positive feelings of warmth and cooperation were able to find expression.[9]

So Abraham wakes up in time. God (Elohim, who gave the order) removes his mask of harsh judgment and puts on His compassionate one (Adonai, who rescinded the order). Isaac steps down from the altar . . . into his father's embrace?

Conclusion

This chapter presents several workshops based on the text of Genesis 12–22, which deals with the trials of Abraham as stages in his adult development as defined by Henry Abramovitch's psychobiography, *Abraham: Psychology of a Spiritual Revolutionary and His Hebrew Chroniclers,* and by Erik Erikson's *Childhood and Society.* In the latter, the last four stages of adult life correspond to the Bible's disclosure of Abraham's mature years: identity versus role confusion; intimacy versus isolation; generativity versus stagnation; integration versus despair. We also noted Jung's method, in which each element of the story is interpreted as an integral part of the whole truth that the psyche is presenting, independent of the history and tradition of text analysis.

It seems, however, that the skeletal midrashic citations of these ten trials have been waiting for the visual artist to flesh them out for our generation. Applying Betty Edwards's *Drawing on the Artist Within,* we have used the pre-verbal "language of lines" to make visible the feeling life suppressed in the laconic narratives, first through abstract penciled lines and collage, then by verbal interpretation. Untutored in art, participants have created visual midrash, so that Abraham's trials have become our own. What does it mean to be a lover, a parent, a believer? How are the tensions of intimacy versus privacy balanced? Where is the courage to both accept and question authority? How are we to confront separation, loss, and age?

None of the midrashic lists cites as a trial Abraham's arbitration on behalf of Sodom and Gomorrah, in which he voices the outrageous notion that the Judge of all the earth might be guilty of injustice in condemning the just together with the wicked. The rabbinic consensus is that social ethics are inescapable, constituting no personal test. Joanna identified a different trial. Abraham was testing how far he could argue with God, a quality dearly cherished and cultivated by seekers of justice and compassion throughout history. In the end he backs off. We have seen and puzzled elsewhere how the complexities of family relationships can blur the clarity of ethical vision and behavior.

Facing the last trial, Abraham mystifies us even more. Confronted with the loss of his future, he utters not a word of protest. In awe of his faith and with bewilderment at his behavior, we turn now to the riddle of the Akedah.

The Lech-Lecha *Workshop: Summary*

OBJECTIVES

To understand how structure conveys meaning through a close reading of the only two *lech-lecha* passages in the Bible; to appreciate *lech-lecha* as the universal experience of leaving one's past; to understand the relationship between exile from Eden and *lech-lecha*; to place the *lech-lecha* pattern into the context of adult development; to perceive the trials of Abraham within the literary brackets formed by the pair of *lech-lechas*; to move from the rational knowledge to the experiential *lech-lecha* through handmade midrash and the language of lines; to appreciate the candor of the text in its exposure of the human failings of the founding father and mother.

PRIMARY TEXTS

Genesis 12–22.

A complete midrashic narrative on the life and trials of Abraham in Louis Ginzberg, *Legends of the Jews,* vol. 1, pp. 183–291.

RECOMMENDED READINGS

Henry Abramovitch, *Abraham: Psychology of a Spiritual Revolutionary and His Hebrew Chroniclers,* Part 1 on the tests, pp. 9–80 (see note 1).

Betty Edwards, *Drawing on the Artist Within,* pp. 49–123.

ART WORKS FOR DISCUSSION

Rembrandt, *Dismissal of Hagar* (four versions), in Hans-Martin Rotermund (ed.), *Rembrandt's Drawings and Etchings for the Bible,* 44–47.

MATERIALS REQUIRED

For the language of lines: initially, pencil, erasers, and white paper; finally, any writing or coloring tool.

For handmade midrash: colored construction paper and glue, with encouragement to add collage elements from found materials and to incorporate the language of lines into the collage.

PROCEDURE (Over Several Sessions)

1 Participants do a personal Lech-Lecha in the language of lines after a close reading of the two occurrences of *lech-lecha* in the Bible.

2 Study of text, Genesis 12–22 (after preparation and reading at home).

3 Participants search the text for Abraham's trials before seeing official versions.

4 Discussion of participants' lists of trials in light of the official versions.

5 Participants translate their choice of trials into the language of lines.

6 Discussion of Rembrandt's several versions of the Dismissal of Hagar, noting Rembrandt's use of the language of lines.

7 Individual presentations of personal trials, visual and verbal. Show and discuss development from the first language of lines Lech-Lecha done at Step 1.

8 Discussion and feedback.

1. Henry Abramovitch, "Abraham: Psychology of a Spiritual Revolutionary and His Hebrew Chroniclers," Ph.D. diss., Yale University, 1977. See his view of the tests, Part 1, pp. 9–80. Also, Erik Erikson, *Childhood and Society* (New York: Norton, 1950).

2. Moses Maimonides (Rambam), *Perush L'Masechet Avot* (Jerusalem: Mosad Harav Kook, 1961), 174. Rambam alone, to my knowledge, identifies two of the trials with Hagar, the first being the upheaval wrought in Abraham's household by the introduction of the second wife.

3. Moshe Greenberg, "NSH in Exodus and the Purpose of the Sinaitic Theophany," *Journal of Biblical Literature* 79, no. 3 (1960): 273–276; also Rivka Kluger, *Psyche and the Bible* (New York: Spring Publications, 1974), 37–39.

4. Edward Edinger, *The Bible and the Psyche: Individuation Symbolism in the Old Testament* (Toronto: Inner City Books, 1986), 25.

5. Betty Edwards, *Drawing on the Artist Within* (New York: Simon & Schuster, 1986), 49–123; figures on 75.

6. Ephraim Speiser, "Abraham and Sarah in Egypt," *Genesis: The Anchor Bible* (Chicago: Doubleday, 1964), 90–94.

7. Ibid., "The Birth of Ishmael", 116–121.

8. Hans-Martin Rotermund (ed.), *Rembrandt's Drawings and Etchings for the Bible* (Philadelphia: Pilgrim Press, 1969), 44–47.

9. Dorothy Zeligs, *Psychoanalysis and the Bible* (New York: Bloch, 1974), 1–34.

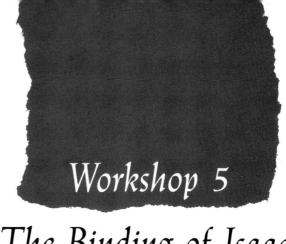

Workshop 5

The Binding of Isaac

One of the most compelling and enigmatic narratives in the Bible is the binding of Isaac, known as the Akedah. Elie Wiesel has noted that every persistent issue in Judaism can be traced to it: the need to both obey and rebel; to be bound as well as free; the dread of conflict between morality and religion; the fear of asserting freedom of will in the face of Divine encounter; the yearning for a future and a purity of purpose as against drifting with glorious memories.[1]

In two thousand years of literature, a universe of meaning for Judaism and Christianity has been expanded from those nineteen stark verses of Genesis 22 about the implications of this trial. The history of Western art has been equally endowed with visual interpretations of the Akedah.[2]

The literary and visual traditions of the Akedah usually have been taught separately, except for special studies by art historians. My own work in this area has shown that art and text can be taught together because word and visual image complete each other. This chapter draws on my doctoral research,[3] out of which the concept of hand-made midrash was born. It advances the innovative methodology in which participants make visible the inner turmoil evoked by the terror of this text. In a larger sense, the collective unconscious revealed in these simple exercises is none other than the core of shared archetypes that lie at the base of the great works of art.

A Close Reading

In brief, Genesis 22 is an encounter fraught with background. An old man and his son, at the bidding of God, go without protest to an unknown place of vision where the younger man unknowingly aids in his own sacrifice. In the end, God changes his mind and reaffirms to Abraham the promise of seed, victory, and blessing. But the father, it seems, returns home alone.

A close reading of the text discloses cues that evoke the universal human issues behind the narrative. Perhaps the most poignant of these occurs in God's drawn-out words to Abraham in verse 2, where purposeful repetition occurs in startling contrast to the sparse, staccato, and artful omission that characterizes these nineteen short verses. Pointed out earlier in the Lech-Lecha Workshop, these verses are repeated here, in their climactic context:

> Take please
> your son . . . your special/only one . . . the one you love
> Isaac
> and *lech-lecha,* go forth
> to the land of Moriah
> and offer him up there as a burnt offering
> on one of the mountains that I will tell you.

fig. 5.1. Moshe Mizrachi, *The Akedah.* (*From* the Jewish Museum/Art Resource, New York City; 1888. Reprinted with permission.)

How strangely human and tentative is the word *please* at the outset of that awful command, as if God knows what chutzpah it takes, and gulps before speaking, almost pleading.

Then comes the intensifying triplicate: "your son, your only one, the one you love." A clue to the form and meaning of this phrase comes to us via the one that immediately follows; it is the imperative "*lech-lecha*," which occurs in only one other biblical passage (Gen. 12), at the beginning of Abraham's calling. It is also an intensifying triplicate.

Lech-lecha, go forth
from your land, from your next of kin, from your father's house
to the land that I will show you
I will make you a great nation.

A closer examination of these two parallel passages enables us to view them as a pair of giant brackets enclosing the Abraham narrative. Each calls for a separation. The earlier passage focuses on the pain of departure from one's past: first, from one's familiar countryside, then one's extended family, and finally from the constellation of familiar sights, sounds, and smells in the parental home. In the second passage, each successive reference to the son emphasizes the singular relationship of this father and his offspring and heightens what appears to be the imminent threat to Abraham's future. There is both an echo confirming the promise and a perplexing reversal in these passages:

Genesis 22:2		Genesis 12:1–2
"The land of Moriah"	parallels	"the land that I will show you."
"Offer him there"	reverses	"I will make you a great nation."

The universal aspect of the narrative is clear, for each one of us has countless experiences of *lech-lecha*: Get thee, go forth, go to yourself, go for your own sake, go to yours, as it is variously translated. It is the challenge of leaving the past behind. Nor do we identify less with the terror of future loss.

The universal import of this episode is enhanced by two stylistic principles of the biblical narrative, purposeful repetition, which is illustrated here and subsequently, and artful omission, which we see here, in the deliberate absence of detail concerning the personality and age of Isaac. Visual artists portray him variously from infancy to young adulthood. The text tells us that Isaac was born to Sara at age ninety. Her death is recorded in the next chapter at age 127. Logically, a number of postbiblical sources render Isaac's age as thirty-seven (e.g., Targum Jonathan, sixth century, and Rashi, eleventh century). The Targum version was painted with charm and fervor in 1888 by folk artist Moshe Mizrachi (fig. 5.1). Here, the bearded Isaac is a younger image of his father. Although the chronological evidence is easily deduced, the shadowy identity of Isaac invites us to view him as every child in all possible relationships with his or her parents.[4]

Finally, when the ram has been substituted and father and son are blessed, verse 19 is thrown in our face, "Abraham then returned to his servants, and they departed together for Beer-sheba." Did Abraham return alone? Where was Isaac?

The narrative is so sparse, so much is left unsaid, said ambiguously, or, at the other extreme, mysteriously repeated, that we are bewildered and unsatisfied. We can readily see why, from the very beginning, seeds were being sown in those painful lacunae. And we can see how those seeds sprouted the legends and the art of the Akedah through the millennia. For example, that thorny little detail at the end of verse 19 suggests that at the happy ending of the trial, Isaac was no longer there. What shall we make of that? Targum Jonathan amusingly suggests that Isaac was whisked away to school, to the mythic academy of Shem and Eber, a safe enough haven where an eligible bachelor could absorb himself in Torah until his marriage to Rebecca was arranged, three years later. In fact, this is how the midrash accounts for the genealogy that immediately follows the Akedah. It subtly reviews and advances the story with the little detail that Bethuel had begotten Rebecca, and it focuses us on the old hometown where Eliezer, Abraham's steward, will find Isaac's bride.

Graduate school, however, is not the only option. A less graceful and more chilling solution to Isaac's disappearance is that he was actually sacrificed. Indeed, such a legend was current in the Middle Ages and is the subject of a monograph by Shalom Spiegel, *The Last Trial*. He offers not only that Isaac was sacrificed but also that he was resurrected by the dew of resurrection! Spiegel suggests that this legend developed in order to deny that the sacrifice of Isaac was in any way less than that of Jesus. Or perhaps it is a reflection of the historical experience of Jewish martyrdom, which demanded a more tragic model than that of merely intended sacrifice.[5]

Still another sacrifice is possible: the father and son relationship itself. Alienated from each other by the Akedah, they no longer walk together. This psychological component is one that is fleshed out by handmade midrash. Here is a parade example of the "grain of sand in the oyster that creates the pearl." An irritant in the text works the imagination until some kind of satisfaction is achieved. This kind of hermeneutic (search for meaning) comes from an abiding respect for the text. It was not an error or an oversight that Isaac wasn't there. It was intentional, if ambiguous. It was meant for each generation to deal with in its own contemporary midrashic mode.

Thus personal relationships and one's religious orientation are two categories that embrace both the midrashic and visual texts of the Akedah. The latter, value-vision, focuses on perception, or lack thereof, which permeates our story consistently. The Hebrew root for *vision* is so pervasive that midrash is compelled to see and hear it even when it isn't there. Thus, for example, in an eighteenth-century copper engraving, the Akedah displays its central motif like the legend of a comic strip: two large words hang over Abraham's head, *yareh* and *yireh*. To Isaac's only question (v. 8), "Where is the lamb for the offering?" Abraham's answer is *yireh*, "God will see/provide." Central to the narrative, *yireh* occurs a second time in verse 14, in which Abraham renames Moriah (which already bears the same root) as "the place where God will see/provide."

The other word, *yareh*, meaning "fear," is equally complex. The angel stops the action, acknowledging, "Now I know you are God *fearing*, because you did not withhold your son" (v. 12). Now *fear* and *see* are homonyms in Hebrew. They look and sound alike. Midrash would like us to think of "God-fearing" as part of the "seeing/vision" complex, therefore the words are juxtaposed to deliver an unequivocal message: God provides for those who are God fearing.[6]

The other motif is that of relationships, feelings. Again, a close reading reveals some surprising aspects of the father/child relationship. The word *love* occurs here for the first time in the Bible, when God puts his heavy hand on Isaac: "Take your son, your only one, the one you love" (v. 2). Imagine the trembling power of that word, *love*, addressed to a man who has a history of difficulties with those closely related to him (see Workshop 4, on the trials).

The critical point of the story occurs in the only interchange between father and son (vv. 6–8): In verse 6, Abraham took the wood for the burnt offering and put it on his son, Isaac. He himself took the firestone and the knife, and the two of them went together. Isaac then said to his father Abraham, "My father!" And he answered, "Here I am, my son." And he said, "Here are the firestone and the wood; but where is the lamb for the burnt offering?" In verse 8, Abraham said, "God will see to the lamb for the burnt offering, my son," and the two of them went together.

We already know that this pair is a father and son. Yet the verbal relationship is repeated five times within three verses. The hardest part comes when Abraham answers Isaac with *hineni*, Here I am, my son. *Hineni* means readiness. That was Abraham's answer to God's call at the outset. How, then, could Abraham be ready for what God was asking and also be present for Isaac's needs? In that sense, the story can be understood as the binding and sacrifice of Abraham as well. These three verses are framed by the phrase, "and the two of them went together." The text suggests that despite the question and the answer, or because of the question and answer, the relationship between father and son remains intact.

But this laconic dialog is so sparse and restrained as to suppress both thought and feeling. Again, it is the reading between the lines that fills volumes. Is it possible, we wonder, that Isaac doesn't really know what is going on? One midrash suggests a change in the punctuation of verse 8 so that it reads, "God will see to [it]; the lamb for the burnt

fig. 5.2. Rembrandt, *Abraham and Isaac Before the Sacrifice* (pen and ink). (*From* the Metropolitan Museum of Art, New York, Robert Lehman Collection; 1645. Reprinted with permission.)

offering [is] my son; and the two of them went together." Thus Isaac, the ready martyr, does know, and still they go together.

The concept that Isaac knows more after Abraham's answer, though probably unknown to Rembrandt as midrash, was etched by him (fig. 5.2) in 1645. Father and son have arrived at Mt. Moriah. Isaac sets down the wood and fingers it restlessly as he asks, "Where is the lamb?" Abraham answers and gestures. His index finger, pointing to God, is midpoint on the diagonal of the direct gaze between father and son. Does Isaac really understand? The background behind Abraham is normal and natural, branches, leaves, and brush; but Isaac is etched against rapid, dark lines, expressive of turmoil (Rembrandt's unmatched language of lines). Isaac stands at the edge of a precipice; his eyes have become dark holes in his face. The seeing and feeling motifs merge. In Rembrandt's etching, Isaac also sees.[7]

Preparation for Handmade Midrash

The foregoing is sufficient introduction to the issues of the Akedah to create a suitable atmosphere for the handmade midrash activity. Participants are then invited to select three or four sheets of colored construction paper from which they will tear five forms: Abraham, Isaac, the ram, the altar, and the Divine Presence. They will then arrange and paste them in a relationship. One of the papers may serve as the background upon which the forms are pasted, or the collage may be sculptural, independent of a base. In some settings participants add outside collage elements such as fragments of fabric or yarn or photos. The work is to be done quietly, without conversation, for its meditative effect. Appropriate background music can be helpful in sustaining the atmosphere. Despite the seriousness of the subject, participants are urged to allow themselves to "play" with the forms as a young child would do and not to think of the exercise as an aesthetic or a moral trial. The aim is to process the forms through dialog and writing: What the rational mind may view as absurd, the soul may rank with symbolic value. Participants are given the option to add a sixth form of their own choosing. In the dialog and writing that follow, each is asked to confront the question, Where am I in my Akedah? Other focusing questions for the dialog and writing are found in the basic recipe for a handmade midrash in the Introduction.

One of the desired effects of this paper-tearing exercise, which will become a handmade midrash, is to lift the participant from the enclosure of historical sequence and to free the imaginal life. The resulting images concretize one's emotions, opening the individual to the intelligence of the heart, to the realization that linear, logical thought is not the only real framework of our lives. Imaginal seeing is a vision that allows one to get outside of one's personal self from a nonhabitual vantage point. What is thus seen brings with it the power to alter one's habitual relationships.

In his seminal work, *Waking Dream Therapy,* Gerald Epstein writes:

> It is well known that many religious and spiritual experiences which convey knowledge to the individual are not describable in words and frequently are attainable only when the content of linear thought is slowed, stopped, emptied. . . . It is only when such nonlinear thinking is embraced that a holistic [incorporates the concept of holy, healthy] experience can happen. . . . If therapy tries to invalidate man's relationship to God, it does so at the expense of dissipating our fundamental wholeness.[8]

Over the years the Akedah Workshop has been presented to various groups, youth and adult, Christian and Jew, lay and professional, in both the United States and Israel. Some Israelis and Jews continue to relive the Akedah as an element of national and religious identity.

Some Christians easily relate the binding of Isaac to the crucifixion. Some high school students and not a few adults address tensions between children and parents. The variables of age, sex, and education do not make as much difference as emotional maturity and the circumstances of one's life, which are not necessarily factors of age or education. These are all random samples and single voices, with no statistical value. The common element is that the method fosters the development of creative metaphor in dealing with problems and speaks to the nonsectarian education of the heart and mind.

One of the surprises for me has been the evolution of successful interfaith Christian-Jewish dialog from the Akedah Workshop. Christians educated to view the crucifixion as the fulfillment, or the completion, of the Akedah, gradually understood and respected how the text and its theology could stand independently in its own right in Judaism. They could allow for a separate and equal mode of understanding. It was in dealing with the common questions of rebellion, freedom, choice, and pain that the Akedah Workshop brought Christians and Jews together—first in the text study but most powerfully in the handmade midrash.[9]

An Israeli Workshop

Sources for the Martyr Model

I will start with Israel, bringing the Akedah back home, so to speak, to its point of origin, to the people who originally had to deal with it. The first tremor I felt was the shocked reaction of a friend with whom I discussed my procedure: "People don't play around with that text in this country. The altar is the land, and everyone is either Abraham or Isaac or both." Precisely for that reason, I was determined to do handmade midrash with them. Through play, it would be more than play. It would be a quest for creative (synectic) analogy to unlock access to the mythic dimensions of that narrative beyond the pious, obedient responses of both synagogue and church. I hoped that it would lead to an even greater commitment to its ultimate values. Hebrew was the language of the workshop and the lore around the Akedah was the milk—or venom—on which these people had been nourished from infancy. We would need to shake free of cliché and stereotype.

I repeated my focus on vision, an example of purposeful repetition in the text. What is "seen" in an episode so devoid of realia that even the single dialog suppresses rather than expresses thought? Does "see" mean the apprehension of an inner reality? The story begged for an experiential, visual, and visible treatment, so unknown to this verbal, intellectual "people of the book."

When martyrdom became a fact of Jewish life, the Akedah became a recurring motif in Jewish life and literature. Holocaust literature, which survived the war years or came into existence through survivors, bears ample evidence of a motif that was first recorded post-biblically during the first century of the Common Era, in the Book of Maccabees. There Isaac is established as the martyr model.

Seven martyred brothers, sons of Hannah, use Isaac as a model of piety and courage: "Let us die on behalf of the Law. . . . Let us not show cowardice. . . . Remember whence ye come, and at the hands of what father Isaac endured immolation for religion's sake" (4 Macc. 13:9–12). Not only does Isaac emerge as the emblem of the willing martyr but his binding in Genesis 22 becomes in 4 Maccabees his actual sacrifice.

Hannah speaks:

> Remember that it is because of God that you have a share in the world and have enjoyed life. For this reason you are bound to endure any hardship for the sake of God. For his sake also was our father Abraham zealous to immolate his son Isaac, the father of a nation, nor did Isaac flinch when he saw his father's hand, armed with a sword, descending upon him (4 Macc. 16:18–20).[10]

Since its rebirth in 1948, the modern State of Israel has fought a series of survival wars that again evoked the Akedah motif. Among sensitive Israelis the Isaac-Ishmael rivalry is also being tragically repeated in the continuing Arab-Israeli violence. It is no surprise that the art work of this group of teachers expresses not only sadness and fear but also militant anger and rebellion against the traditional theological position. But, then, Jews have always argued with God. Perhaps that is even the more authentic Jewish response. It is Abraham's silence on behalf of his son that we find so bewildering.[11]

What once worked as a model of martyrdom among Jews is not uncontested in this workshop. Noam, an observant Diaspora Jew, has brought his allegiance and his Torah learning to the modern State of Israel, but his Akedah is not the expression of unquestioning belief. Sara, who once expressed relief that the big ram would be the sacrifice, letting everyone off the hook, suddenly realizes that her own son may be that ram. In Shira's work, everyone changes for the better—except Abraham, against whom she has greater anger than even against God. Rina's Akedah family is central in a world shrunken against the inscrutable rage of time, suspended in conflict and silence. Bracha thinks God is enjoying the Akedah. Nava says that only the orthodox are "holy" people, people with that kind of commitment. Hayyim alone makes a monument to the inevitability of sacrifice.

NOAM:

*God Is Not
in This Picture*

The background is a dull army green. The singular "Son No. 1" is red, a color he shares with the squiggle of a ram, the other sacrifice, lower left, waiting in the wings. Isaac is bound in fire-orange ropes. Abraham is the tiny little triangle in the corner brandishing a monstrous saw-toothed knife, many times his own size, which is suspended diagonally over Isaac. Noam recalls that the word for knife in this narrative is *ma-achelet,* "the devourer." He declares that God is not to be found in this picture.

The only male in the group, Noam creates brazenly iconoclastic work that gives courage to his less assertive female colleagues: first, the absence of God; then the revealing proportions—a severely diminished Abraham represented only by his enormous lethal weapon. Noam has little to say and less to write; his anger and disillusion are smoldering.

SARA:

*Pierced by
God's Presence*

(fig. 5.3)

Sara identified four areas in which she had been affected by handmade midrash: in understanding the text, the art, the human condition, and her own self-perception. She writes:

God is shining yellow, dominating all. The smooth, finished edges of the entire sheet have been torn unevenly to emphasize God's infinity. Abraham is white, striving for wholeness and purity. Tortured, his color melts into the yellow of God, yet he seems closed, impervious

fig. 5.3. Sara, *Pierced by God's Presence.*

to the presence of God, who pierces his heart like a knife. The altar is earthen, a neutral brown. Isaac is red, the sacrifice. He lies on his back, recalling the victims of Pompeii, petrified for eternity in the postures of their suffering. The black [the sixth and optional element] that surrounds him is the tragedy, the suffering. The divine yellow penetrates him also, like a blunted sword. The white robe of Abraham is spotted with black: suffering and sin. The ram comes from above, a harbinger of freedom, redemption. Its color is green, the calming color of nature. He hardly has a black spot. Perhaps he is not conscious of his fate, but who knows, who can say the ram doesn't know suffering?

The discovery was myself, the black in everything, not at peace with myself. I worked at first with forms and colors, not thinking about proportions till I saw Noam's huge knife. Then I knew why my ram was so large and central. Once we have the sacrifice, we are free of guilt and responsibility. How shocking to think that the offering is usually another person who dies in place of you.

Only now as I write do I fully realize the absence of the fourth figure, the mother, Sara. What happened could not have happened had God brought her into the trial. Midrash accounts for this absence by telling of her death. I used to think death was a rather extreme emotional response. Now I think it is entirely fitting, nonromantic realism. Is Isaac my son? The day of his mobilization draws near and with it the fear and trembling. . . . The knife is raised and stabbing my heart. Do I identify with Sara because I am a mother, or because I too am named Sara?

Initially, Sara refuses to confront the contemporary Israeli military symbolism of the Akedah. However, through the art exercise and its processing, and stimulated by the courage of her colleague, Noam, she becomes fully and poignantly aware of her own identification with the biblical Sara and the many possible roles Sara might have played.

Sara in the Midrash and Art of the Akedah

True, Sara is almost invisible in the official version of the Akedah. But the power of midrash and art to discern sensitivities between the lines rescues her from oblivion and assigns her a variety of roles. The textual provocation for Sara's place in midrash is the fact of her death abruptly following the Akedah. We are given to wonder whether there is a connection. Midrash conjures up Satan, the adversary, who tells her that Isaac has not exactly gone to study Torah, the deceit used by Abraham to get Isaac out of the house. She cries out in terror and anguish and dies. Some say her cries halt the Akedah and echo in the six urgent and broken calls of the shofar on Rosh Hashanah. Since the Akedah in synagogue art replaces the appearance of the shofar because of the association with the ram, it makes doubly good sense that the often-questioned figure before the tent in the Dura-Europos Synagogue be identified as Sara, also associated with the shofar.

fig. 5.4.
E. R. Goodenough, *Jewish Symbols in the Greco-Roman Period*. (Princeton University Press, Princeton, New Jersey: Bollingen Series 37, Vol. 11, Plate III; 245–256 C.E. Reprinted with permission of the Yale University Art Gallery, Dura Europos Collection.)

fig. 5.5. Henry Wilson, *Angel of the Moon*. (*From* the bronze doors of the Cathedral of St. John the Divine, New York City; 1935. Photo reprinted by permission of the author.)

Sara's presence in this earliest recorded visual Akedah in Jewish art is striking. She stands before her tent in the unique iconography of this Akedah scene over the Torah niche. Nobody faces the viewer. They are all turned in the direction of "vision," either the hand of God or the future temple to be built on Mt. Moriah. Dura was a small Roman Diaspora town on the Euphrates River in Syria, not a mainstream Jewish community. Its amazing synagogue endured twelve years (244–256 C.E.) before the city was destroyed by a Sassanian invasion. To my knowledge, this feminist consciousness and other aspects of its visual originality have not appeared elsewhere to date in synagogue art (fig. 5.4).

A contemporary version of the tradition that the saving female angel may be Sara can be seen in the Akedah on the bronze doors of the Cathedral of St. John the Divine in New York City (fig. 5.5).

God is a looming, threatening presence [uppermost rectangle]. Abraham, is a being, form, object, vessel, filled with tremendous rage that becomes smaller, turning into resigned acceptance [center rectangle]. Isaac is filled with growing fear and struggles with Abraham's resigned acceptance [lower left rectangle]. The altar is also a large, looming presence for Abraham, connected to God, not for Isaac [square, right]. Finally, the ram comes directly from God in the

SHIRA:
Everything Changes
(fig. 5.6)

fig. 5.6. Shira, *Everything Changes.*

form of a shaft of lightning and negates the altar. God also becomes a yellow presence, more positive, more hopeful. I share Abraham's rage. How could God ask this of anyone? Why does he feel it necessary to test this way? Are there not other ways of showing one's devotion? I do not share Abraham's acceptance. I could not and would not make that "Divine sacrifice." I believe it is permissible to question God's actions.

The Bible records almost no dialog between father and son during the fateful three-day journey. Shira, in her graphic study of process, illustrates what is not spoken, the diminishing resistance of the father and the growing terror of the son. The horizontal rectangles that look like coffins further represent her preoccupation with final questions. God is also processed. His threatening black presence lightens ["yellow . . . more positive, more hopeful"]. In her concluding remarks, Shira identifies herself with Abraham's rage against God. But Isaac's problem is not God. "Isaac struggles with Abraham's resigned acceptance." Isaac's problem is his father. The tiny patch of Abraham's resistance meets and barely overlaps the enormity of Isaac's fear at the altar; it is but small comfort and protection.

Shira did not know the extent of her feelings until she made them visible. By bringing poet Wilfred Owen, painter Caravaggio, and theologian Søren Kierkegaard to the class, we were able to explore the motif of the cruel father in a larger, more comprehensive context.

Wilfred Owen, the young British poet who died at the front during World War I, left in his legacy a poem based on Genesis 22 called "The Parable of the Old Man and the Young." In the posthumous edition of his poems, editor Edmund Blunden records a comment the poet had penned by that poem: "The willingness of the older generation to sacrifice the younger."[12]

> So Abram rose, and clave the wood and went,
> And took the fire with him, and a knife.
> And as they sojourned both of them together,
> Isaac the first-born spake and said, My Father,
> Behold the preparations, fire and iron,
> But where the lamb for this burnt-offering?
> Then Abram bound the youth with belts and straps,
> And builded parapets and trenches there,
> And stretched forth the knife to slay his son.
> When lo! an angel called him out of heaven,
> Saying, Lay not thy hand upon the lad,
> Neither do anything to him. Behold
> A ram, caught in a thicket by its horns,
> Offer the Ram of Pride instead of him.
> But the old man would not so, but slew his son,—
> And half the seed of Europe, one by one.

One can hear Isaac's screams in a powerful image of the cruel Abraham in Caravaggio's turbulent painting, *The Sacrifice of Isaac*. Numerous visual images of the Akedah, expressing a range of emotions, have been assembled by Theodor Ehrenstein in *Das Alte Testament Im Bilde*.[13] The motif of the cruel father takes a startling turn in one of the "midrashic" vignettes found in Kierkegaard's *Fear and Trembling*. Isaac, uncomprehending of his father:

> Embraces Abraham's knees, pleads for his young life, for the fair hope of his future . . . then for an instant he turned away from him, and when Isaac again saw Abraham's face . . . his glance was wild, his form was horror. He seized Isaac by the throat, threw him to the ground and said, "Stupid boy, dost thou then suppose that I am thy father? I am an idolator. Dost thou suppose that this is God's bidding? No, it is my desire." Then Isaac trembled and cried out in his terror, "O God in heaven, have compassion upon me. God of Abraham have compassion upon me. If I have no father upon earth, be Thou my father." But Abraham in a low voice said to himself, "O Lord in Heaven, I thank thee. After all it is better for him to believe that I am a monster than to lose faith in thee."[14]

The motif of the father protectively masking God goes back at least to the talmudic period:

> At that moment Isaac agreed with his mouth, but in his heart he said "Who will save me from my father? I have no salvation other than the Holy One, blessed be He, as it is written, 'My help is from God who made heaven and earth (Ps. 121).' "
>
> *Avot of Rabbi Nathan*

The background is red. This is The Day, the great Day, stormy, full of emotion. The world, in white, is dwarfed in comparison to the awesome Day. Abraham and Isaac are bound to each other like the branches of a tree to the trunk. Abraham casts looks to the day, in the distance, and searches for Light. Perhaps an angel, perhaps an order that will focus, direct, help him execute this difficult mission, or perhaps delay it.

The Light is yellow, also the altar, symbolizing evil. The altar is ready, but part of it extends out beyond the world expressing struggles, misgivings. The ram so palpable at the foot of the altar almost leaps up in its desire, but Abraham doesn't turn to him. The command must come from out there.

I find myself within the conflict, awesome conflict of a loving father about to destroy his son, his future, and in this way to be worthy of being a Divine child. How shall he choose? How would I choose?

RINA:

The World Pales Before the Demands of This Day

Rina sets the round white world against the requirements of the red background, The Day, that is, the inscrutable demands of time. She does not mention God. Abraham and Isaac are centered with the axis of the world because their dilemma of commitment, love, obedience, morality, and free will is also central to an ordered universe. Those elements that deal with sacrifice, namely Light (or God) and the altar, are pushed to the limits of time, half out of the world, and labeled "evil" because they represent the crux, the terrible cost, the riddle of God's dark side. All the parts touch, engaged in relationship. Only Abraham's looks don't reach Light.

The ram is eager. Contrary to traditional iconography in which Abraham turns in the direction of the help—the ram, the hand of God, the angel—Abraham turns away from the easy answer. He challenges the distant Light. Rina's work is suspended in this moment, in the awesome conflict and the expectant silence.

Conclusions: The Inevitability of Sacrifice

One of the most important discoveries of these workshops is that dialog and self-disclosure can and do take place among teachers of diverse religious and secular backgrounds. There is an opportunity to express torment and to grapple with the nature of commitment and the tensions present in an examined life.

Thus, for example, Bracha's Akedah shows a conflict between God and the altar. The altar "does not absorb," she writes, alluding to the story of Cain and Abel in which the earth painfully absorbs Abel's blood and cries out to God as a witness to the crime (Gen. 4:11). Here, by contrast, the altar refuses to go along with God, who is smiling with pleasure.

In another bittersweet example, commitment is heroically present only among the very orthodox. Writing about her Abraham who is large and black, Nava explains that "black is my association with maximum commitment." She was referring to the ultra-orthodox Jews, whose garb is mainly black. The discussion raises questions about being "holy" without being ritually observant and about the narrow line between maximum commitment and fanaticism, returning us to those very examples from 4 Maccabees with which we began.

One of the most poignant examples comes from Hayyim (see fig. 5.7, Color Section 3), an art student at the community college in the Negev frontier town of Yerucham. The deceptive simplicity of his abstract forms carries the personal vision of the Akedah as an event that happens wholly inside Abraham. God is the primary element, the ominous black background. Abraham is the color of blood, anger, vitality, strength, life. Within him is the breach, the tear, in which are layered the blue and green of Isaac and the altar. The small, upright white monument, the sacrifice, begins internally (an ulcer? a pearl?) and grows to external visibility. Does the nature of life oblige the continual presence of sacrifice in its pure shrinelike verticality?

Without eliminating dissonance, Hayyim achieves harmony, integration, and a balance of tensions. His work has evocative power, inner consistency (a union of form and content), and economy of artistic means—all characteristics of good art. He has succeeded in linking an emotional state to a pictorial idea with similar qualities, out of which he creates an image that contains and symbolizes his emotions.

A Day-School Workshop

I also conducted the Akedah Workshop with high school students in a prominent day school of a large metropolitan Jewish community on the East Coast.[15] About thirty students, aged fourteen to sixteen, participated in the lesson, presenting me with a different kind of challenge. First, there was the exuberant adolescent energy that is so different from a graduate school class or a teacher's seminar, and there was the need for a tight and fast structure to suit the smaller unit of time (much less than the normal two and a half to three hours that I prefer). Then there was the elitist spirit to deal with. These students know they are among the best, and when it comes to a popular biblical passage, they are convinced that they know everything there is to know. Their individual uniqueness promised a dramatic range of responses.

Why single out a group of traditional Jewish high school students? Two additional factors deserve comment. First, adolescence is an age of passionate and/or idealistic commitment, whether it be to social causes, love, religion, drugs, or the military. Second, this particular religious school is sufficiently enlightened so as not to isolate itself from the larger secular American community, unlike more orthodox and fundamentalist institutions. The workshop provides an opportunity to examine religious and moral issues and intrafamilial relationships, allowing for faith-struggle, criticism, and rebellion to be expressed and heard through creative art play. Thus faculty who participate are prompted to ask themselves whether the formal curriculum affirms the place of affective response in young people who are being educated to assume leadership in the larger communities.

From the handmade midrashim created by this group, I have chosen those of conceptual and visual interest. Jeff is a proto-martyr, fiercely loyal yet struggling with the desire to live. Aaron's Abraham is heroic but keeps his distance from thoughts and feelings. David's concern is not God but his father. Trust my parents? No way. Marie is direct and honest. She knows the Akedah is central and painful. Dave says God knows everything, but Abraham still can choose. Naomi is most disturbed about reconciliation after the Akedah. Reflections on the workshop and issues of religious education follow the presentation.

Bind Me Well?

(see fig. 5.8,
Color Section 3)

The ram is at a distance and can't see his fate. Only his horn survives (as a shofar). The altar is a plain altar shape to which Isaac is tightly bound. Isaac is still and unmoving, willing to sacrifice himself to God out of life, fear for God, and love of his father. Abraham is represented as an arm holding a knife straightforward in his answer to God's call. I am not in this picture, but it represents my feelings. I feel that the Bible is eternal because of the fact it is undying. My picture shows the simplicity of the story on the surface and invites people to look into it and see what they want. (It is important to remember that what actually is in it is what I intended; what other people add is garbage. What I meant can be transmitted only by me and those who I tell explicitly what I mean.)

Of the five requested forms, only the altar and Isaac are complete. Abraham is represented as an arm with the knife, solely an executioner. The ram is present, not as a substitute sacrifice but as the remote symbolic association with the shofar of the future. God is absent—or at least not specifically present—in the black background. The altar is hardly a simple shape but is specifically designed to fit Isaac and to accommodate the ropes.

Jeff wants to reflect honor on his education in the tradition of the willing sacrifice, but his forms tell more. How willing is an Isaac so tightly bound? Jeff denies his identification with Isaac yet admits that the work represents his feelings, which are barely suppressed beneath the garbled commercial: "I feel that the Bible is eternal because of the fact it is undying." "What other people add is garbage" may be a further denial of feelings too difficult to face. Isaac is willing, out of contradictory fear and love; the strong ropes witness a fierce conflict. Yet how else can an old man bind a young man, if not with the slender cord of love?

Jeff's work bears an uncanny resemblance to Isaac's statement in the sixth-century commentary Targum-Jonathan, a composite of early rabbinic thinking. "Bind me well," says the proto-martyr, "so that I don't inadvertently move and blemish the [perfection of] the sacrifice."[16] Here the youth's reluctant willingness is disguised by cultic requirements. In both, the desire to live struggles with the obedience and faith conditioning required by the tradition.

AARON:

No Biblical Feelings

(see fig. 5.9,
Color Section 3)

My work is full of forms and interactions. However, I found it difficult to ascribe to them the forms intended, as I cannot see the biblical historical story as containing emotions describable through this medium. Biblical and talmudic as well as later scholars have studied and commented on the causes and effects of this Akedah for centuries and have run the gamut of its results on Abraham, Isaac, and the entire Jewish people. I am part of these people and therein lies my personal involvement with the story. The scars our patriarchs have

fig. 5.7. Hayyim,
Inevitable Sacrifice
(p. 130).

fig. 5.8. Jeff, *Bind Me
Well?* (p. 132).

fig. 5.9. Aaron, *No Biblical Feelings* (p. 132).

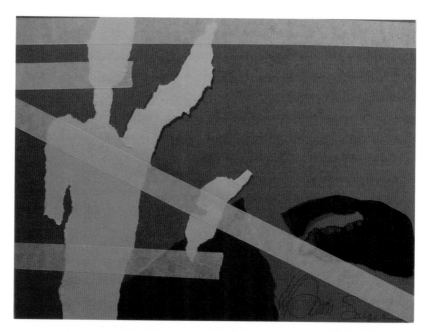

fig. 5.11. Marie, *Isaac Is a Small Thing with a Huge Head* (p.134).

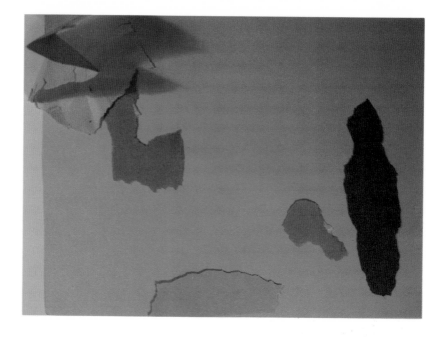

fig. 5.12. Naomi, *The Ram Is on the Altar, but the Story Is Not Over* (p. 136).

fig. 5.16. Duane, *Abraham and Isaac Are Mirror Images* (p. 142).

fig. 5.17. Susan C., *The Split Between Head and Heart* (p. 144).

fig. 5.18. Doris, *Mountain of Vision* (p. 147).

borne have changed Jewish history, and I am only I, one Jew, not ready to ascribe these feelings to pieces of construction paper. I agree that I am not explaining this well or even adequately, but I am unable to do this project with any depth of feeling.

Aaron claims that he cannot do this exercise with any depth of feeling, but in fact he has done just that. His Abraham is a heroic figure. Not sad or weeping, he is a giant, filling the entire vertical space. The most intriguing forms are the stripes of masking tape that represent the Divine Presence. His declared use of them, I was told privately, was to obscure the human image, representing his struggle with the so-called image prohibition. Stripes (as emanations) have been a clear expression of the Divine Presence throughout the history of religious art, particularly diagonal emanations.[17] These stripes do more than simply provide divine light to Abraham. The horizontal stripes, which are static, act as restrainers on Abraham, two of them on his head, one on the lower abdomen. Thus do the commands of God block both Abraham's perception and his feeling impulses. Still, there is an emotional connection between father and son. The one diagonal line goes from God through Abraham to Isaac, going through Abraham's heart.

The viewer may ask, Isn't the placement of the stripes accidental? The gluing process lessens the possibility of chance. Casual or rapid placement of parts is delayed by the gluing, allowing for deliberate if not conscious choice. Aaron's statement is the rationalization, the intellectualization that gives him distance from what he has done and helps him not to see it. Thus do the faithful take orders. Since one does not question on high, one is excused from feeling. Sometimes psychological truth surfaces despite one's conscious intentions. It is both self-expression and self-disclosure.

God is above man; He has nothing to do with the real scene. The ram is also peripheral, being only an afterthought and a convenient substitution after the real drama is resolved. The main components are Abraham and Isaac and the altar. Isaac is on the altar, completely subject to Abraham's whims. The altar holds him there under Abraham, who stands over him in judgment. I feel a certain kinship for Isaac, but there is no way I can truly identify with him since he trusted his parents enough to get on an altar. Never!

DAVID:

Trust My Parents— No Way

(fig. 5.10)

Here an adolescent boy takes the biblical story personally in an open and explicit rebellion against his parents. We have seen how students may speak in one vein but express conflict through their art. Here we have the opposite; defiance is expressed verbally, whereas the art transparently reveals the youth's need for trust and protection.

fig. 5.10. David, *Trust My Parents—No Way.*

Isaac lies secure and stable as the sacrifice, without ropes, although in a defensive posture, his knees up. Contrasting with the tiny Isaac, Abraham is huge, extending beyond the edge of the paper. Despite what David says about Abraham standing in judgment, the form of the father is not destructive. He is a tree, which is protective and life-sustaining, from whom the child can draw strength. The ram is hardly peripheral as he states; surely David will be replaced by this huge animal for which there is hardly a place on the altar.

David does not provide a form for the Divine Presence, about whom he says: "He has nothing to do with the real scene." David's concerns are clearly father and son. He does not raise the question of faith in God. His question is whether to have faith in the father, even as he is so small and the father so large and powerful.

MARIE:

Isaac Is a Small Thing with a Huge Head

(see fig. 5.11, Color Section 3)

The Divine Presence is 3-D [three-dimensional]. He overlooks all. The color, orange-yellow, shows light and greatness. The ram is coming out of the form showing that God gave the ram to Abraham. The ram is spring green because this shows renewed life. The pale green altar touching the bottom is in the middle of the page. Its color shows a draining of life. Isaac is a small thing with a huge head, showing that he is going through a huge ordeal though he is so young. The deep purple Abraham is large, and his features are all proportioned. He has no hands to show he is really at a loss to do anything about it.

Marie's statements are clear, without judgment or doubt. She is able to give herself final answers yet does not deny her feelings. She recognizes Isaac's trial as well as Abraham's. She has faith in God, who provides the great ram. She speaks directly of the altar as that which drains the life strength; without being judgmental, she simply places it centrally.

Marie shows unusual consistency and harmony between her verbal statement and visual imaging. Unspoken, but clearly evident, is the fact that father and child are not alienated from each other by the trial. Elsewhere, we see where the altar separates Abraham and Isaac, where Isaac turns away from his father for salvation, or where the image of the father is wholly aggressive. Here Abraham is without hands, at a loss, by Marie's admission, but the child is with him in his dilemma. "And the two of them went together." Or is the disarming of Abraham nevertheless a safeguard against that irrational moment of evil?

Abraham has progressed to a point of belief with God such that he, however emotional for him, will do God's every wish. The ram and Isaac therefore are the same color. They are the two "victims," so to speak, of the command. They surround Abraham, who is reaching out his hand to his son above the altar. The altar itself is independent and neutral; no one touches it. The presence is blue; it surrounds all and can be seen through all but Abraham. God controls all the factors except for Abraham, who must make up his own mind. This is where I see my place in the Akedah. Almost everyone can pinpoint a time when they feel as if they were being tested; when all their surroundings were beyond their control but their own success was in their own hands.

DAVE:
God Controls It All, Except for Abraham

Is Abraham as dispassionately neutral as Dave announces? Red is well chosen for Abraham. If Abraham is angry, his anger is suppressed in passive silence. Red is also life, strength, and vitality. The red hand that reaches out to the son will not be so quick to cut off his future as he was to leave his past with the call, "Go forth." Dave is at pains to emphasize, both verbally and visually, that the altar is (almost) unoccupied.

Each of the figures bears a sign of God's presence—except Abraham, as if to say God has withdrawn in order to give Abraham complete freedom of choice. Nachmanides, the thirteenth-century exegete whose work may have been known to this student, accounts for God's test of Abraham as an opportunity for him to demonstrate his freedom of will. A thousand years earlier, Rabbi Akiba had written, "Everything is known in advance, but the option is yours." In other words, God knows what the choices are, but He surrenders some of His omniscience to permit the individual to be fully human by making his or her own decision. Dave places himself at that point in the Akedah.

Censure of Abraham turns up early on. In the second century,

Rabbi Akiba criticizes Abraham by defining the responses to aggression of four personality types: "The King (God) has four sons. One is beaten and remains silent; one is beaten and kicks back; one is beaten and pleads for mercy; one is beaten and says 'hit me again.' Abraham is the one who is beaten and remains silent, as it is written. Take your son . . . Isaac, and offer him up as a burnt offering. He should have spoken up [in protest] saying 'yesterday You said to me through Isaac will your seed be called' " (Semahot, ch. 8).

NAOMI:

The Ram Is on the Altar, but the Story Is Not Over

(see fig. 5.12, Color Section 3).

This is the final scene of the Akedah. The ram has already been placed on the altar in Isaac's place. Yet the story is not over. Isaac remains pleading and Abraham's emotions are still depressed. The Divine Presence is in motion. It touches every inch in the scene. It binds the picture together, tying the emotions of Isaac and his father. I feel the continuity of the Presence. It extends beyond the scene into everyday life. The turmoil and anxiety of the event extend beyond the Akedah, beyond this portion of Bereshit into my own life. My relation with my parents is a good one, yet there are times when there is anguish. As there is never ceasing turmoil in the picture, there is never a complete calm in my life.

The form of God is unusual in this aesthetic composition. Though all-encompassing, as Naomi writes, God is not embracing but, rather, grasping with a grotesque hand. The trial is over, but there is no resolution between father and son. If Abraham is relieved, his pale sagging form reveals no joy. Kierkegaard wrote that Abraham's face was darkened and he knew joy no more. Centuries earlier, Rembrandt's last treatment of the Akedah, an etching done in 1655 (fig. 5.13), created an Abraham whose eyes are black hollows in his head, whose mouth is a gaping hole. And why is Isaac still pleading? Things can never be the same. "The two of them went together," twice repeated in the text, has dissolved into the singular subject and verb of verse 19, "And Abraham returned [alone?] . . . to Beer-sheba."

Color selection and placement emphasize Abraham's aloneness. God and the ram are paired in color and conceptual identity, a dark and foreboding presence, as are Isaac and the altar in bloody association,[18] leaving Abraham central, strangely pallid and ungrounded. Of the twenty-three examples in this class, Naomi's alone deals with the issue of post-Akedah reconciliation and alienation.

Of the three moments of the Akedah—before, during, and after—the last appears least frequently among the hundreds of examples in the history of art and in the commentaries as well. But the earliest Jewish examples are among the most original. Thus we can identify Sara in the unusual iconography of the Dura-Europos Akedah, 245–

fig. 5.13. Rembrandt, *The Sacrifice of Isaac* (etching). (*From* the Metropolitan Museum of Art, New York; 1655. Reprinted with permission.)

fig. 5.14. *Akedah.* (*From* the Beth Alpha mosaic floor, Beth Alpha, Israel; 6th century. Photo reprinted by permission of the author.)

256 C.E., and we can identify Isaac in the least frequently found posture of the Akedot, namely, being rescued from the altar, in the sixth-century Beth Alpha mosaic floor (fig. 5.14).[19]

Conclusions: Denial and Alienation

The students were learning the tradition well, I observed. Since I often encounter Jewish illiteracy in all strata of the Jewish community, I was thrilled to find American high school students who could read a talmudic text and were familiar with the theology of the medieval exegetes. But I also found that for all its sophistication, the curriculum seemed not to have made space for heart, for students to engage in honest disclosure, to express fear, doubt, and protest without invoking censure. It is commonplace that such dialog can foster self-confidence and build faith more firmly founded.

The creative art play of the Handmade Midrash Workshop gave support to the honest disclosure of conflict. Jeff ridiculed us for looking deeply into his work: "What others say is garbage." His value statement is rhetoric garbled by conflicted feelings: "I feel the Bible is eternal because of the fact it is undying." So he bravely ties himself to the altar with choking bonds to suppress his fear and block his flight. Aaron gives us an eloquent rundown of the importance of the Akedah in Jewish history—too big to be understood by means of anything as trivial as an art-play exercise. His concluding statement admits defeat in doing this project with any depth of feeling. But we have already seen his heroic representation of Abraham, whose mind and gut are restrained by strips of masking tape. This is precisely what Aaron so vigorously denies—his own great depth of feeling.

Denial was a recurring motif in the day-school workshop. The problem with denial coupled with unquestioning practice is that it breeds alienation. Denial creates the impression that religion isn't strong enough to deal honestly with ultimate issues.

The following effective and affective closing activity places the Akedah in a larger context and gives courage for individual action. The group is divided into small groups, each having to deal with one of these concepts as it relates to the Akedah: (1) People are constantly on trial by life because they are human. (2) It's the loneliest thing in the world to be standing up when everyone else is sitting down. (3) An idea is always on trial somewhere. (4) There are few words that everyone understands the same way. (5) The most important questions in life can never be answered by anyone except yourself. (6) One man's suffering doesn't count, no matter what he is suffering. In this manner, a valued traditional text is connected to ultimate human concerns. And a particular religious issue achieves universal stature.

The graduate students in the Akedah Workshop would soon be occupying church pulpits or would be continuing academic, theological studies. Two principles marked the differences between handmade midrashim of Christians and those of Jewish students. Both Jewish midrash (Genesis Rabbah) and the church fathers articulate the Christian position that the crucifixion is seen as the completion of the Akedah and, second, that the sacrificed ram and Isaac are both seen as the "lamb of God" (see Margaret's typology subsequently). Traditional Christians were at peace with the full and unquestioning readiness for sacrifice, as are most orthodox Jews. But there is a strong tradition among Jews to argue with God, to question even God's authority. We must not forget that martyrology notwithstanding, the bottom line of the Akedah is that Isaac walks away from the altar.

Among other motifs are the deep probing into the nature of sacrifice (Duane), the dual sacrifice of father and son (Kin Wan), Isaac as Oedipus (Kyle), parallels (namely the typology) between Abraham and Job as well as Isaac and Jesus (Margaret), and the larger typology of the Akedah as parallel to the receiving of the Torah. Feminists speak to the absence and presence of Sara and the symbolic sacrifice of sexuality by Christianity (Rose, Susan C.). Finally, this section concludes with the transformation of Abraham—and of God—as indicated by a close reading of the text, together with a Jungian approach to symbol, leading us to the concept of reconciliation and t'shuva ("turning" or "repentance").

Handmade midrash was adopted by my colleague, Duane Christensen, in his own teaching, and he also recommends its use in Christian-Jewish dialog (see note 9). Christensen shared with me the response of one of our participants in her meeting with faculty: "If I heard Lou correctly, she put the experience of the Akedah Workshop in the same sentence and the same category as her religious conversion experience. She described how reluctant she was to enter into the experience at the outset. But once she let go, it was a bit like entering what she envisions a hypnotic state to be like. That moment is apparently one that she knows she will be going back to again and again."

One sentence in Lou's description took my breath. "I discovered that as an observer, I would be confined to interpretation, but as a participant, I was open to God's power." Here was clear affirmation of the basic idea of handmade midrash: that the word needs its personal visual analog in order to engage both mind and heart.

ROSE:

Isaac Is Green—
She Is My
Daughter

(fig. 5.15)

The white form is the Divine Presence. It originally filled up the whole
page, and I had to tear it smaller to make room for anyone/thing
else. It was meant to fill all the space. It cannot be resisted.

Isaac is green—she is my daughter, now twenty-one. Isaac
welcomes the Divine Presence with gladness. She does not know all
that is involved. She has recently decided to be a counselor and is
employed at a home for battered women while finishing her
undergraduate work.

I am the black altar—the instrument of her sacrifice. She would
not be entering a life of service to the hurting people of this world if it
weren't for me. I have not led her to this, or pushed her, or
encouraged her. I have just been there in her life doing those kinds of
jobs since before she was born. She has seen my tears over other
people's problems too many times, watched me give time and energy
and money above what I had to give. It is my own sacrifice that has

fig. 5.15. Rose, *Isaac Is*
Green—She Is My
Daughter.

brought her to her own point of sacrifice. But she does not know the price of forty years of doing this. She does not understand the sacrifice.

Abraham is the dark figure in the foreground. He is helpless in the face of such a scene. He can do nothing. He is mute. I am partly in Abraham, but Abraham does not have an active role. This sacrifice is freely chosen, but without knowing its consequences. Isaac, alive and growing, green and vibrant, chooses it for herself. To welcome the Divine Presence is to choose the sacrifice. To welcome the Presence is to place oneself beyond choice—for the Divine Presence is irresistible.

Is there a lamb in the picture? Only as part of the Divine Presence. The experience of the Divine Presence is the lamb, but Isaac does not escape the sacrifice.

Rose becomes the matriarch Sara, wholly absent from the text of Genesis 22, and Abraham, who is absent in this interpretation. Central to Rose's mother-daughter presentation is the concept of the willing sacrifice that we have seen in the Targum Jonathan (cf. Jeff, fig. 5.8). In addition, Rose unhesitatingly affirms the inevitability of sacrifice. However, she has completely turned the tables on the "expected" sacrifice. Her sacrifice embodies the literal meaning of the word, "to make holy," in the sense that *holy* in the Hebrew Bible stands for the forces of life. Her altruistic behavior has created a model for her daughter, not of sacrifice and martyrdom in death, but of giving oneself in life for improving the lot of the less fortunate. As in the literal text of Genesis 22, Isaac does not die; Rose's daughter, Isaac, lives also, and she lives to nurture others as she was nurtured on the altar of the mother. The one puzzling and negative feature in Rose's art and statement is that the self-altar is black and the accompanying statement, though filled with generous giving and tearful empathy, seems lacking in joy. One wonders whether, in giving all to others, the self has really been fulfilled. (See Rose's work in Tearing Out of Eden, [fig. 3.3]. Until now an assistant, behind the scenes, to her pastor husband, Rose is completing her divinity degree. In mid-life, they will now seek a new position as co-pastors.)

It is instructive at this point to complement Rose's work with that of Flo, a continuing education student at a Berkeley synagogue. Flo represents God as an infinity sign hovering over all. Isaac, composed of all the elements (altar, ram, divinity), rests within Abraham, who is a uterus. Thus Abraham becomes the missing Sara and, as a mother, has the power to bring to life and to death. Rose and Flo, unknown to each other, geographical neighbors, orbit respectively in the Baptist and Jewish worlds. How extraordinary it would be to bring them, and not only their biblical interpretations, into dialog.

FLO:
Abraham Is a Uterus

SUSAN:

Three Moments in the Akedah

There are three traditional "moments" depicted in the art of the Akedah: the three-day journey to Moriah, the crisis at the altar, and the afterward or reconciliation. The second is the moment that occurs most often in the history of art. Susan has chosen the third moment in her work and has integrated Jesus' resurrection with Isaac set free.

Abraham is bowed not only in suffering and potential loss but also in awe and worshipful thanksgiving to God. Especially he is bowed in respect to the ram. (The thought just occurred to me as I see the bound ram looking directly into Abraham's face; similar perhaps to American Indians thanking trees that they cut down, and corn that they harvested, and buffalo that they shot.)

. . . I reasoned that if the ram were already in the picture, then he might as well already be on the altar, and Isaac unbound, set free. But it wasn't my reasoning that swayed me, so much as my feelings. My own unbinding is still so recent; I did not want him bound! I wanted to picture the story after God's provision had been recognized, while it was in fact being celebrated.

From the beginning white had seemed the only color I could use for Isaac . . ."pure" and "holy" came to mind. . . . I deliberately extended his arms so that he stands hovering, a human in the shape of a cross.

. . . Isaac's placement on the paper was not quite so deliberate. I intended for him to be separated from Abraham by the altar and to be free of the altar, which is shaped like a cupped hand or a nest, cradling the sacrifice. I did not realize until later that he is also higher than the other figures, rejoicing that he is free, blessing the whole scene. I feel in this picture a sense of hope, trust, peace, and exuberance, a celebration of life. I feel affirmed and uplifted by this experience. God meets our needs in surprising and unexpected ways.

DUANE:

Abraham and Isaac Are Mirror Images

(see fig. 5.16, Color Section 3)

Why did I make Abraham and Isaac mirror images of each other? And what is the significance of the line of separation between them? Is it an established fact describing something both past and present? Or is it the beginning of a new reality in the relationship between them? Are the two figures both me? I think so. I am the one sacrificed and the sacrificer. And that fact feels strange. Abraham should be the other figure—the authority to which I have been bound. But Abraham is not someone or something external. Abraham and Isaac are indeed bound. Somehow both of those figures represent me—even with the line of separation between them. I am somehow being set free from myself.

God's hand is not so much extended to prevent the sacrifice as it is to indicate the necessity of the separation—almost to bless it.

The parent is the child and the parent. Edinger quotes Jung:

Let us try for a moment to look into Abraham's soul when he was commanded to sacrifice his only son. Quite apart from the compassion he felt for his child, would not a father in such a position feel himself as the victim, and feel that he was plunging the knife into his own breast? He would be at the same time the sacrificer and the sacrificed.[20]

The separation between the two figures is both their distinct realities and the cutting and ragged edges of their constantly shifting relationships. By seeing ourselves as both generations, we are set free from the confinement of role definition, set free to experience the paradoxes of binder and bound. And yes, God blesses the separation as the only means for consciously coming together once again.

But Kin Wan made two altars—the big black one for Abraham, the little red one for Isaac. They are both sacrificed, he said; the son because the father wants to obey God's will and the father because he must choose between God and his son.

KYLE:

The Son Is the Father Is the Lover

My Akedah is very disturbing to me. I am both the Isaac kneeling over the altar, a compliant victim, and the other Isaac on the left of the gray Abraham (my father), who is ready to strike back. My angry Isaac is leaning out to the left to move his whole body into the striking of the father so that he will surely be destroyed. But the father, poised to sacrifice, seems helpless, looking up God and saying, Must I do this?

Now I see Abraham as another, third Isaac, a transition between the sacrifice and the terrible figure of Isaac the murderer. The altar is Sara (mother), and Isaac is willing to sacrifice himself to save her. He has not been placed on the altar but places himself over it protectively.

This is a scene I thought I had worked through in my own life, but it is still there. Things have changed. I know that I no longer have to be the victim or sacrificial lamb to my parents' relationship. Nor must I kill my father to have a relationship with my mother.

In a way my parents and my struggle with them and between them has been my God, but now I see that I must leave. But where do I go? There were many good things in my father's house. Where do I find them again? In the scene, God is the same color as my parents, and from his cloud he beckons to me to find him in my own way. I will find love as I have known before, and I will find a self (both humble and angry), but not a murderer and not a victim.

Healing often takes place through the process art of handmade midrash. It is not necessary for the instructor to be a therapist. The forms themselves speak to their maker. One of the aims of midrash is to create a two-way avenue between the Bible and the individual in which, through counterpoint, the hoary text becomes comprehensible and the individual's life acquires meaning and perspective. Mid-rash also serves as a kind of therapy: It permits expression of wild and raw impulses, for "imaginary enactment of an illicit act permits a certain discharge of emotion without harmful social consequences."[21]

SUSAN C.:
The Split Between Head and Heart

(see fig. 5.17, Color Section 3)

I took the form of Abraham to be dark and tortured. The whole experience centered on Abraham, who became the real sacrifice—a sacrifice of head and heart. Isaac is a small figure that became the heart of Abraham. The altar is a spiral form that moves and changes and somehow represents life to me. The presence of God is just a finger holding up the head of Abraham. His head has been separated from his body during this experience but is connected by an orange life force. The ram surprisingly became the largest figure. Brown is earthy to me, and the ram seems to be all the earthy desires sacrificed in the name of God and spirituality. The ram is also a guillotine shape because, traditionally, sensuality or sexuality is the instrument that supposedly takes one away or kills our spirituality.

Integrating the use of art with reading of Scripture has helped me see many more symbolic meanings in the Scripture. The first paper cut was a spontaneous expression of my subconscious awareness, and the meaning of the art only became clear after actually sitting down and writing about it. The Akedah became a representation of Western culture's split between heart and mind. What got sacrificed in the split was the body, and this has come to be the real split between spirituality and sexuality apparent in Christianity. I would never have made the connection between the scriptural story and the symbolic story had it not been for art.

In the language of lines drawing, the idea of every character being a part of Abraham came to me while reading the text. What the art did was formulate a graphic representation of how all the parts were Abraham, which crystallized the whole idea in one symbol. Now when I look at it, the entire idea comes to me at once without having to read my explanation. This has deepened the richness of Scripture for me, by seeing how one biblical symbol can have many personal meanings quite apart from the traditional interpretation.

MARGARET'S TYPOLOGY:
Abraham Is Job, Isaac Is Jesus

As a prelude to Margaret's typological midrash, we need to know something about "types" as a midrashic concept. Typology is a form of biblical interpretation that deals with the correspondences between persons, events, and institutions. Thus there are traditions concerning the acts of God that are analogous to events that happened earlier in biblical history or that foreshadow what will come later. Concerning the Akedah, the New Testament interprets Jesus as the fulfillment of major traditions from the Hebrew Bible. So Isaac becomes a "type" of

Jesus. Genesis Rabbah, one of the major collections of midrash, comments on the verse in which Abraham places the wood on Isaac's shoulders, "Isaac carries the wood like the one who carried the cross" (Gen. Rabbah 56:3). How did Jesus get into Genesis Rabbah? Genesis Rabbah was written during the early Christian centuries by a community aware of Christian doctrine. By the second century, Melito, the church father, already referred to the steps of Jesus' suffering in terms of Isaac's experience. Thus both the New Testament and the church fathers see the crucifixion as a completion of the binding of Isaac, and the midrash knew it. Similarly, the sufferings of Abraham make him a type of Job in the midrash.[22]

In her presentation, Margaret is unquestioning "that God is in charge, that Abraham is his man, that His purpose is being fulfilled." "Everything is in readiness," she writes in an impeccable hand, "the altar, the flame, the ram hiding in the thicket, unseen by the figures. Above the mountaintop, God waits in the cloud, directing the figures to the chosen place for the sacrifice." She is with the figures approaching the altar; she also observes in the lower lefthand corner, "I don't want to look, but I can't stop."

Isaac and Abraham, hand in hand, approach the mountain and the altar. But they are not alone. Abraham is accompanied by the (shadow) spirit of Job, a kinship between them because of their suffering. Isaac is accompanied by Christ, both only sons, both sacrificed by a loving father. The figures approach hand in hand because there is love and understanding of the task ahead and a simple trust between them. They know destiny calls them to this place.

The Christian model of unquestioning sacrifice has been well assimilated. Happy is the one whose faith is so secure and free of doubt.

Another example of typology relates to the Akedah. Abraham is a "type" of Moses, and the Akedah is a "type," or a "prefiguring," of Mattan Torah, the moment when Israel is given the Torah and is chosen by virtue of choosing a special destiny. As a mathematical proportion it looks like this: Abraham and Isaac : Akedah = All of Israel : Mattan Torah. Verbally it reads, "Abraham and Isaac relate to the Akedah and its trial of faith, as All of Israel relate to Mattan Torah and its trial of deeds." What are the parallel clues that reveal this prefiguring pattern? Most are biblical, and some are reinforced by midrash.

The Typology of Chosenness

1 Abraham and Moses are both born outside Canaan.
2 Both are threatened in their infancy by kings who feared their

potential. Thus Pharaoh decreed the death of newborn Israelite boys, and Abraham hid from Nimrod for thirteen years in a cave.

3   Both leave an environment of idolatry to lead their people across a river to the Promised Land: Abraham, to the call of "go forth" to a covenant and the promise of seed and land (Gen. 12:1; Josh. 24:2–4); and Moses, leading Israel out of Egypt, across the Red Sea to a covenant and a land of promise (Exod. 13ff.).

4   God uses the same rescue formula with both: To Abraham, "I am Yahweh who took you out of Ur" (Gen. 15:7); to Moses, "I am Yahweh who took you out of Egypt" (Exod. 20:2).

5   To the Divine call, both men answer in readiness, *hineni*, "Here I am"—Abraham on Moriah (Gen. 22:1), and Moses at the burning bush that is Sinai (Exod. 3:4, 12).

6   Both Abraham and Moses experience God's appearance at the sacred center of the world, Abraham at Moriah in Jerusalem, and Moses at Sinai, which the midrash identifies as part of Moriah! "Because their father Isaac lay upon this mountain, bound as a sacrifice, it is fitting that upon it his children receive the Torah."[23]

Other verbal parallels between Moriah and Sinai are the ram and shofar, the third-day motif, the "seeing" motif, and, most crucial, the test/experience motif. As Abraham and Isaac test/experience this trial of faith, so all of Israel experiences the test of coming to consciousness of a special destiny and commitment to Torah. Could this be what the Akedah is all about? It is, at the very least, yet another layer of meaning.

T'shuva *and* Change

If, as Jung might say, the altar is the place where a person comes to communicate with God, then the whole journey to this place contains keys to psychological and spiritual truths essential to becoming a whole person. But the truths are necessarily hidden in the puzzling details, disclosing themselves to each of us only when we are ready to act on them. Each element presents itself to the inner being, waits for response, and sculpts itself into a personal symbol.

For me there is only one comfort in the Akedah. True, God changes his mind in the end; that is a relief but not really a comfort. The comfort is that the puzzling details of the chapter begin to disclose a pattern of change.

"After these things," our story begins. This means that things don't happen in isolation, without preparation. So Abraham completed tasks or experiences to reach this point where *"God put him to the test."* We noted earlier that in Middle English the word for "test" is associated with the vessel in which metals were assayed, where precious metals were separated from lead (which weighs one down?). In Jungian terms we might say that the test can produce psychic transformation. Thus the nineteen short sentences of our text are like a crucible, an intense enclosed place where death and rebirth are to take place.

The land of Moriah is the way "to one of the mountains I will show you." The way is also the teacher. *Mori Yah:* "God is my teacher." Let us see how the way instructs. The destination is at first indeterminate. At the outset, vision has poor visibility. *He got up early in the morning.* One sees the light, a literal metaphor. Daybreak, dawn, or first light means illumination, hope, and a willingness to do God's will.

He lifted up his eyes and saw the place from afar. He lifted up his eyes and saw the ram behind. Perhaps the place and the ram are connected. The word *place* in Hebrew, *maqom*, is also one of the names of God. This seems to denote a special kind of seeing—perhaps the inner seeing or knowing that the East connects with the third eye (see Doris, fig. 5.18, Color Section 3, where the altar contains the eye).

He put the wood for the offering on Isaac and took in his hand the fire and the knife. Isaac is burdened with the *prima materia,* the basic material out of which all things are made. Abraham's hand, the tool that extends one's body, carries the symbols of transformation, illumination (fire), and freeing and severance (the knife, Heb. *ma-achelet,* "the devourer"). Note these very elements in Doris's work, the hand that carries the fire to the all-seeing mountain-ram-altar.

Sandwiched between the identical and weighty sentences in verses 6 and 8, *and the two of them went together,* Isaac says, "Here is the fire and the wood, but where is the lamb for the burnt offering?" Percival suggests that the lamb represents gentleness, young innocence, meekness, purity, and mystic rebirth and that Isaac is pointing out that transformation requires complete surrender of the ego and isolation from its previous experience. Isaac wonders if this is possible in such an old man as Abraham. His father replies, "God will see himself (will choose) the lamb," the innocence and gentleness needed for this surrender. Curiously, when Abraham lifts his eyes, his vision falls upon a ram, not a lamb. Edinger says:

> The ram signifies unregenerate archetypal energy which must be extracted from the unconscious and sacrificed. Abraham is participating in a process of divine transformation by permitting himself to entertain murderous impulses against Isaac. This brings the ram-energy into consciousness where it can then be sacrificed under the aegis of the more differentiated aspect of God. Psychologically one might say that Abraham's test deter-mined whether he was willing to risk a conscious encounter with his primitive affects, in the faith that they are capable of transformation.[24]

The lamb presages the change in Abraham and in God. The text of Genesis 22 supports this divine transformation. It is Elohim, the stern aspect of God, who issues the command in verse 1, whereas it is the angel of Yaweh, the compassionate aspect of God in verses 11 and 12, who rescinds the order: "Now I know that you fear Elohim"; that is, now I know you know the dark side of God and did not withhold your son, the complete surrender of your ego, the required sacrifice.

The Akedah is central to the Rosh Hashanah liturgy, in which the core concept is *t'shuva,* the need to change and repair one's personal relationships. The hope for humanity is that the parent and child who do not return together in verse 19 will soon turn and heal the tear in this closest of bindings.

Conclusion: *The Internal Journey*

The foregoing textual analysis, with selections from the midrash, accompanied by many richly imaginative illustrations of handmade midrash, constitutes a new approach to the teaching of the Akedah, integrating intellect and emotion, mind and heart, verbal and nonverbal modes. It has not been my purpose to solve the insoluble riddle of the Akedah. I have wanted only to air as many different angles as possible. Reviewing the material now, I can only echo *Pirke Avot,* the sages' expression of wondrous admiration for the layered complexity of Torah: "Turn it over, turn it over again, because everything is in it."

Like the sages, I can also say that I have learned most from my students, one of whom wrote the final selection. I recalled when rereading it that many pages ago I spoke about the call to Abraham that occurs at the beginning and at the end of his cycle, the *lech-lecha,* which is variously translated as "get thee, go forth, go to yourself, go for yourself, go to yours." What is suggested in that "go forth" is that two journeys are about to take place, an external journey and an internal journey. All external journeys, as every tourist knows, are infinitely richer if the traveler also fully recognizes the internal journey that is happening simultaneously.

In addition to creating the handmade midrash, Susan Cafarelli did a language of lines drawing on several specific passages of the Akedah. During her reading of the text, the idea came to her that every character was a part of Abraham. The lines became a graphic formulation of how all the parts were Abraham, which crystallized into a single symbol. It is the final example of a Jungian interpretation wherein each element presents itself to the "inner being," waits for response, and transforms itself into a personal symbol. It seems fitting to end this workshop summary with this most healing selection in Abraham's inward *lech-lecha.*

SUSAN C.:

All the Parts Are Abraham

(fig. 5.19)

The passages I have chosen (Gen. 22:1, 2, 5, 10, 12, 13, 17, 19) stand out to me in yet another meaning. The entire story can be taken with all the characters playing parts of Abraham. Isaac becomes the part of ourselves that needs to be healed. The servants take the parts of whatever helps us along the road to our own self-discovery. God is the ever-loving providence that leads us to the strange place where all

fig. 5.19. Susan C., *All the Parts Are Abraham.*

this can happen. Through trust, we offer a part of ourselves that we love to hold onto, mistakenly thinking it is really part of our being. Abraham's eyes are opened in Moriah, and he sees that what was really the sacrifice is outside of himself. He is meant to sacrifice, not his own flesh and blood, but something that has caught itself in the thicket by the wayside. The ram is caught itself in a thicket just like parts of our psyche are caught in webs that prevent us from being whole. God never intends for us to sacrifice ourselves but to let go of that which is not of our true selves. So the ram represents all those things that get entangled in our lives and that we relate to as part of us. The blessing of God is our own growth that takes place when we realize this and is signified by the "descendents as plentiful as the stars and sand." The final gift is that our wholeness is passed on to future generations by our inner awareness of personal blocks to wholeness (Abraham's descendents shall possess the gate of their enemies). Abraham returns to his servants alone because he has now integrated more of himself, and what was not himself, he has discarded.

The Akedah Workshop: Summary

OBJECTIVES

To identify the compelling issues of Judaism that are found in the Akedah; to examine how purposeful repetition and artful omission reveal and conceal critical elements of the narrative; to understand how the narrative moves into symbol, and how the art of the Akedah is also both narrative and symbolic; to show how difficulties in the text continually create midrash; to create midrash through the handmade methodology.

PRIMARY TEXTS

Genesis 22.

Targum Jonathan on Genesis 22, as presented in Jo Milgrom, *The Binding of Isaac (The Akedah): A Primary Symbol in Jewish Thought and Art.*

RECOMMENDED READINGS

Shalom Spiegel, *The Last Trial.*

Jo Milgrom, *The Binding of Isaac (The Akedah): A Primary Symbol in Jewish Thought and Art.*

ART WORKS FOR DISCUSSION

Moshe Mizrachi, "The Akedah," lithograph.

Selections from Jo Milgrom, *The Binding of Isaac.*

Note: This workshop functions well with handmade midrash as the only visual part. I have found that presenting the art of the Akedah results in supersaturation in a single workshop and is therefore better utilized in follow-up workshops.

MATERIALS REQUIRED

Colored construction paper and glue.

PROCEDURE

1 Close reading and discussion of the biblical text.

2 Comparison of biblical text with expansion in Targum Jonathan.

3 Examine the Moshe Mizrachi lithograph as "visual midrash" based on the Targum. Note how the visual imagination expands the verbal.

4 Participants choose four or five sheets of paper in different colors and tear five forms: Abraham, Isaac, the ram, the altar, and God's presence and paste them *in a relationship*. A sixth form may be added, by individual choice.

5 Discuss in small groups. Allow troubling issues to be raised. Write. Follow the basic recipe in the Introduction.

Alternate procedure: Save steps 2 and 3 for a subsequent workshop. The Moshe Mizrachi lithograph is visually related to Targum Jonathan not only in regard to the age of Isaac but also in regard to the centrality of the altar going back to Adam (*see* v.9, App. 4, p. 172) and the staged "supernatural" ram (v.13 p. 172). More details in the uses of midrash, the martyr model, and extensive art historical materials can be found in Milgrom, *The Binding of Isaac (The Akedah),* above, under PRIMARY TEXTS and RECOMMENDED READINGS.

1. Elie Wiesel, *Messengers of God* (New York: Random House, 1976), 69.

2. The Catalogue of Christian Art, at Princeton University and at UCLA, boasts 1,475 separate entries on the Akedah, up to the year 1500; it is not a book but a large research section of these libraries.

3. Jo Milgrom, *The Binding of Isaac (The Akedah): A Primary Symbol in Jewish Thought and Art* (Berkeley, Calif.: Bibal Press, 1988).

4. Yona Fischer (ed.), *Art and Craft in the Land of Israel in the Nineteenth Century* (Heb.) (Jerusalem: Israel Museum, 1979), 88–109.

5. Shalom Spiegel, *The Last Trial* (New York: Schocken, 1967).

6. Bernard Bamberger, "Fear and Love in the Old Testament," *Hebrew Union College Annual* 6 (1929):39–53. Bamberger concludes that when they appear in the same document, fear and love of the Lord mean the same thing. For example, Deuteronomy 10:12, where fear and love appear as parallel and synonymous, "Now Israel, what does the Lord your God require of you, but to *fear* the Lord your God, to walk in all his ways, and to *love* him and to serve the Lord your God with all your heart and with all your soul."

7. Hans-Martin Rotermund (ed.), *Rembrandt's Drawings and Etchings for the Bible* (Philadelphia: Pilgrim Press, 1969), 50.

8. Gerald Epstein, *Waking Dream Therapy* (New York: Human Sciences Press, 1981), 51. Epstein restores the healing perspectives of religion within psychology as handmade midrash affirms the neglected function of psychology and art in the study of religious texts and experience.

9. Duane Christensen, "The Akedah in Genesis 22:1–19: An Invitation to Jewish-Christian Dialogue," *American Baptist Quarterly* IV, no. 4 (1985):340–347. Christensen's article developed out of my Handmade Midrash Workshop given in his class at the American Baptist Seminary of the West, Berkeley, California.

10. The Books of Maccabees are not part of the Hebrew Bible. Books 1 and 2 are in the Apocrypha, which has been preserved in the Catholic Bible; 3 and 4 are in the *Old Testament Pseudepigrapha,* vol. 2, J. H. Charlesworth (ed.) (New York: Doubleday, 1983).

11. Since the War of Independence in 1948, the modern state of Israel has fought four additional wars: the Sinai campaign in 1956, the Six-Day War in 1967, the Yom Kippur War in 1973, the War in Lebanon in 1982. An extensive literature and art of protest has been growing since 1948. A 1988 exhibition catalog of *The Akedah in Modern Israeli Art* by Gideon Ofrat at the Museum of Modern Israeli Art in Ramat Gan shows the visual work of forty-four contemporary Israeli artists and quotes from countless writers and poets who address the Akedah in wholly nontraditional terms.

12. Edmund Blunden (ed.), *The Poems of Wilfred Owen* (New York: Viking, 1931), 122. See also reference to this work and the midrashic process in Shalom Spiegel, *The Last Trial,* xii–xiii.

13. Theodor Ehrenstein, *Das Alte Testament Im Bilde* (Vienna: 1923), for extensive visual images from the Hebrew Bible.

14. Søren Kierkegaard, *Fear and Trembling* (Princeton: Princeton University Press, 1945), 26–29.

15. Invaluable assistance in analyzing these art works was given by Ofra Bruno, lecturer in art therapy at the David Yellin Teacher's Seminar, Jerusalem.

16. John Bowker, *The Targums and Rabbinic Literature* (Cambridge: Cambridge University Press, 1969), 224–225. Targum Jonathan is officially called Targum Pseudo-Jonathan.

17. Hans-Martin Rotermund, "The Motif of Radiance in Rembrandt's Biblical Drawings," *Journal of the Warburg Courtauld* 29 (1966):101–121.

18. I. B. Jaffe (ed.), *The Sculpture of Leonard Baskin* (New York: Viking, 1980), shows contemporary sculpture in which Isaac becomes the altar. Permanently in the Jewish Museum, Fifth Avenue at Ninety-Second Street, New York.

19. Rachel Hachlili, *Ancient Jewish Art and Archaeology in the Land of Israel* (Leiden, Holland: Brill, 1988), 291.

20. Edward Edinger, *The Bible and the Psyche: Individuation Symbolism in the Old Testament* (Toronto: Inner City Books, 1986), 35.

21. K. J. Kaplan, M. W. Schwartz, and M. Markus-Kaplan (eds.), "The Family: Biblical and Psychological Foundations," *Journal of Psychology and Judaism* 8, no. 2 (1984); also, E. Wellisch, *Isaac and Oedipus* (London: Routledge & Kegan Paul, 1954), 27–52.

22. "Typology," *Interpreter's Dictionary of the Bible,* supplementary volume (Nashville: Abingdon, 1976), 926; for Abraham as Job, see Louis Ginzberg, *Legends of the Jews* (Philadelphia: The Jewish Publication Society, 1909), vol. 1, 305, 421, and vol. 5, 248, 383, 389.

23. Ginzberg, *Legends of the Jews,* vol. 3, 84.

24. Edinger, *The Bible and the Psyche,* 34.

Appendix of Sources

1 *Reflections on Light*

Sight is an absolutely spiritual phenomenon; accurately and only to be so defined; and the "Let there be Light" is as much, when you understand it, the ordering of intelligence as the ordering of vision.

John Ruskin, *The Eagle's Nest*

The history of Genesis or the old mythology repeats itself in the experience of every child. He too is a demon or god thrown into a particular chaos, where he strives to lead things from order into disorder.

Ralph Waldo Emerson,
Nature—Addresses and Lectures: The Method of Nature

Can the man say *Fiat Lux*, Let there be Light, and out of chaos make a world? Precisely as there is light in himself, will he accomplish this.

Thomas Carlyle, *On Heroes, Hero-Worship, and the Heroic in History*, III

Say not, let there be light, but darkness visible.

William Hazlitt, *On Reading New Books*

The splendid discontent of God with chaos made the world; and from the discontent of man the world's best progress springs.

Ella Wheeler Wilcox, *Discontent*

It is written, "God said, 'Let there be light,' and there was light." Rabbi Yosi said, "That light was hidden away, and it is reserved for the righteous in the world to come, as they (the Rabbis of the Talmud) have explained, based on the verse, 'Light is sown for the righteous' (Psalm 97:11). Indeed, [it is sown] for the righteous. That light never shone except for the First Day; afterwards it was hidden away and shone no more."

Rabbi Yehuda said, "If it were completely hidden away, the world would not exist for even a moment. Rather, it was hidden away and sown like a seed, which then gives birth and produces seeds and fruits. Thus the world is maintained. Every single day a ray of that light shines into the world and keeps everything alive, for with that ray the Holy One, may He be blessed, feeds the world.

"And in every place where Torah is studied at night, one thread-thin ray comes out from that hidden light and flows down to those studying . . . .

"Since the First Day the light has never been fully revealed, but it does indeed function in the world. Every day it renews the act of Creation."

Zohar II, 148b–149a;
translated from the Aramaic by Daniel Matt (reprinted with permission)

I have been taught by my teacher that Adam somehow resembled that first light which was hidden away. Afterwards, a thread-thin ray appeared to give "breath (or "soul"; Hebrew, *neshamah*) to the people on earth and life to those who walk thereon" (Isaiah 42:5).

Understand this, for the secret is essentially one.

I cannot expand this, for thus I have been commanded.

Shimon Lavi, *Ketem Paz, p. 121b;*
translated by Daniel Matt (reprinted with permission)

For with the appearance of the light, the universe expanded;
With the concealment of the light,
all individually existing things came into being . . .
This is the mystery of the Act of Creation.
One who is able to understand will understand.

Shimon Lavi, *Ketem Paz, p. 124c;*
translated by Daniel Matt (reprinted with permission)

The light which God created during the Six Days of Creation—with that light Adam could see from one end of the world to the other. However, God hid that light away from the righteous to enjoy in the life to come.

Where did he hide it? In the Torah. Therefore, when I open the Zohar I see the entire world.

Israel ben Eliezer, the Baal Shem Tov;
translated by Daniel Matt (reprinted with permission)

בְּרֵאשִׁית בָּרָא אֱלֹהִים אֵת הַשָּׁמַיִם וְאֵת הָאָרֶץ: 2 וְהָאָרֶץ הָיְתָה תֹהוּ וָבֹהוּ וְחֹשֶׁךְ
עַל־פְּנֵי תְהוֹם וְרוּחַ אֱלֹהִים מְרַחֶפֶת עַל־פְּנֵי הַמָּיִם: 3 וַיֹּאמֶר אֱלֹהִים יְהִי אוֹר וַיְהִי־
אוֹר: 4 וַיַּרְא אֱלֹהִים אֶת־הָאוֹר כִּי־טוֹב וַיַּבְדֵּל אֱלֹהִים בֵּין הָאוֹר וּבֵין הַחֹשֶׁךְ:
5 וַיִּקְרָא אֱלֹהִים ׀ לָאוֹר יוֹם וְלַחֹשֶׁךְ קָרָא לָיְלָה וַיְהִי־עֶרֶב וַיְהִי־בֹקֶר יוֹם אֶחָד:

פ   6 וַיֹּאמֶר אֱלֹהִים יְהִי רָקִיעַ בְּתוֹךְ הַמָּיִם וִיהִי מַבְדִּיל בֵּין מַיִם לָמָיִם:
7 וַיַּעַשׂ אֱלֹהִים אֶת־הָרָקִיעַ וַיַּבְדֵּל בֵּין הַמַּיִם אֲשֶׁר מִתַּחַת לָרָקִיעַ וּבֵין הַמַּיִם
אֲשֶׁר מֵעַל לָרָקִיעַ וַיְהִי־כֵן: 8 וַיִּקְרָא אֱלֹהִים לָרָקִיעַ שָׁמָיִם וַיְהִי־עֶרֶב וַיְהִי־בֹקֶר יוֹם
שֵׁנִי: פ 9 וַיֹּאמֶר אֱלֹהִים יִקָּווּ הַמַּיִם מִתַּחַת הַשָּׁמַיִם אֶל־מָקוֹם אֶחָד
וְתֵרָאֶה הַיַּבָּשָׁה וַיְהִי־כֵן: 10 וַיִּקְרָא אֱלֹהִים ׀ לַיַּבָּשָׁה אֶרֶץ וּלְמִקְוֵה הַמַּיִם קָרָא
יַמִּים וַיַּרְא אֱלֹהִים כִּי־טוֹב: 11 וַיֹּאמֶר אֱלֹהִים תַּדְשֵׁא הָאָרֶץ דֶּשֶׁא עֵשֶׂב
מַזְרִיעַ זֶרַע עֵץ פְּרִי עֹשֶׂה פְּרִי לְמִינוֹ אֲשֶׁר זַרְעוֹ־בוֹ עַל־הָאָרֶץ וַיְהִי־כֵן: 12 וַתּוֹצֵא
הָאָרֶץ דֶּשֶׁא עֵשֶׂב מַזְרִיעַ זֶרַע לְמִינֵהוּ וְעֵץ עֹשֶׂה־פְּרִי אֲשֶׁר זַרְעוֹ־בוֹ לְמִינֵהוּ
וַיַּרְא אֱלֹהִים כִּי־טוֹב: 13 וַיְהִי־עֶרֶב וַיְהִי־בֹקֶר יוֹם שְׁלִישִׁי: פ שֵׁנִי 14 וַיֹּאמֶר
אֱלֹהִים יְהִי מְאֹרֹת בִּרְקִיעַ הַשָּׁמַיִם לְהַבְדִּיל בֵּין הַיּוֹם וּבֵין הַלָּיְלָה וְהָיוּ לְאֹתֹת

2   *Genesis* 1:1–4:2*

1 When God began to create[a] heaven and earth—[2]the earth being unformed and void, with darkness over the surface of the deep and a wind from[b] God sweeping over the water—[3] God said, "Let there be light"; and there was light. [4]God saw that the light was good, and God separated the light from the darkness. [5]God called the light Day, and the darkness He called Night. And there was evening and there was morning, a first day.[c]

[6]God said, "Let there be an expanse in the midst of the water, that it may separate water from water." [7]God made the expanse, and it separated the water which was below the expanse from the water which was above the expanse. And it was so. [8]God called the expanse Sky. And there was evening and there was morning, a second day.

[9]God said, "Let the water below the sky be gathered into one area, that the dry land may appear." And it was so. [10]God called the dry land Earth, and the gathering of waters He called Seas. And God saw that this was good. [11]And God said, "Let the earth sprout vegetation: seed-bearing plants, fruit trees of every kind on earth that bear fruit with the seed in it." And it was so. [12]The earth brought forth vegetation: seed-bearing plants of every kind, and trees of every kind bearing fruit with the seed in it. And God saw that this was good. [13]And there was evening and there was morning, a third day.

From TANAKH: The Holy Scriptures. Philadelphia: The Jewish Publication Society, 1985; with permission.
[a] *Others "In the beginning God created."*
[b] *Others "the spirit of."*
[c] *Others "one day."*

וּלְמוֹעֲדִ֔ים וּלְיָמִ֖ים וְשָׁנִֽים: ¹⁵ וְהָי֤וּ לִמְאוֹרֹת֙ בִּרְקִ֣יעַ הַשָּׁמַ֔יִם לְהָאִ֖יר עַל־הָאָ֑רֶץ
וַֽיְהִי־כֵֽן: ¹⁶ וַיַּ֣עַשׂ אֱלֹהִ֔ים אֶת־שְׁנֵ֥י הַמְּאֹרֹ֖ת הַגְּדֹלִ֑ים אֶת־הַמָּא֤וֹר הַגָּדֹל֙
לְמֶמְשֶׁ֣לֶת הַיּ֔וֹם וְאֶת־הַמָּא֤וֹר הַקָּטֹן֙ לְמֶמְשֶׁ֣לֶת הַלַּ֔יְלָה וְאֵ֖ת הַכּוֹכָבִֽים: ¹⁷ וַיִּתֵּ֥ן
אֹתָ֛ם אֱלֹהִ֖ים בִּרְקִ֣יעַ הַשָּׁמָ֑יִם לְהָאִ֖יר עַל־הָאָֽרֶץ: ¹⁸ וְלִמְשֹׁל֙ בַּיּ֣וֹם וּבַלַּ֔יְלָה
וּֽלֲהַבְדִּ֔יל בֵּ֥ין הָא֖וֹר וּבֵ֣ין הַחֹ֑שֶׁךְ וַיַּ֥רְא אֱלֹהִ֖ים כִּי־טֽוֹב: ¹⁹ וַֽיְהִי־עֶ֥רֶב וַֽיְהִי־בֹ֖קֶר י֥וֹם
רְבִיעִֽי: פ ²⁰ וַיֹּ֣אמֶר אֱלֹהִ֔ים יִשְׁרְצ֣וּ הַמַּ֔יִם שֶׁ֖רֶץ נֶ֣פֶשׁ חַיָּ֑ה וְעוֹף֙ יְעוֹפֵ֣ף עַל־
הָאָ֔רֶץ עַל־פְּנֵ֖י רְקִ֥יעַ הַשָּׁמָֽיִם: ²¹ וַיִּבְרָ֣א אֱלֹהִ֔ים אֶת־הַתַּנִּינִ֖ם* הַגְּדֹלִ֑ים וְאֵ֣ת כָּל־
נֶ֣פֶשׁ הַֽחַיָּ֣ה | הָֽרֹמֶ֡שֶׂת אֲשֶׁר֩ שָׁרְצ֨וּ הַמַּ֜יִם לְמִֽינֵהֶ֗ם וְאֵ֤ת כָּל־ע֤וֹף כָּנָף֙ לְמִינֵ֔הוּ
וַיַּ֥רְא אֱלֹהִ֖ים כִּי־טֽוֹב: ²² וַיְבָ֧רֶךְ אֹתָ֛ם אֱלֹהִ֖ים לֵאמֹ֑ר פְּר֣וּ וּרְב֗וּ וּמִלְא֤וּ אֶת־
הַמַּ֙יִם֙ בַּיַּמִּ֔ים וְהָע֖וֹף יִ֥רֶב בָּאָֽרֶץ: ²³ וַֽיְהִי־עֶ֥רֶב וַֽיְהִי־בֹ֖קֶר י֥וֹם חֲמִישִֽׁי: פ
²⁴ שְׁלִישִֽׁי וַיֹּ֣אמֶר אֱלֹהִ֗ים תּוֹצֵ֨א הָאָ֜רֶץ נֶ֤פֶשׁ חַיָּה֙ לְמִינָ֔הּ בְּהֵמָ֥ה וָרֶ֖מֶשׂ וְחַֽיְתוֹ־
אֶ֖רֶץ לְמִינָ֑הּ וַֽיְהִי־כֵֽן: ²⁵ וַיַּ֣עַשׂ אֱלֹהִים֩ אֶת־חַיַּ֨ת הָאָ֜רֶץ לְמִינָ֗הּ וְאֶת־הַבְּהֵמָה֙
לְמִינָ֔הּ וְאֵ֛ת כָּל־רֶ֥מֶשׂ הָֽאֲדָמָ֖ה לְמִינֵ֑הוּ וַיַּ֥רְא אֱלֹהִ֖ים כִּי־טֽוֹב: ²⁶ וַיֹּ֣אמֶר אֱלֹהִ֗ים
נַֽעֲשֶׂ֥ה אָדָ֛ם בְּצַלְמֵ֖נוּ כִּדְמוּתֵ֑נוּ וְיִרְדּוּ֩ בִדְגַ֨ת הַיָּ֜ם וּבְע֣וֹף הַשָּׁמַ֗יִם וּבַבְּהֵמָה֙
וּבְכָל־הָאָ֔רֶץ וּבְכָל־הָרֶ֖מֶשׂ הָֽרֹמֵ֥שׂ עַל־הָאָֽרֶץ: ²⁷ וַיִּבְרָ֨א אֱלֹהִ֤ים | אֶת־הָֽאָדָם֙
בְּצַלְמ֔וֹ בְּצֶ֥לֶם אֱלֹהִ֖ים בָּרָ֣א אֹת֑וֹ זָכָ֥ר וּנְקֵבָ֖ה בָּרָ֥א אֹתָֽם: ²⁸ וַיְבָ֣רֶךְ אֹתָם֮ אֱלֹהִים֒
וַיֹּ֨אמֶר לָהֶ֜ם אֱלֹהִ֗ים פְּר֥וּ וּרְב֛וּ וּמִלְא֥וּ אֶת־הָאָ֖רֶץ וְכִבְשֻׁ֑הָ וּרְד֞וּ בִּדְגַ֤ת הַיָּם֙
וּבְע֣וֹף הַשָּׁמַ֔יִם וּבְכָל־חַיָּ֖ה הָֽרֹמֶ֥שֶׂת עַל־הָאָֽרֶץ: ²⁹ וַיֹּ֣אמֶר אֱלֹהִ֗ים הִנֵּה֩ נָתַ֨תִּי
לָכֶ֜ם אֶת־כָּל־עֵ֣שֶׂב | זֹרֵ֣עַ זֶ֗רַע אֲשֶׁר֙ עַל־פְּנֵ֣י כָל־הָאָ֔רֶץ וְאֶת־כָּל־הָעֵ֛ץ אֲשֶׁר־בּ֥וֹ
פְרִי־עֵ֖ץ זֹרֵ֣עַ זָ֑רַע לָכֶ֥ם יִֽהְיֶ֖ה לְאָכְלָֽה: ³⁰ וּֽלְכָל־חַיַּ֣ת הָ֠אָרֶץ וּלְכָל־ע֨וֹף הַשָּׁמַ֜יִם
וּלְכֹ֣ל | רוֹמֵ֣שׂ עַל־הָאָ֗רֶץ אֲשֶׁר־בּוֹ֙ נֶ֣פֶשׁ חַיָּ֔ה אֶת־כָּל־יֶ֥רֶק עֵ֖שֶׂב לְאָכְלָ֑ה וַֽיְהִי־כֵֽן:
³¹ וַיַּ֤רְא אֱלֹהִים֙ אֶת־כָּל־אֲשֶׁ֣ר עָשָׂ֔ה וְהִנֵּה־ט֖וֹב מְאֹ֑ד וַֽיְהִי־עֶ֥רֶב וַֽיְהִי־בֹ֖קֶר י֥וֹם
הַשִּׁשִּֽׁי: פ

ב וַיְכֻלּ֛וּ הַשָּׁמַ֥יִם וְהָאָ֖רֶץ וְכָל־צְבָאָֽם: ² וַיְכַ֤ל אֱלֹהִים֙ בַּיּ֣וֹם הַשְּׁבִיעִ֔י מְלַאכְתּ֖וֹ
אֲשֶׁ֣ר עָשָׂ֑ה וַיִּשְׁבֹּת֙ בַּיּ֣וֹם הַשְּׁבִיעִ֔י מִכָּל־מְלַאכְתּ֖וֹ אֲשֶׁ֥ר עָשָֽׂה: ³ וַיְבָ֤רֶךְ אֱלֹהִים֙
אֶת־י֣וֹם הַשְּׁבִיעִ֔י וַיְקַדֵּ֖שׁ אֹת֑וֹ כִּ֣י ב֤וֹ שָׁבַת֙ מִכָּל־מְלַאכְתּ֔וֹ אֲשֶׁר־בָּרָ֥א אֱלֹהִ֖ים
לַעֲשֽׂוֹת: פ רביעי [שני לספרדים] ⁴ אֵ֣לֶּה תוֹלְד֧וֹת הַשָּׁמַ֛יִם וְהָאָ֖רֶץ בְּהִבָּֽרְאָ֑ם*
בְּי֗וֹם עֲשׂ֛וֹת יְהוָ֥ה אֱלֹהִ֖ים אֶ֥רֶץ וְשָׁמָֽיִם: ⁵ וְכֹ֣ל | שִׂ֣יחַ הַשָּׂדֶ֗ה טֶ֚רֶם יִֽהְיֶ֣ה בָאָ֔רֶץ וְכָל־

¹⁴God said, "Let there be lights in the expanse of the sky to separate day from night; they shall serve as signs for the set times—the days and the years; ¹⁵and they shall serve as lights in the expanse of the sky to shine upon the earth." And it was so. ¹⁶God made the two great lights, the greater light to dominate the day and the lesser light to dominate the night, and the stars. ¹⁷And God set them in the expanse of the sky to shine upon the earth, ¹⁸to dominate the day and the night, and to separate light from darkness. And God saw that this was good. ¹⁹And there was evening and there was morning, a fourth day.

²⁰God said, "Let the waters bring forth swarms of living creatures, and birds that fly above the earth across the expanse of the sky." ²¹God created the great sea monsters, and all the living creatures of every kind that creep, which the waters brought forth in swarms, and all the winged birds of every kind. And God saw that this was good. ²²God blessed them, saying, "Be fertile and increase, fill the waters in the seas, and let the birds increase on the earth." ²³And there was evening and there was morning, a fifth day.

²⁴God said, "Let the earth bring forth every kind of living creature: cattle, creeping things, and wild beasts of every kind." And it was so. ²⁵God made wild beasts of every kind and cattle of every kind, and all kinds of creeping things of the earth. And God saw that this was good. ²⁶And God said, "Let us make man in our image, after our likeness. They shall rule the fish of the sea, the birds of the sky, the cattle, the whole earth, and all the creeping things that creep on earth." ²⁷And God created man in His image, in the image of God He created him; male and female He created them. ²⁸God blessed them and God said to them, "Be fertile and increase, fill the earth and master it; and rule the fish of the sea, the birds of the sky, and all the living things that creep on earth."

²⁹God said, "See, I give you every seed-bearing plant that is upon all the earth, and every tree that has seed-bearing fruit; they shall be yours for food. ³⁰And to all the animals on land, to all the birds of the sky, and to everything that creeps on earth, in which there is the breath of life, [I give] all the green plants for food." And it was so. ³¹And God saw all that He had made, and found it very good. And there was evening and there was morning, the sixth day.

2 The heaven and the earth were finished, and all their array. ²On the seventh day God finished the work that He had been doing, and He ceased^d on the seventh day from all the work that He had done. ³And God blessed the seventh day and declared it holy, because on it God ceased from all the work of creation that He had done. ⁴Such is the story of heaven and earth when they were created.

^d *Or "rested."*

עֵשֶׂב הַשָּׂדֶה טֶרֶם יִצְמָח כִּי לֹא הִמְטִיר יְהוָה אֱלֹהִים עַל־הָאָרֶץ וְאָדָם אַיִן
לַעֲבֹד אֶת־הָאֲדָמָה: 6 וְאֵד יַעֲלֶה מִן־הָאָרֶץ וְהִשְׁקָה אֶת־כָּל־פְּנֵי־הָאֲדָמָה: 7 וַיִּיצֶר
יְהוָה אֱלֹהִים אֶת־הָאָדָם עָפָר מִן־הָאֲדָמָה וַיִּפַּח בְּאַפָּיו נִשְׁמַת חַיִּים וַיְהִי
הָאָדָם לְנֶפֶשׁ חַיָּה: 8 וַיִּטַּע יְהוָה אֱלֹהִים גַּן־בְּעֵדֶן מִקֶּדֶם וַיָּשֶׂם שָׁם אֶת־הָאָדָם
אֲשֶׁר יָצָר: 9 וַיַּצְמַח יְהוָה אֱלֹהִים מִן־הָאֲדָמָה כָּל־עֵץ נֶחְמָד לְמַרְאֶה וְטוֹב
לְמַאֲכָל וְעֵץ הַחַיִּים בְּתוֹךְ הַגָּן וְעֵץ הַדַּעַת טוֹב וָרָע: 10 וְנָהָר יֹצֵא מֵעֵדֶן
לְהַשְׁקוֹת אֶת־הַגָּן וּמִשָּׁם יִפָּרֵד וְהָיָה לְאַרְבָּעָה רָאשִׁים: 11 שֵׁם הָאֶחָד פִּישׁוֹן
הוּא הַסֹּבֵב אֵת כָּל־אֶרֶץ הַחֲוִילָה אֲשֶׁר־שָׁם הַזָּהָב: 12 וּזֲהַב הָאָרֶץ הַהִוא טוֹב שָׁם
הַבְּדֹלַח וְאֶבֶן הַשֹּׁהַם: 13 וְשֵׁם־הַנָּהָר הַשֵּׁנִי גִּיחוֹן הוּא הַסּוֹבֵב אֵת כָּל־אֶרֶץ כּוּשׁ:
14 וְשֵׁם הַנָּהָר הַשְּׁלִישִׁי חִדֶּקֶל הוּא הַהֹלֵךְ קִדְמַת אַשּׁוּר וְהַנָּהָר הָרְבִיעִי הוּא
פְרָת: 15 וַיִּקַּח יְהוָה אֱלֹהִים אֶת־הָאָדָם וַיַּנִּחֵהוּ בְגַן־עֵדֶן לְעָבְדָהּ וּלְשָׁמְרָהּ:
16 וַיְצַו יְהוָה אֱלֹהִים עַל־הָאָדָם לֵאמֹר מִכֹּל עֵץ־הַגָּן אָכֹל תֹּאכֵל: 17 וּמֵעֵץ
הַדַּעַת טוֹב וָרָע לֹא תֹאכַל מִמֶּנּוּ כִּי בְּיוֹם אֲכָלְךָ מִמֶּנּוּ מוֹת תָּמוּת:
18 וַיֹּאמֶר יְהוָה אֱלֹהִים לֹא־טוֹב הֱיוֹת הָאָדָם לְבַדּוֹ אֶעֱשֶׂה־לּוֹ עֵזֶר כְּנֶגְדּוֹ:
19 וַיִּצֶר יְהוָה אֱלֹהִים מִן־הָאֲדָמָה כָּל־חַיַּת הַשָּׂדֶה וְאֵת כָּל־עוֹף הַשָּׁמַיִם
וַיָּבֵא אֶל־הָאָדָם לִרְאוֹת מַה־יִּקְרָא־לוֹ וְכֹל אֲשֶׁר יִקְרָא־לוֹ הָאָדָם נֶפֶשׁ חַיָּה
הוּא שְׁמוֹ: [שלישי לספרדים] 20 וַיִּקְרָא הָאָדָם שֵׁמוֹת לְכָל־הַבְּהֵמָה וּלְעוֹף
הַשָּׁמַיִם וּלְכֹל חַיַּת הַשָּׂדֶה וּלְאָדָם לֹא־מָצָא עֵזֶר כְּנֶגְדּוֹ: 21 וַיַּפֵּל יְהוָה אֱלֹהִים
תַּרְדֵּמָה עַל־הָאָדָם וַיִּישָׁן וַיִּקַּח אַחַת מִצַּלְעֹתָיו וַיִּסְגֹּר בָּשָׂר תַּחְתֶּנָּה: 22 וַיִּבֶן
יְהוָה אֱלֹהִים אֶת־הַצֵּלָע אֲשֶׁר־לָקַח מִן־הָאָדָם לְאִשָּׁה וַיְבִאֶהָ אֶל־הָאָדָם:
23 וַיֹּאמֶר הָאָדָם

זֹאת הַפַּעַם

עֶצֶם מֵעֲצָמַי

וּבָשָׂר מִבְּשָׂרִי

לְזֹאת יִקָּרֵא אִשָּׁה

כִּי מֵאִישׁ לֻקֳחָה־זֹּאת:

24 עַל־כֵּן יַעֲזָב־אִישׁ אֶת־אָבִיו וְאֶת־אִמּוֹ וְדָבַק בְּאִשְׁתּוֹ וְהָיוּ לְבָשָׂר אֶחָד:

25 וַיִּהְיוּ שְׁנֵיהֶם עֲרוּמִּים הָאָדָם וְאִשְׁתּוֹ וְלֹא יִתְבֹּשָׁשׁוּ:

When the LORD God made earth and heaven—[5]when no shrub of the field was yet on earth and no grasses of the field had yet sprouted, because the LORD God had not sent rain upon the earth and there was no man to till the soil, [6]but a flow would well up from the ground and water the whole surface of the earth—[7]the LORD God formed man[e] from the dust of the earth.[f] He blew into his nostrils the breath of life, and man became a living being.

[8]The LORD God planted a garden in Eden, in the east, and placed there the man whom He had formed. [9]And from the ground the LORD God caused to grow every tree that was pleasing to the sight and good for food, with the tree of life in the middle of the garden, and the tree of knowledge of good and bad.

[10]A river issues from Eden to water the garden, and it then divides and becomes four branches. [11]The name of the first is Pishon, the one that winds through the whole land of Havilah, where the gold is. ([12]The gold of that land is good; bdellium is there, and lapis lazuli.[g]) [13]The name of the second river is Gihon, the one that winds through the whole land of Cush. [14]The name of the third river is Tigris, the one that flows east of Asshur. And the fourth river is the Euphrates.

[15]The LORD God took the man and placed him in the garden of Eden, to till it and tend it. [16]And the LORD God commanded the man, saying, "Of every tree of the garden you are free to eat; [17]but as for the tree of knowledge of good and bad, you must not eat of it; for as soon as you eat of it, you shall die."

[18]The LORD God said, "It is not good for man to be alone; I will make a fitting helper for him." [19]And the LORD God formed out of the earth all the wild beasts and all the birds of the sky, and brought them to the man to see what he would call them; and whatever the man called each living creature, that would be its name. [20]And the man gave names to all the cattle and to the birds of the sky and to all the wild beasts; but for Adam no fitting helper was found. [21]So the LORD God cast a deep sleep upon the man; and, while he slept, He took one of his ribs and closed up the flesh at that spot. [22]And the LORD God fashioned the rib that He had taken from the man into a woman; and He brought her to the man. [23]Then the man said,

> "This one at last
> Is bone of my bones
> And flesh of my flesh.
> This one shall be called Woman,[h]
> For from man[i] was she taken."

[24]Hence a man leaves his father and mother and clings to his wife, so that they become one flesh.

[e] *Heb.* 'adam.
[f] *Heb.* 'adamah.
[g] *Others "onyx"; meaning of Heb.* shoham *uncertain.*
[h] *Heb.* 'ishshah.
[i] *Heb.* 'ish.

ג וְהַנָּחָשׁ הָיָה עָרוּם מִכֹּל חַיַּת הַשָּׂדֶה אֲשֶׁר עָשָׂה יְהוָה אֱלֹהִים וַיֹּאמֶר אֶל־
הָאִשָּׁה אַף כִּי־אָמַר אֱלֹהִים לֹא תֹאכְלוּ מִכֹּל עֵץ הַגָּן: 2 וַתֹּאמֶר הָאִשָּׁה אֶל־הַנָּחָשׁ
מִפְּרִי עֵץ־הַגָּן נֹאכֵל: 3 וּמִפְּרִי הָעֵץ אֲשֶׁר בְּתוֹךְ־הַגָּן אָמַר אֱלֹהִים לֹא תֹאכְלוּ מִמֶּנּוּ
וְלֹא תִגְּעוּ בּוֹ פֶּן־תְּמֻתוּן: 4 וַיֹּאמֶר הַנָּחָשׁ אֶל־הָאִשָּׁה לֹא־מוֹת תְּמֻתוּן: 5 כִּי יֹדֵעַ
אֱלֹהִים כִּי בְּיוֹם אֲכָלְכֶם מִמֶּנּוּ וְנִפְקְחוּ עֵינֵיכֶם וִהְיִיתֶם כֵּאלֹהִים יֹדְעֵי טוֹב וָרָע:
6 וַתֵּרֶא הָאִשָּׁה כִּי טוֹב הָעֵץ לְמַאֲכָל וְכִי תַאֲוָה־הוּא לָעֵינַיִם וְנֶחְמָד הָעֵץ
לְהַשְׂכִּיל וַתִּקַּח מִפִּרְיוֹ וַתֹּאכַל וַתִּתֵּן גַּם־לְאִישָׁהּ עִמָּהּ וַיֹּאכַל: 7 וַתִּפָּקַחְנָה עֵינֵי
שְׁנֵיהֶם וַיֵּדְעוּ כִּי עֵירֻמִּם הֵם וַיִּתְפְּרוּ עֲלֵה תְאֵנָה וַיַּעֲשׂוּ לָהֶם חֲגֹרֹת: 8 וַיִּשְׁמְעוּ
אֶת־קוֹל יְהוָה אֱלֹהִים מִתְהַלֵּךְ בַּגָּן לְרוּחַ הַיּוֹם וַיִּתְחַבֵּא הָאָדָם וְאִשְׁתּוֹ מִפְּנֵי
יְהוָה אֱלֹהִים בְּתוֹךְ עֵץ הַגָּן: 9 וַיִּקְרָא יְהוָה אֱלֹהִים אֶל־הָאָדָם וַיֹּאמֶר לוֹ אַיֶּכָּה:
10 וַיֹּאמֶר אֶת־קֹלְךָ שָׁמַעְתִּי בַּגָּן וָאִירָא כִּי־עֵירֹם אָנֹכִי וָאֵחָבֵא: 11 וַיֹּאמֶר מִי
הִגִּיד לְךָ כִּי עֵירֹם אָתָּה הֲמִן־הָעֵץ אֲשֶׁר צִוִּיתִיךָ לְבִלְתִּי אֲכָל־מִמֶּנּוּ אָכָלְתָּ:
12 וַיֹּאמֶר הָאָדָם הָאִשָּׁה אֲשֶׁר נָתַתָּה עִמָּדִי הִוא נָתְנָה־לִּי מִן־הָעֵץ וָאֹכֵל:
13 וַיֹּאמֶר יְהוָה אֱלֹהִים לָאִשָּׁה מַה־זֹּאת עָשִׂית וַתֹּאמֶר הָאִשָּׁה הַנָּחָשׁ
הִשִּׁיאַנִי וָאֹכֵל: 14 וַיֹּאמֶר יְהוָה אֱלֹהִים אֶל־הַנָּחָשׁ

כִּי עָשִׂיתָ זֹּאת
אָרוּר אַתָּה מִכָּל־הַבְּהֵמָה
וּמִכֹּל חַיַּת הַשָּׂדֶה
עַל־גְּחֹנְךָ תֵלֵךְ
וְעָפָר תֹּאכַל
כָּל־יְמֵי חַיֶּיךָ:
15 וְאֵיבָה אָשִׁית בֵּינְךָ וּבֵין הָאִשָּׁה
וּבֵין זַרְעֲךָ וּבֵין זַרְעָהּ
הוּא יְשׁוּפְךָ רֹאשׁ
וְאַתָּה תְּשׁוּפֶנּוּ עָקֵב: ס
16 אֶל־הָאִשָּׁה אָמַר
הַרְבָּה אַרְבֶּה עִצְּבוֹנֵךְ וְהֵרֹנֵךְ
בְּעֶצֶב תֵּלְדִי בָנִים

^{25}The two of them were naked,^{j} the man and his wife, yet they felt no shame. ^{1}Now the serpent was the shrewdest of all the wild beasts that 3 the LORD God had made. He said to the woman, "Did God really say: You shall not eat of any tree of the garden?" ^{2}The woman replied to the serpent, "We may eat of the fruit of the other trees of the garden. ^{3}It is only about fruit of the tree in the middle of the garden that God said: "You shall not eat of it or touch it, lest you die.'" ^{4}And the serpent said to the woman, "You are not going to die, ^{5}but God knows that as soon as you eat of it your eyes will be opened and you will be like $^{k-}$divine beings who know^{-k} good and bad." ^{6}When the woman saw that the tree was good for eating and a delight to the eyes, and that the tree was desirable as a source of wisdom, she took of its fruit and ate. She also gave some to her husband, and he ate. ^{7}Then the eyes of both of them were opened and they perceived that they were naked; and they sewed together fig leaves and made themselves loincloths.

^{8}They heard the sound of the LORD God moving about in the garden at the breezy time of day; and the man and his wife hid from the LORD God among the trees of the garden. ^{9}The LORD God called out to the man and said to him, "Where are you?" ^{10}He replied, "I heard the sound of You in the garden, and I was afraid because I was naked, so I hid." ^{11}Then he asked, "Who told you that you were naked? Did you eat of the tree from which I had forbidden you to eat?" ^{12}The man said, "The woman You put at my side—she gave me of the tree, and I ate." ^{13}And the LORD God said to the woman, "What is this you have done!" The woman replied, "The serpent duped me, and I ate."
^{14}Then the LORD God said to the serpent,

"Because you did this,
More cursed shall you be
Than all cattle
And all the wild beasts:
On your belly shall you crawl
And dirt shall you eat
All the days of your life.
^{15}I will put enmity
Between you and the woman,
And between your offspring and hers;
They shall strike at your head,
And you shall strike at their heel."

^{16}And to the woman He said,

"I will make most severe
Your pangs in childbearing;
In pain shall you bear children.

---

^{j} Heb. 'arummim, play on 'arum "shrewd" in 3.1.
$^{k\text{-}k}$ Others "God, who knows."

וְאֶל־אִישֵׁךְ תְּשׁוּקָתֵךְ

וְהוּא יִמְשָׁל־בָּךְ: ס

17 וּלְאָדָם אָמַר כִּי־שָׁמַעְתָּ לְקוֹל אִשְׁתֶּךָ וַתֹּאכַל מִן־הָעֵץ אֲשֶׁר צִוִּיתִיךָ

לֵאמֹר לֹא תֹאכַל מִמֶּנּוּ

אֲרוּרָה הָאֲדָמָה בַּעֲבוּרֶךָ

בְּעִצָּבוֹן תֹּאכֲלֶנָּה

כֹּל יְמֵי חַיֶּיךָ:

18 וְקוֹץ וְדַרְדַּר תַּצְמִיחַ לָךְ

וְאָכַלְתָּ אֶת־עֵשֶׂב הַשָּׂדֶה:

19 בְּזֵעַת אַפֶּיךָ תֹּאכַל לֶחֶם

עַד שׁוּבְךָ אֶל־הָאֲדָמָה

כִּי מִמֶּנָּה לֻקָּחְתָּ

כִּי־עָפָר אַתָּה

וְאֶל־עָפָר תָּשׁוּב:

20 וַיִּקְרָא הָאָדָם שֵׁם אִשְׁתּוֹ חַוָּה כִּי הִוא הָיְתָה אֵם כָּל־חָי: 21 וַיַּעַשׂ יְהוָה

אֱלֹהִים לְאָדָם וּלְאִשְׁתּוֹ כָּתְנוֹת עוֹר וַיַּלְבִּשֵׁם: פ חמישי [רביעי לספרדים]

22 וַיֹּאמֶר | יְהוָה אֱלֹהִים הֵן הָאָדָם הָיָה כְּאַחַד מִמֶּנּוּ לָדַעַת טוֹב וָרָע וְעַתָּה | פֶּן־

יִשְׁלַח יָדוֹ וְלָקַח גַּם מֵעֵץ הַחַיִּים וְאָכַל וָחַי לְעֹלָם: 23 וַיְשַׁלְּחֵהוּ יְהוָה אֱלֹהִים

מִגַּן־עֵדֶן לַעֲבֹד אֶת־הָאֲדָמָה אֲשֶׁר לֻקַּח מִשָּׁם: 24 וַיְגָרֶשׁ אֶת־הָאָדָם וַיַּשְׁכֵּן

מִקֶּדֶם לְגַן־עֵדֶן אֶת־הַכְּרֻבִים וְאֵת לַהַט הַחֶרֶב הַמִּתְהַפֶּכֶת לִשְׁמֹר אֶת־

דֶּרֶךְ עֵץ הַחַיִּים: ס

ד וְהָאָדָם יָדַע אֶת־חַוָּה אִשְׁתּוֹ וַתַּהַר וַתֵּלֶד אֶת־קַיִן וַתֹּאמֶר קָנִיתִי אִישׁ אֶת־

יְהוָה: 2 וַתֹּסֶף לָלֶדֶת אֶת־אָחִיו אֶת־הָבֶל וַיְהִי־הֶבֶל רֹעֵה צֹאן וְקַיִן הָיָה עֹבֵד

אֲדָמָה:

Yet your urge shall be for your husband,
And he shall rule over you."
¹⁷To Adam He said, "Because you did as your wife said and ate of the tree about which I commanded you, 'You shall not eat of it,'

Cursed be the ground because of you;
By toil shall you eat of it
All the days of your life:
¹⁸Thorns and thistles shall it sprout for you.
But your food shall be the grasses of the field;
¹⁹By the sweat of your brow
Shall you get bread to eat,
Until you return to the ground—
For from it you were taken.
For dust you are,
And to dust you shall return."

²⁰The man named his wife Eve,[l] because she was the mother of all the living.[m] ²¹And the LORD God made garments of skins for Adam and his wife, and clothed them.

²²And the LORD God said, "Now that the man has become like one of us, knowing good and bad, what if he should stretch out his hand and take also from the tree of life and eat, and live forever!" ²³So the LORD God banished him from the garden of Eden, to till the soil from which he was taken. ²⁴He drove the man out, and stationed east of the garden of Eden the cherubim and the fiery ever-turning sword, to guard the way to the tree of life.

4 Now the man knew[n] his wife Eve, and she conceived and bore Cain, saying, "I have gained[o] a male child with the help of the LORD." ²She then bore his brother Abel. Abel became a keeper of sheep, and Cain became a tiller of the soil.

^l *Heb.* ḥawwah.
^m *Heb.* ḥay.
ⁿ *Heb.* yada', *often in a sexual sense.*
^o *Heb.* qanithi, *connected with* "Cain."

כ״ב וַיְהִ֗י אַחַר֙ הַדְּבָרִ֣ים הָאֵ֔לֶּה וְהָ֣אֱלֹהִ֔ים נִסָּ֖ה אֶת־אַבְרָהָ֑ם וַיֹּ֥אמֶר אֵלָ֖יו
אַבְרָהָ֖ם וַיֹּ֥אמֶר הִנֵּֽנִי: 2 וַיֹּ֡אמֶר קַח־נָ֠א אֶת־בִּנְךָ֨ אֶת־יְחִֽידְךָ֜ אֲשֶׁר־אָהַ֗בְתָּ
אֶת־יִצְחָ֔ק וְלֶךְ־לְךָ֔ אֶל־אֶ֖רֶץ הַמֹּרִיָּ֑ה וְהַעֲלֵ֤הוּ שָׁם֙ לְעֹלָ֔ה עַ֚ל אַחַ֣ד הֶֽהָרִ֔ים אֲשֶׁ֖ר
אֹמַ֥ר אֵלֶֽיךָ: 3 וַיַּשְׁכֵּ֨ם אַבְרָהָ֜ם בַּבֹּ֗קֶר וַֽיַּחֲבֹשׁ֙ אֶת־חֲמֹר֔וֹ וַיִּקַּ֞ח אֶת־שְׁנֵ֤י נְעָרָיו֙
אִתּ֔וֹ וְאֵ֖ת יִצְחָ֣ק בְּנ֑וֹ וַיְבַקַּע֙ עֲצֵ֣י עֹלָ֔ה וַיָּ֣קָם וַיֵּ֔לֶךְ אֶל־הַמָּק֖וֹם אֲשֶׁר־אָֽמַר־ל֥וֹ
הָאֱלֹהִֽים: 4 בַּיּ֣וֹם הַשְּׁלִישִׁ֗י וַיִּשָּׂ֨א אַבְרָהָ֧ם אֶת־עֵינָ֛יו וַיַּ֥רְא אֶת־הַמָּק֖וֹם מֵֽרָחֹֽק:
5 וַיֹּ֨אמֶר אַבְרָהָ֜ם אֶל־נְעָרָ֗יו שְׁבוּ־לָכֶ֥ם פֹּה֙ עִֽם־הַחֲמ֔וֹר וַאֲנִ֣י וְהַנַּ֔עַר נֵֽלְכָ֖ה עַד־
כֹּ֑ה וְנִֽשְׁתַּחֲוֶ֖ה וְנָשׁ֥וּבָה אֲלֵיכֶֽם: 6 וַיִּקַּ֨ח אַבְרָהָ֜ם אֶת־עֲצֵ֣י הָעֹלָ֗ה וַיָּ֙שֶׂם֙ עַל־
יִצְחָ֣ק בְּנ֔וֹ וַיִּקַּ֣ח בְּיָד֔וֹ אֶת־הָאֵ֖שׁ וְאֶת־הַֽמַּאֲכֶ֑לֶת וַיֵּלְכ֥וּ שְׁנֵיהֶ֖ם יַחְדָּֽו: 7 וַיֹּ֨אמֶר
יִצְחָ֜ק אֶל־אַבְרָהָ֤ם אָבִיו֙ וַיֹּ֣אמֶר אָבִ֔י וַיֹּ֖אמֶר הִנֶּ֣נִּֽי בְנִ֑י וַיֹּ֗אמֶר הִנֵּ֤ה הָאֵשׁ֙ וְהָ֣עֵצִ֔ים
וְאַיֵּ֥ה הַשֶּׂ֖ה לְעֹלָֽה: 8 וַיֹּ֙אמֶר֙ אַבְרָהָ֔ם אֱלֹהִ֞ים יִרְאֶה־לּ֥וֹ הַשֶּׂ֛ה לְעֹלָ֖ה בְּנִ֑י וַיֵּלְכ֥וּ
שְׁנֵיהֶ֖ם יַחְדָּֽו: 9 וַיָּבֹ֗אוּ אֶֽל־הַמָּקוֹם֮ אֲשֶׁ֣ר אָֽמַר־ל֣וֹ הָאֱלֹהִים֒ וַיִּ֨בֶן שָׁ֤ם אַבְרָהָם֙
אֶת־הַמִּזְבֵּ֔חַ וַֽיַּעֲרֹ֖ךְ אֶת־הָעֵצִ֑ים וַֽיַּעֲקֹד֙ אֶת־יִצְחָ֣ק בְּנ֔וֹ וַיָּ֤שֶׂם אֹתוֹ֙ עַל־הַמִּזְבֵּ֔חַ
מִמַּ֖עַל לָעֵצִֽים: 10 וַיִּשְׁלַ֤ח אַבְרָהָם֙ אֶת־יָד֔וֹ וַיִּקַּ֖ח אֶת־הַֽמַּאֲכֶ֑לֶת לִשְׁחֹ֖ט אֶת־בְּנֽוֹ:
11 וַיִּקְרָ֨א אֵלָ֜יו מַלְאַ֤ךְ יְהֹוָה֙ מִן־הַשָּׁמַ֔יִם וַיֹּ֖אמֶר אַבְרָהָ֣ם ׀ אַבְרָהָ֑ם וַיֹּ֖אמֶר
הִנֵּֽנִי: 12 וַיֹּ֗אמֶר אַל־תִּשְׁלַ֤ח יָֽדְךָ֙ אֶל־הַנַּ֔עַר וְאַל־תַּ֥עַשׂ ל֖וֹ מְא֑וּמָה כִּ֣י ׀ עַתָּ֣ה
יָדַ֗עְתִּי כִּֽי־יְרֵ֤א אֱלֹהִים֙ אַ֔תָּה וְלֹ֥א חָשַׂ֛כְתָּ אֶת־בִּנְךָ֥ אֶת־יְחִֽידְךָ֖ מִמֶּֽנִּי: 13 וַיִּשָּׂ֨א

3 *Genesis* 22:1–19

22 Some time afterward, God put Abraham to the test. He said to him, "Abraham," and he answered, "Here I am." ²And he said, "Take your son, your favored one, Isaac, whom you love, and go to the land of Moriah, and offer him there as a burnt offering on one of the heights that I will point out to you." ³So early next morning, Abraham saddled his ass and took with him two of his servants and his son Isaac. He split the wood for the burnt offering, and he set out for the place of which God had told him. ⁴On the third day Abraham looked up and saw the place from afar. ⁵Then Abraham said to his servants, "You stay here with the ass. The boy and I will go up there; we will worship and we will return to you."

⁶Abraham took the wood for the burnt offering and put it on his son Isaac. He himself took the firestone[a] and the knife; and the two walked off together. ⁷Then Isaac said to his father Abraham, "Father!" And he answered, "Yes, my son." And he said, "Here are the firestone and the wood; but where is the sheep for the burnt offering?" ⁸And Abraham said, "God will see to the sheep for His burnt offering, my son." And the two of them walked on together.

⁹They arrived at the place of which God had told him. Abraham built an altar there; he laid out the wood; he bound his son Isaac; he laid him on the altar, on top of the wood. ¹⁰And Abraham picked up the knife to slay his son. ¹¹Then an angel of the LORD called to him from heaven: "Abraham! Abraham!" And he answered, "Here I am." ¹²And he said, "Do not raise your hand against the boy, or do anything to him. For now I know that you fear God, since you have not withheld

---

ᵃ *Lit. "fire."*

אַבְרָהָם אֶת־עֵינָיו וַיַּרְא וְהִנֵּה־אַיִל אַחַר נֶאֱחַז בַּסְּבַךְ בְּקַרְנָיו וַיֵּלֶךְ אַבְרָהָם
וַיִּקַּח אֶת־הָאַיִל וַיַּעֲלֵהוּ לְעֹלָה תַּחַת בְּנוֹ: ¹⁴ וַיִּקְרָא אַבְרָהָם שֵׁם־הַמָּקוֹם הַהוּא
יְהוָה ׀ יִרְאֶה אֲשֶׁר יֵאָמֵר הַיּוֹם בְּהַר יְהוָה יֵרָאֶה: ¹⁵ וַיִּקְרָא מַלְאַךְ יְהוָה אֶל־
אַבְרָהָם שֵׁנִית מִן־הַשָּׁמָיִם: ¹⁶ וַיֹּאמֶר בִּי נִשְׁבַּעְתִּי נְאֻם־יְהוָה כִּי יַעַן אֲשֶׁר
עָשִׂיתָ אֶת־הַדָּבָר הַזֶּה וְלֹא חָשַׂכְתָּ אֶת־בִּנְךָ אֶת־יְחִידֶךָ: ¹⁷ כִּי־בָרֵךְ אֲבָרֶכְךָ
וְהַרְבָּה אַרְבֶּה אֶת־זַרְעֲךָ כְּכוֹכְבֵי הַשָּׁמַיִם וְכַחוֹל אֲשֶׁר עַל־שְׂפַת הַיָּם וְיִרַשׁ
זַרְעֲךָ אֵת שַׁעַר אֹיְבָיו: ¹⁸ וְהִתְבָּרֲכוּ בְזַרְעֲךָ כֹּל גּוֹיֵי הָאָרֶץ עֵקֶב אֲשֶׁר שָׁמַעְתָּ
בְּקֹלִי: ¹⁹ וַיָּשָׁב אַבְרָהָם אֶל־נְעָרָיו וַיָּקֻמוּ וַיֵּלְכוּ יַחְדָּו אֶל־בְּאֵר שָׁבַע וַיֵּשֶׁב
אַבְרָהָם בִּבְאֵר שָׁבַע: פ

your son, your favored one, from Me." [13]When Abraham looked up, his eye fell upon a[b] ram, caught in the thicket by its horns. So Abraham went and took the ram and offered it up as a burnt offering in place of his son. [14]And Abraham named that site Adonai-yireh,[c] whence the present saying, "On the mount of the LORD there is vision."[d]

[15]The angel of the LORD called to Abraham a second time from heaven, [16]and said, "By Myself I swear, the LORD declares: Because you have done this and have not withheld your son, your favored one, [17]I will bestow My blessing upon you and make your descendants as numerous as the stars of heaven and the sands of the seashore; and your descendants shall seize the gates of their foes. [18]All the nations of the earth shall bless themselves by your descendants, because you have obeyed My command." [19]Abraham then returned to his servants, and they departed together for Beer-sheba; and Abraham stayed in Beer-sheba.

---

[b] *Reading 'eḥad with many Heb. mss. and ancient versions; text 'aḥar "after."*
[c] *I.e., "the Lord will see"; cf. v. 8.*
[d] *Heb. Behar Adonai yera'eh.*

4 *Targum Jonathan on Genesis 22*

The entire text of the Akedah is included here, interwoven with the Masoretic text so that the reader can fully enjoy the religious imagination that created it as well as the ingenious organic situations into which postbiblical theological problems are set.[*]

V. 1 AND IT WAS AFTER THESE THINGS when Isaac and Ishmael argued, that Ishmael said, It is right that I should inherit Father since I am his first born. But Isaac said, It is right for me to inherit Father because I am the son of Sarah his wife and you are the son of Hagar my mother's maid. Ishmael answered saying, I am more worthy than you because I was circumcised at age 13; if it had been my will to hold back I would not have risked my life to be circumcised. But you were circumcised when you were 8 days old; had you known what it was all about you would not have risked your life. Isaac replied, Today I am 36 years old. If the Holy One, blessed be He, were to ask for all my limbs I would not hold back. Immediately these words were heard before the Lord of the universe and immediately the word of THE LORD TESTED ABRAHAM AND SAID TO HIM, ABRAHAM!

2 AND HE SAID, HERE I AM. AND HE SAID, TAKE YOUR SON, THE ONLY ONE THAT YOU LOVE, ISAAC, AND GO TO THE LAND OF worship, AND OFFER HIM THERE AS A BURNT OFFERING ON ONE OF THE MOUNTAINS THAT I WILL TELL YOU.

3 AND ABRAHAM AROSE EARLY IN THE MORNING, SADDLED HIS ASS, TOOK TWO OF HIS YOUNG MEN, Eliezer and Ishmael, WITH HIM, AND ISAAC HIS SON, AND HE SPLIT chips and young shoots and fig and palm WOOD which are fit FOR THE BURNT OFFERING: AND HE ROSE AND WENT TO THE PLACE WHICH THE LORD HAD TOLD HIM.

[*] *Genesis 22—Masoretic text in uppercase letters; Targum Jonathan in lowercase letters. The official name for Targum Jonathan is Targum Pseudo-Jonathan.*

4   ON THE THIRD DAY ABRAHAM LIFTED HIS EYES AND SAW the cloud of glory smoking on the mountain and he recognized it FROM AFAR.

5   AND ABRAHAM SAID TO THE YOUNG MEN, STAY HERE WITH THE ASS; I AND THE LAD WILL GO THAT FAR to test whether the joyful thing I was promised . . . "so shall your seed be" will be established; WE WILL WORSHIP the Lord of the universe AND WILL RETURN TO YOU.

6   AND ABRAHAM TOOK THE WOOD OF THE BURNT OFFERING AND LAID IT UPON ISAAC HIS SON: AND HE TOOK IN HIS HAND THE FIRE AND THE KNIFE: AND THE TWO OF THEM WENT TOGETHER (as one).

7   AND ISAAC SAID TO ABRAHAM HIS FATHER, Abba, AND HE SAID, HERE I AM, MY SON; AND HE SAID, HERE IS THE FIRE AND THE WOOD; WHERE IS THE LAMB FOR THE OFFERING?

8   AND ABRAHAM SAID, THE LORD will choose FOR HIMSELF THE LAMB FOR THE OFFERING, MY SON. AND THE TWO OF THEM WENT with a whole heart TOGETHER (as one).

9   AND THEY CAME TO THE PLACE THAT GOD HAD TOLD HIM; AND ABRAHAM BUILT THERE THE ALTAR which Adam had built, which had been destroyed by the flood, which Noah had again built and which had been destroyed by the generation of the division; HE ARRANGED THE WOOD ON IT, AND BOUND ISAAC HIS SON, AND LAID HIM ON THE ALTAR ON TOP OF THE WOOD.

10 AND ABRAHAM STRETCHED FORTH HIS HAND AND TOOK THE KNIFE TO SLAY HIS SON. Isaac answered and said to his father, Bind me well, lest I struggle in mortal agony, and be thrown into the pit of destruction, and there be found a blemish in your sacrifice. (Now) the eyes of Abraham looked at the eyes of Isaac; but the eyes of Isaac looked at the angels on high. Isaac saw them but Abraham did not. And the angels on high answered, Come, see these unique people in the world, one slaying and the other being slain; the one who slays does not withhold and the one to be slain stretches out his neck.

11 AND AN ANGEL OF THE LORD CALLED TO HIM FROM THE HEAVENS AND SAID TO HIM, ABRAHAM! ABRAHAM! AND HE SAID, HERE I AM.

12 AND HE SAID TO HIM, DON'T STRETCH OUT YOUR HAND TO THE LAD AND DON'T DO ANYTHING evil TO HIM BECAUSE NOW it is clear to me THAT YOU FEAR THE LORD AND YOU HAVE NOT WITHHELD YOUR SON, YOUR ONLY ONE, FROM ME.

13 AND ABRAHAM LIFTED HIS EYES AND SAW, BEHOLD a certain RAM that was created in the twilight of the completion of the world, CAUGHT IN THE THICKET of a tree BY ITS HORNS; AND ABRAHAM WENT AND TOOK him AND OFFERED HIM UP INSTEAD OF HIS SON.

14 AND ABRAHAM gave thanks and prayed there, IN THAT PLACE and said, When I prayed for your mercy O Lord, it was clear to you that there was no guile in my heart, and I turned to perform your decree with joy, so that when the children of Isaac my son come to a time of suffering, let this be a remembrance for them, and answer them and save them, that all the generations to come may say, ON THIS MOUNTAIN Abraham bound Isaac his son, and there the Shekhina of THE LORD WAS REVEALED to him.

15 AND THE ANGEL OF THE LORD CALLED TO ABRAHAM A SECOND TIME FROM THE HEAVENS.

16 AND SAID by my word HAVE I SWORN SAID THE LORD, BECAUSE YOU HAVE DONE THIS THING AND HAVE NOT WITHHELD YOUR SON, YOUR ONLY ONE.

17 THAT IN BLESSING I WILL BLESS YOU AND IN MULTIPLYING, I WILL MULTIPLY YOUR children LIKE THE STARS OF THE HEAVENS AND THE SAND ON THE SEASHORE, and your children WILL INHERIT cities in the presence of THEIR ENEMIES.

18 AND ALL THE NATIONS OF THE EARTH WILL BE BLESSED BECAUSE of the merit of your son; because you accepted my words.

19 And the angels on high took Isaac and brought him to the school of Shem the Great and he was there for three years. The same day ABRAHAM RETURNED TO THE YOUNG MEN AND THEY AROSE AND WENT TOGETHER TO BEER SHEBA; AND ABRAHAM LIVED IN BEER SHEBA.

20 AND IT WAS AFTER THESE THINGS, after Abraham had bound Isaac, that Satan came and told Sarah that Abraham had killed Isaac. Sarah rose up and cried out and choked and died because of the anguish.

(Now) Abraham came and was resting on the way AND IT WAS TOLD TO ABRAHAM, MILCAH TOO HAS GIVEN BIRTH; she has been blessed with many children through the merit of her sister, to bring forth sons TO NAHOR YOUR BROTHER.

Bibliography

Abramovitch, Henry. "Abraham, Psychology of a Spiritual Revolutionary and His Hebrew Chroniclers." Ph.D. Diss., Yale University, 1977.

Blunden, Edmund (ed.). *The Poems of Wilfred Owen*. New York: Viking, 1931.

Bowker, John. *The Targums and Rabbinic Literature*. Cambridge: Cambridge University Press, 1969.

Buber, Martin. *Hasidism and Modern Man*. Maurice Friedman (trans. and ed.) New York: Horizon, 1957.

Christensen, Duane. "The Akedah in Genesis 22:1–19: An Invitation to Jewish-Christian Dialogue." *American Baptist Quarterly* IV, no. 4 (1985): 340–347.

Cook, Roger. *The Tree of Life*. London: Thames & Hudson, 1974.

Dan, Joseph. "Samael, Lilith and the Concept of Evil." *Association of Jewish Studies Review* 5 (1980): 17–40.

Dowling, Terence. "The Psychological Significance of the Placenta." Paper presented at the Third International Congress on Pre- and Perinatal Psychology: Nurturing the Possible Human, San Francisco, July 9–12, 1987.

Dillenberger, Jane. *Style and Content in Christian Art*. Nashville: Abingdon, 1963.

Edinger, Edward. *The Bible and the Psyche: Individuation Symbolism in the Old Testament*. Toronto: Inner City Books, 1986.

———. *Ego and Archetype*. New York: Penguin, 1974.

Edwards, Betty. *Drawing on the Artist Within*. New York: Simon & Schuster, 1986.

Ehrenstein, Theodor. *Das Alte Testament Im Bilde*. Vienna: A. Kende, 1923.

Eliade, Mircea. "The Myth of Alchemy." *Parabola* III, no. 3 (1978): 28.

———. *The Sacred and the Profane*. New York: Harcourt, Brace and World, 1959.

Encyclopedia Judaica. Jerusalem: Keter, 1971.

Epstein, Gerald. *Waking Dream Therapy*. New York: Human Sciences Press, 1981.

Erikson, Erik. *Childhood and Society.* New York: Norton, 1950.

Fischer, Yona (ed.). *Art and Craft in the Land of Israel in the Nineteenth Century* (Heb.). Jerusalem: Israel Museum, 1979.

Freedman, H., and Simon, M. (eds.). *Midrash Rabbah.* 10 vols. London: Soncino, 1939.

Ginzberg, Louis. *Legends of the Jews.* 7 vols. Philadelphia: The Jewish Publication Society, 1909.

Goodenough, E. R. *Jewish Symbols in the Greco-Roman Period.* 13 vols. Princeton, N.J.: Bollingen, 1965.

Gordon, William J. J. *Synectics.* New York: Harper & Row, 1961.

Greenberg, Moshe. "NSH in Exodus and the Purpose of the Sinaitic Theophany." *Journal of Biblical Literature* 79, no. 3 (1960): 273–276.

Greenspan, Jay Seth. *Hebrew Calligraphy.* New York: Schocken, 1981.

Henderson, Joseph, and Oakes, Maud. *The Wisdom of the Serpent.* New York: Brazilier, 1963.

Interpreter's Dictionary of the Bible. 5 vols. Nashville: Abingdon, 1976.

Jaffe, I. B. (ed.). *The Sculpture of Leonard Baskin.* New York: Viking, 1980.

Kaplan, K. J., Schwartz, M. W., and Markus-Kaplan, M. (eds.). "The Family: Biblical and Psychological Foundations." *Journal of Psychology and Judaism* 8, no. 2 (1984).

Kaunfer, A. "Synectics: An Approach to Teaching Midrash." *Melton Research Center Newsletter* 11 (Fall, 1980): 2–5.

Keel, Othmar. *Symbolism of the Biblical World.* New York: Crossroads, 1978.

Keyes, Margaret Frings. *Inward Journey.* LaSalle, La.: Open Court, 1983.

Kierkegaard, Søren. *Fear and Trembling.* Princeton: Princeton University Press, 1945.

Kluger, Rivka. *Psyche and the Bible.* New York: Spring Publications, 1974.

Knowles, Charles. *The Psalm Book of Charles Knowles.* New York: Viking & Pinnacle Press, 1959.

Kushner, Lawrence. *The Book of Letters.* New York: Harper & Row, 1975.

Leach, Edmund. *Genesis as Myth.* London: Jonathan Cape, 1960.

Mellinkoff, Ruth. *The Horned Moses in Medieval Art and Thought.* Berkeley and Los Angeles: University of California Press, 1970.

Meyer, Franz. *Marc Chagall.* New York: Harry N. Abrams.

Milgrom, Jo. *The Binding of Isaac (The Akedah): A Primary Symbol in Jewish Thought and Art.* Berkeley, Calif.: Bibal Press, 1988.

———. "Handmade Midrash." *Melton Journal* 17 (Winter 1984): 16–18.

———. "Some Consequences of the Image Prohibition in Jewish Art." In E. Firmage, B. Weiss, and J. W. Welch (eds.), *Religion and Law.* Winona Lake, Wis.: Eisenbrauns, 1990.

———. "Some Second Thoughts About Adam's First Wife." In Gregory A. Robbins (ed.), *Genesis 1–3 in The History of Exegesis.* Lewiston, New York: Mellen, 1988.

———. "The Tree of Life Springs from the Threshold." In Doug Adams and Diane Apostolos-Cappadona (eds.), *Art as Religious Studies.* New York: Crossroads, 1987.

Ofrat, Gideon. *The Akedah in Modern Israeli Art* (Heb.). Ramat Gan: Museum of Modern Israeli Art, 1988.

Robertson, Seonid M. *Rosegarden and Labyrinth.* Dallas: Spring Publications, 1982.

Rollins, Wayne G. *Jung and the Bible.* Atlanta: John Knox, 1983.

Rosenberg, Joel W. "The Garden Story Forward and Backward." *Prooftexts,* vol. 1, no. 1 (Jan. 1981): 1–27.

Rotermund, Hans-Martin (ed.). *Rembrandt's Drawings and Etchings for the Bible*. Philadelphia: Pilgrim Press, 1969.

————. "The Motif of Radiance in Rembrandt's Biblical Drawings." *Journal of the Warburg Courtauld* 29 (1966): 101–121.

Sacks, Robert. *The Lion and the Ass*. Santa Fe, N.Mex.: St. John's College, 1976.

Scholem, Gershom. *On the Kabbalah and Its Symbolism*. New York: Schocken, 1974.

————. "The Names of God and the Linguistic Theory of the Kabbalah." *Diogenes* 79 (1972): 59–70.

————. *Mada'e Ha-Yahadut II* (Heb.). Jerusalem: 1927.

Speiser, Ephraim. *Genesis: The Anchor Bible*. Chicago: Doubleday, 1964.

Spiegel, Shalom. *The Last Trial*. New York: Schocken, 1967.

Swartz, Beth Ames. *Israel Revisited*. Scottsdale, Ariz.: B. Swartz, 1981.

von Oech, Roger. *A Whack on the Side of the Head*. New York: Warner, 1988.

Walton, Anna (ed.). *Tent of Meeting*. Santa Fe, N.Mex.: The Tent of Meeting, 1985.

Wellisch, E. *Isaac and Oedipus*. London: Routledge & Kegan Paul, 1954.

Wiesel, Elie. *Messengers of God*. New York: Random House, 1976.

————. *The Golem*. New York: Summit, 1983.

Williams, Arnold. *The Common Expositor*. Chapel Hill, N.C.: University of North Carolina, 1948.

Zeligs, Dorothy. *Psychoanalysis and the Bible*. New York: Bloch, 1974.